*class politics
in the information age*

class politics
in the information age

Donald Clark Hodges

University of Illinois Press

Urbana and Chicago

© 2000 by the Board of Trustees of the University of Illinois
All rights reserved
Manufactured in the United States of America
♾ This book is printed on acid-free paper.

Library of Congress Cataloging-in-Publication Data
Hodges, Donald Clark, 1923–
Class politics in the information age / Donald Clark Hodges.
     p.   cm.
Includes bibliographical references and index.
ISBN 0-252-02583-0 (cloth : alk. paper)
1. Professions—Social aspects—United States. 2. Expertise—Social
aspects—United States. I. Title.
HT690.U6H63   2000
305.5'53—dc21   99-050925

c 5 4 3 2 1

To
the heroes and heroines
of the
end of millennium battle in Seattle
for protesting
against the lies, half-truths, and hypocrisy
of the
Age of Information

Now that people are classified by ability, the gap between the classes has inevitably become wider. . . . Today the eminent know that success is just reward for their own capacity, for their own efforts, and for their own undeniable achievement. They deserve to belong to a superior class.

—Michael Young, *The Rise of the Meritocracy, 1870–2033*

The simple truth is that the professional classes of our modern bureaucratized societies are engaged in a class struggle with the business community for status and power.

—Irving Kristol, *Two Cheers for Capitalism*

Organized labor has its fair share of fighters. But what it needs is general, faithful lieutenants, and an army. The question is: Where are the leaders?

—Jack Seddon, president of PATCO New York from 1977 to 1979 and leader of the Professional Air Traffic Controllers' strike against the U.S. government in 1981

contents

preface

FIRST POLITICAL SCIENTIST: "Political science has come a
  long way since Machiavelli."
SECOND POLITICAL SCIENTIST: "On the contrary, it has yet
  to catch up to him."
—Conversation at the Twentieth World Congress of Philosophy,
  Boston, August 1998

This is a book on the political economy of expertise; it scrutinizes the
actions of professionals in the spirit of Machiavelli's *Prince*—but without glo-
rifying expedience or worldly success. Intended as a counterpart of Milovan
Djilas's *New Class*—an exposure of the revolutionary vanguard of professionals in the former Soviet Union and his native Yugoslavia—it examines the
origins, development, aims, and means of the new class in the United States.
As a critique of the ideology of professional workers, it reveals their economic dogmatism, political hypocrisy, and intellectual tyranny. It lays bare the
sources of professional pelf, power, and privilege at the cost of the underlying
population. It shows that a dissection of professionalism unlocks secrets unknown to Marxism—for the innocent who do not know but need to know in
self-defense.

That income inequalities have not been reduced with the advent of the
"knowledge society" indicates that the new class of knowledge workers is not
the benign group of public-spirited citizens they imagine themselves to be. Like
professionals in the countries of actually existing socialism, they congratulate
themselves on representing the public interest but fail to face up to the common role of professionals in both free societies and single-party states. The
irony is that professionals in the United States agree with Djilas's critique of
their counterparts under Marxist-Leninist regimes, but they do not turn his
critique back on themselves.

It is now widely recognized that expertise has replaced capital as the decisive asset in the U.S. economy. But pending further investigation, this does not

tell us how the economic surplus is distributed. The consensus is that capitalists are still pocketing the lion's share. Since they lack the decision-making powers that are currently in the hands of managers and other professional workers, however, the United States is no longer capitalist in the full sense of the word. Professionals are in the driver's seat, and labor struggles are directed not against the monied interests but against a new class enemy.

To understand class politics in the knowledge society, a change of focus from the political economy of capital to the political economy of expertise is required. At the heart of postcapitalist society is the conflict between labor and the owners of expertise. But why a conflict with labor? Because, like capital, expertise is the private property of a privileged class. Expertise enables its owners to command an above-average share of the national income.

To judge from the existing literature, the condition of labor in corporate America is an uncharted territory in the Information Age. Radical political economists are to be credited with virtually the only existing in-depth studies, but their geodesy of labor is antiquarian. They have only remodeled Marx's conceptual apparatus in response to twentieth-century monopoly capitalism, even though, as I argue in the following pages, the postcapitalist order has been dominant for the past three decades. The critical and revolutionary mantle is thus worn by dinosaurs.

From a Marxist perspective, the "new class" is not new, it is not a class, and it is not important. To be sure, professionals in the role of wage earners are not peculiar to the contemporary world; what is new about them is their massive growth and their leading role in the Information Age. If land, labor, and capital were the sole factors of production, professionals might qualify as labor or as human capital or as both; but if one adds expertise to this list, they constitute not only a separate class but also a great and influential one. Marxist categories of analysis are outdated in the Information Age, and post-Marxist ones are required. As will be seen, not capital and not labor but expertise calls the tune in today's new economic order.

As the statistical abstracts show, the surplus concealed in wages and salaries has reached a level such that capitalists, while still individually the biggest, are no longer collectively the principal beneficiaries of the economic surplus. The long-heralded "managerial revolution" has been consummated. The "new class"—the class of college graduates-turned-professionals—not only occupies the emperor's throne but also carries off most of the tribute. In the United States, you do not need a socialist party or a revolutionary vanguard to make a revolution.

The social pact between labor and the professional class has become a dead letter. The New Deal, the Fair Deal, the New Frontier, and the Great Society all testified to its acceptance. By the mid-fifties, however, it was already being challenged by the rapidly expanding and flourishing army of college graduates.

As long as America's plutocrats, the descendants of the "robber barons," still held sway and enjoyed the lion's share of economic privileges, professionals had need of organized labor to transform the status quo. But with capitalists becoming increasingly marginalized, labor emerged as the professionals' enemy, while taxes for funding the welfare state became the principal threat to their newly won status.

In 1905, a book appeared in Geneva that was to revolutionize our understanding of the professional worker. Written by the Polish revolutionary Waclaw Machajski (1866–1926) under the pen name A. Volski, *The Intellectual Worker* proclaimed to the world the following theses: educated or professional workers constitute a class distinct from Marx's proletariat; higher education is their specific "capital," the source of their privileged wages; this class is destined to replace the capitalists not only politically but also as the principal beneficiary of the economic surplus. Professionals may be slaves to their careers, but they are hardly "wage-slaves."

In the United States, Machajski's scenario of professional workers as a potentially new ruling class was disseminated by his disciple Max Nomad and by such prominent figures in the educational establishment as the political scientist Harold Lasswell, the political philosopher James Burnham, and the political sociologists Daniel Bell and Alvin Gouldner. Largely because of them, the theory of a new class of knowledge workers and of a postindustrial, postcapitalist information society gained currency in American academic circles. However, neither the master himself nor any of his acolytes put together an agenda of leading questions whose answers would enable one to calculate either the relative or the absolute size of the surplus pocketed in any given year by professional workers. Moreover, they were at a loss to know if and when the emerging new order had replaced the old, except in countries where capitalists were forcibly expropriated, such as the Soviet Union, the Eastern Europe countries, and China.

The present work is the sequel to *America's New Economic Order* (1996), in which I first developed a yardstick for calculating surplus wages and estimating the magnitude of professional exploitation. In the following pages, I address several new leading questions. How does one go about measuring different intensities of work, scaling them, and matching wages and hours? Or does the market do it? Is there a middle class between knowledge workers and the laboring masses? Are cooperatives the vanguard or the rear guard of the new order? Does finance capital dominate the new global order, or are professionals in the driver's seat internationally as well as nationally? Does it make sense to talk of capitalism without capitalists, socialism without socialists, and fascism without fascists? How do both the Republican and the Democratic parties cater to professional interests? Is there a basic difference between neoliberalism and neoconservatism in class politics? Such questions have a bearing on the role of professionals in corporate America and on the politics of who gets what, when, and how.

Among the most consequential political theorists in the modern world, Niccolò Machiavelli and Karl Marx stood head and shoulders above their contemporaries—Machiavelli as the political historian and strategist par excellence and Marx as the classic example of a political philosopher turned political economist. The present work owes a major intellectual debt to each.

For encouragement and help in completing this study, I thank Professor Ray Canterbery of the Economics Department at Florida State University; Professor James K. Galbraith of the Lyndon B. Johnson School of International Affairs, University of Texas at Austin; Professor Larry Lustig at the University of Maryland University College, Asian Division, Seoul, Korea, who pored over early and later versions of the manuscript; and Jane Mohraz, associate editor at the University of Illinois Press, who contributed to the manuscript's present shape.

class politics
in the information age

1.

the politics of political economy

The problems of economics were always at bottom political.
—David Bazelon, *Power in America: The Politics of the New Class* (1964)

The modern intellectual separation of economics from politics has made both spheres strangely unbalanced.
—Robert B. Reich, *The Next American Frontier* (1983)

Class struggle is a political phenomenon best understood within the framework of political theory and political economics in particular—that is, political economy. Class struggle is central to both because its object is a bigger slice of the available income over and above subsistence, or what is required to feed, clothe, house, transport, and pacify the laboring population, and because the ways and means of conducting this struggle are political.

The history of modern political theory is pertinent to understanding class struggles in the modern world, that is to say, from the dawn to the dusk of the capitalist era. But our world is a postcapitalist one that can be fully understood only through a political theory of its own.

What are the contours of this new political theory? As in the political theories it displaces, political economy plays a leading role. Political economy is not economics, and we need to know how these two fields of inquiry differ and what a postcapitalist political theory may offer.

Postcapitalist Political Theory

I am not alone in campaigning for a new political science that goes beyond the ken of mainstream political scientists, but the Caucus for a New Political Science, a national organization of radical teachers, students, researchers, and activists organized in the late 1960s, has yet to make a complete break with outlived stereotypes. The Caucus is committed to developing an understanding and critique of capitalist society and to helping create the social changes needed to transcend it, but capitalism is already on the margins of a new economic order. Inadvertently, the Caucus has played into the hands of a new ruling class in the name of an alternative political science and an alternative politics aimed at creating a socialist center of gravity within the political science profession. Making room for Marxist analyses in a profession that until recently was solidly anti-Marxist was no mean accomplishment, but it was precisely at a moment when post-Marxist analyses were called for.

Founded in 1968, the Union for Radical Political Economics advances a similar agenda for the economics profession. Its members consist of academics and activists who share an interest in radical analyses of political and economic issues and in advancing solutions to the social question. In spite of its marked interest in labor matters, it has yet to focus on the new class of professionals as labor's fundamental enemy. Like the Caucus for a New Political Science, it has contributed to making Marxist analyses acceptable in a profession with a pronounced anti-Marxist bias. But even as the left wing of the economics profession, it has inadvertently become the voice of the new class of professionals in a struggle to curb the privileges of the so-called monied interests.

On the questionable premise that we are still living under late capitalism, these new political theories take as their starting point the deconstruction of the values and shibboleths legitimizing new forms of oppression under conditions of globalization. Suppose, however, that we are no longer living under late capitalism and that globalization is symptomatic of a new postcapitalist order. Then the accepted definitions that look backward instead of forward belong to a past era. Besides the deconstruction of the values and shibboleths of early and late capitalism, postcapitalist political theory leads to a critique of postcapitalist society.

By the modern or capitalist world, I mean the era ushered in by the cultural Renaissance of the fifteenth and sixteenth centuries, the new humanism opposed to medievalism, the Protestant work ethic, the scientific and industrial revolutions, the emergence of nationalism and the system of nation-states, the rule of law through representative government, and, economically, the displacement of a landed aristocracy by businesspeople. By the postcapitalist world, I mean the new era that arose after World War I with the Bolshevik Revolution, the end of laissez faire, the new system of totalitarian regimes, the welfare state, the rise of the professions, and, in the wake of World War II, a new economic order.

So understood, political theory has yet to catch up with what is happening in the world. A new conceptual framework with a new set of definitions is required if this challenge is to be met—a new probing and systematic reflection in response to questions concerning the distribution of political power, pelf, and privilege. If politics is about who gets what, when, and how, then political theory attempts to explain why people receive different shares. Since these shares hinge on the production as well as the distribution of an economic surplus, it is a matter of both political theory and political economy.

Basic to modern political theory was its focus on the agents of the modern world and their enemies or competitors for political power. From Machiavelli, the father of modern political theory, through Hobbes, Rousseau, Burke, and Tocqueville to Marx, Sorel, Lenin, Mussolini, and Hitler, class struggle became the key to political understanding. The historians of the French and Russian revolutions echoed this established wisdom that was more than merely conventional.

The class structure of postcapitalist societies diverges from that in the modern world, however. In the modern world, the principal contestants consisted of an aristocracy of landowners who were progressively displaced by a class of upstart capitalist entrepreneurs ostensibly representing the interests of the "people," the motley Third Estate. In postcapitalist societies, the key players are capitalists and a new class of professional workers, including management—the cream of a loosely labeled "working class," or Fourth Estate. Just as capitalists leapfrogged into positions of prominence over the backs of other classes belonging to the Third Estate—the petty bourgeoisie and workers on their own account, such as small shopkeepers, artisans, and peasants—so professional workers leapfrogged their way to pelf and privilege over the backs of manual and clerical workers.

In postcapitalist societies, as in capitalist ones, an underlying population provides the wherewithal for the overlying privileged layer. Such is the condition of exploited wage earners—human livestock, albeit lords over other animals they in turn domesticate. They, too, are engaged in a class struggle, but one they periodically lose. Today they are lackeys of the new class of professionals in times of peace, cannon fodder in times of war.

The mortal struggle between the old and the new world orders began with the Bolshevik Revolution in 1917, leading to the establishment of socialism in the Soviet Union during the mid-1930s. This signaled to the major European powers the need to contain the "Red Specter" threatening social peace under conditions in which they were being ravaged by the Great Depression. All the efforts of the Soviet Union to reach an accommodation with the West failed until the 1939 Non-Aggression Pact with Nazi Germany that ended in disaster in 1941.

With the defeat of the Axis powers in World War II, the West was faced with a greatly strengthened Soviet Union owing to the expansion of socialism throughout Eastern Europe followed by Mao's conquest of the Chinese mainland. The cold war ensued with its unforeseen climax—the dissolution of the Soviet Union. As Robert Heilbroner imperiously announced in an article in the *New Yorker* on 23 January 1989, some three years prior to the Soviet collapse, "Less than seventy-five years after it officially began, the contest between capitalism and socialism is over: capitalism has won."[1]

Convinced that the contest was over, the purveyors of this conventional wisdom began arranging trade agreements on a world scale of exploitation that is unprecedented in its level of greed. New methods of extracting and appropriating the global surplus have made the corporations so rich and powerful worldwide that they are behaving like nation-states. A new world order is being made in the image of its key players—as corporate America goes, so goes the world.

But are the new world order and its principal players to be pegged as capitalist? What began as a struggle between capitalism and socialism did not end as such. The convergence of the two systems after World War II led to new depictions of the American economy, variously called "Intellectual Capitalism," "Managerial Capitalism," "Managerial Socialism," "Corporate Socialism," not to mention a system both postcapitalist and postsocialist. These designations are of secondary importance. What is more important is the emergence of a new economic order and its failure to live up to the accepted definitions of either capitalism or socialism.

The forms of capital have altered over time; the forms of socialism have also changed. Alongside the new, giant corporations are the old-fashioned family and medium-sized enterprises that anyone a hundred years ago would have found familiar. Corporate capital has undergone a metamorphosis, having escaped the control of stockholders and having become so large and complex that only the graduates of business schools and their professional staffs possess the expertise required to manage it. A meritocracy of experts has replaced the reign of stockholders as the corporations' principal beneficiaries.

The standard definitions bracket out class struggle and the decisive politico-economic actors at the heart of both capitalism and socialism. They replace these actors with the legal concept of ownership and a deus ex machina consisting of the market in one case and planning in the other—definitions fit for the academy but not for the real world. They provide no clues for identifying the greedy ones. Are the new absentee owners primarily individuals? Or are they institutional investors—the giant corporations, whose returns go to fatten the paychecks of professional workers?

Keynesian and neoclassical economics assume that capitalism is an economic system characterized by private ownership of capital goods. As Paul Samuelson put it, "Our economy has the name 'capitalism' because this capital, or 'wealth,' is primarily the private property of somebody—the capitalist"— unlike a socialist economy that is characterized by collective or government ownership of the means of production.[2] As a result, the political contest between capitalism and socialism is mistakenly reduced to a clash between the private and public sectors.

Common to both definitions is the presumption that the owners of private and public property are the principal beneficiaries. The irony is that this may or may not be the case. Indeed, it has become increasingly atypical for the owners of either private property or public property to command the lion's share of the national income.

Since it has become the exception that the owners under either system are the prime beneficiaries, one needs to ask what is fundamental to each. Is it ownership or preferential treatment in distribution? If ownership, is it the ownership of real property, its paper surrogates, or what is misleadingly called human capital—that is, income-yielding expertise?

Each system is characterized by ownership not for its own sake but for the sake of accumulation: profits from the income-yielding power of capital goods under capitalism, and privileged salaries for expertise under socialism. Marx was right in highlighting the exploitative function of private ownership, but he was wrong in dismissing the role of exploitation under public ownership. A post-Marxist unmasking of the undisclosed realities under each system would have us redefine both.

In the United States, for example, defining our economy on the basis of private ownership of capital goods is obsolete. Capitalism no longer prevails against the invading socialist economy. As will be seen from a close reading of the statistical abstracts, preferential treatment in distribution is today the prerogative of professional workers in the form of surplus wages.

It follows that the private/public antithesis is immaterial to whether the U.S. economy is capitalist or socialist. Whereas the nationalization, municipalization, and collectivization of private property means socialism, it does not follow that the privatization of public ownership—even on a massive scale— signifies a return to capitalism. Also irrelevant is the antithesis of a market economy and centralized planning. Preferential treatment in distribution for the new professional class is possible with or without a planned economy.

In addition to the classical factors of land, labor, and capital common to both systems is the ownership of a fourth factor of production—brainpower or expertise. Thus, capitalism is a system in which the lion's share of the economic surplus goes to the owners of capital, and socialism is the system in which it goes to the owners of expertise. A major defect of the standard definitions is that a revolution may have occurred without our being able to identify it.

The "private sector" is a misnomer when applied to modern corporations, which, as Keynes correctly perceived, represent a quasi-public or semisocialist mode of business organization. Corporations are not private property; they form part of a sector intermediate to government and private business. As in the public sector, professional workers do the hiring and firing in these contemporary Leviathans. Thanks to bonuses, benefits, and above-average wages, managers and their professional staffs suction off ever larger amounts of the gross returns from industry and commerce—at the expense of not just labor but also private stockholders. Granted that we live in a mixed economy that is not fully socialist, in which the capitalist sector is still powerful, the private sector may have ceased to be hegemonic some three decades ago.

What is labor's role in this new dispensation? The same as always—to sow what it cannot reap, to play the part of the fabled goose by laying golden eggs for its master. The principal difference has been the change in bosses. This change points to a class struggle different from the one that characterized the capitalist epoch, to a struggle between labor and the professions, between ordinary workers and the American counterpart of the former Soviet Nomenklatura.

How does the struggle between labor and professionals find expression? We have become so used to visualizing a class struggle motivated from below that we fail to see that class struggle in the United States is initiated also from above. Under capitalism, it was the war against capital that defined the class struggle; but in America's new corporate order, the war against labor—whether through downsizing, restructuring, flexible employment, forced early retirements, violations of labor law, or resettlement in low-wage areas—is decisive. As a result, labor unions are on the defensive, and collective contracts no longer offer workers a shield against management offensives.

Ordinary labor has become increasingly unnecessary to fuel the corporate economy. An enormous mass of economically superfluous humanity is stacking the welfare rolls. At the same time, the new professional elites resent the rising costs of welfare and do not want to feed the underlying population when they cannot be fed by it. Parson Malthus rather than Dr. Marx has become their prophet.

The new economic elites are more knowledgeable than the old. Contrary to preconceived notions, the class struggle begins in America's colleges and universities. It goes by many names: careerism, professionalism, ambition, pursuit of happiness, being a good student, excelling, making something of oneself, or, as a popular U.S. Army advertisement has it, being "all that you can be." Increasingly, the class struggle means the struggle for "class," for specialized knowledge, for the soft job that goes with expertise, and for the fat paycheck that goes with both. There is not much that labor can do about it. The recently renewed interest in extraterrestrial saviors may not be entirely coincidental.

Marxist political theorists have yet to get a handle on these changed circumstances. Bogged down in the conceptual confusion of a working class that includes the new exploiters, they have failed to respond to Marx's call to abandon illusions about life, not to mention his call to abandon a life that requires illusions. They have uncritically accepted Marx's conceptual apparatus instead of investigating the new forms of class struggle targeting both capitalists and working peons.

Marx sought to unmask the illusions of everyday life and their reflection in economic thought, but he only partly succeeded. Even during his time, there were others who, thanks to their reading of *Capital,* had a better grasp of reality. Inspired by Marx's tour de force, they were able to recognize its shortcomings and to go beyond it. This made them post-Marxists. Since they perceived the world through different lenses, they were not content with simply bringing Marxism abreast of the times.

Post-Marxists were the first to acknowledge that the new bosses would use their expertise and control over production to become the new robber barons. But this new order of expertise depended, first, on an economic surplus concealed in wages and, second, on the professionals' share of surplus wages catching up to and surpassing capital income—the sum of private profits, dividends, interest, and rent.

Such are the larger contours of the class struggle over the economic surplus. The old masters continue to appeal to abstinence and to impersonal market forces to justify their incomes; the new bosses prefer to talk of material incentives, productivity bonuses, and premiums for special qualifications and responsibility. Meanwhile, working stiffs engage in unionization, strikes, boycotts, and political action to raise the basic wage to the level of the average wage. In such terms are the old and the new class struggles hidden or glossed over with ideological cosmetics.

As Marx envisioned the transition from capitalism to socialism, the new order would involve not a leveling of wages and salaries but the divesting of capitalists. To be sure, capitalism is still alive and kicking, but it is no longer the principal source of surplus income. Marxists and their fellow travelers have mistaken a new mode of exploitation for the final stage of capitalism.

As evidence for this startling and controversial claim, the first step is to demonstrate that the price exceeds the cost of virtually all grades of skill, the excess consisting of surplus wages. The second is to establish that surplus wages exceed the total income from capital. The third is to show that the surplus wages of experts or professionals alone exceed capital income. The result must come as a shock to Marxist ideologues who take for granted that Americans are still living under capitalism and who have a blind spot for this new chunk of reality. It must also be an embarrassment to working stiffs who, for the past three decades, have been barking up the wrong tree.

As far back as the 1920s, Keynes acknowledged the germs of a new order in the tendency of big enterprises to socialize themselves and to approximate the status of public corporations. In the semisocialism of the giant corporations, he discovered an acceptable alternative to the centralized state socialism of the Bolsheviks and of the Marxist political parties on the Continent. He was among the first to note that managers and their professional staffs make up a self-perpetuating oligarchy beholden to one another rather than to meddling outsiders. What he failed to note is that this corporate elite with its new decentralized socialism and new global enterprises was on the road to becoming labor's fundamental enemy.

Political Economy versus Economics

In broad brushstrokes, political theory may be divided into those branches occupied with ends and means and those concerned with outcomes and their explanations. Political philosophy is a reflection on goals and their justifications; political strategy examines the means and their implementation under conditions in which not everything is under control and luck plays a prominent role. Political history investigates the actions of different agents and attempts to periodize what has happened and is happening, while political economy endeavors to explain why political events have taken one course rather than another.

Political economy is thus a branch of political theory. But it has seldom been recognized as such, and it is more often associated with economics. That is a cardinal mistake, as a review of its history reveals.

Having initially appeared in the eighteenth century as a branch of the art of government concerned with the promotion of wealth as the basis of state power, it evolved in the nineteenth century into a social science comprising the modern science of economics but concerned principally with governmental policy. Today it is an interdisciplinary science concerned with the interrelationship of political and economic processes, alternatively the political branch of economics or the economic branch of political science focusing on the struggle over the economic surplus.

Unlike today's mainstream economics with its built-in mathematical harmonies, classical political economy was called the dismal science because of its gloomy forecasts concerning the laboring poor. Except for periods of rapidly increasing demand for labor in excess of supply, it was assumed that labor power would be priced at its cost of subsistence and that any surplus wages would be eaten up by human reproduction and new mouths to feed.[3] In this dismal science, the poor would be always with us.

Classical gloom, with its iron law of wages and law of population, gave way to neoclassical cheer, however. Impelled by rising standards of living that refuted the classical view, the new science of economics held forth the prospect of both a rising tide that raises all boats and a system of rewards corresponding to each person's contribution to the total product. Increasing productivity meant there would be more for all; and, given the fantastic notion of perfect competition, every commodity (including labor power) would have a value exactly corresponding to its price.

To its credit, Marxist political economy acknowledged that classical political economy was on the right track in holding that working stiffs could expect only a subsistence wage and that neoclassical economics was on the wrong track in denying the reality of human exploitation. But if there could be only gloom in present society, there would be plenty to cheer in the new order destined to replace capitalism. Thus, in view of Marx's forecasts of a virtual paradise in postcapitalist societies, Marxist political economy also became falsified by events.[4]

Both Marxist political economy and conventional economics are responsible for these mistaken forecasts. For the most part, Marxists have been slow to acknowledge their mistakes; when they do, they blame them on obsolete theoretical premises that allegedly need revision. In contrast, the economists reply that science relies on theoretical models; if matters do not turn out according to the model, it is the world, not the model, that is at fault.

What a strange, topsy-turvy view of the world and our place in it. Economics has become increasingly technical and detached, not only from politics but also from the uncertainties that are a defining feature of the buzzing, blooming confusion of everyday life. Such was the departure in both name and substance from the earlier study of political economy from which economics emerged.

Adam Smith, the father of modern political economy, had gone a different route in stressing the political dimension of economics. Since power depends on riches, he wrote, the great object of the political economy of every country is to increase the riches and power of that country. As a branch of the science of legislation, political economy proposes to enrich both the people and the sovereign.[5] Political economy is therefore more than a technical science for unraveling the mysteries of the market place.

The change in perspective from political economy to economics had to wait a full century after Smith to become effective. Although Stanley Jevons's *Theory of Political Economy* appeared as late as 1871, the preface to the first edition made abundantly clear that its mathematically treated pleasure-pain calculus was nonpolitical and that his use of the term *political economy* was only in deference to tradition. Convinced that mathematical economics was the wave of the future, he was among the first to substitute "Science of Economy" for "Political Economy." However, not until the second edition in 1879 did he acknowledge the "substitution for the name Political Economy of the single convenient term Economics." This would become the title of the new discipline.[6]

In an effort to preserve the classical tradition, Alfred Marshall settled for a broad definition of the new science in 1890, designed to make room for political economy alongside Jevons's theory of psycho-mathematical utility. His inclusion of the old with the new made him the father of neoclassical economics. Marshall restored a token significance to politics, but he shifted the focus of the classics from the competition among labor, capitalists, and landowners to the comparatively innocuous competition of individuals and small entrepreneurs in the marketplace.

What did Marshall mean by economics? It is the study of human beings in the ordinary business of life, "the attainment and use of the material requisites of well-being . . . [with] wealth for its subject matter." It is the investigation of "the consumption and production, the distribution and exchange of wealth; the organization of industry and trade; the money market; wholesale and retail dealing; foreign trade; and the relation between employers and employed." While helping legislators formulate policies that bear on business practice, economics "shuns many political issues, which the practical man cannot ignore." It leaves to political science the investigation of such questions and is therefore "better described by the broad term 'Economics' than by the narrower term 'Political Economy'."[7] The narrower term? It might be more accurate to say broader term, since political economy is an interdisciplinary science cutting across both economics and politics.

The same year that Marshall published his *Principles of Economics*, his close friend at Cambridge John Neville Keynes, the leading logician-philosopher of economics among the neoclassicals and the father of John Maynard Keynes, published *The Scope and Method of Political Economy*. Although in fundamental agreement with Marshall, he chose to retain the term *political economy* for a science of choice, of the "reasonable adaptation of means to ends," but defined it more narrowly in connection with the substance of wealth as "activities that direct themselves toward the creation, appropriation, and accumulation of wealth." *Economics* or *economic science* may be preferred to *political economy* for being less ambiguous, but *"political economy* is . . . too firmly established to be altogether discarded; and we, therefore, use all three of the names more or less indiscriminately."[8]

So conceived, economics is concerned not just with quantifying utility, and it does not rely exclusively on model building and a priori formulations of general laws. It is both theory and practice. Politically, according to John Neville Keynes, it is "mainly concerned with the economic activities of the State in its corporate capacity, or of individuals as controlled by the State." Furthermore, its reliance on the facts of economic history gives to economics a historical dimension: "Neither of the two can take the place of the other . . . economic history and economic theory in different ways assist and control one another."[9]

John Maynard Keynes went beyond his father in giving priority to the world of economic reality over Jevons's mathematical models. Although dispensing with the term *political economy,* he restored its substance. "Keynes did not write the *General Theory* in order to solve puzzles about hypothetical conditions, but out of an urgent concern that governments would fail to end the massive unemployment and deprivation of the 1920s and 1930s," E. Ray Canterbury observed. Keynes argued persuasively that the growth of wealth—the paramount concern of Adam Smith—is dependent not on the abstinence of the rich but on raising the wages and consumption of the poor. He might well have agreed with Michael Kalecki: "The workers spend what they get; the capitalists get what they spend."[10]

Joan Robinson, another Cambridge economist, stressed Keynes's unique contribution to the revival of political economy: he "brought back something of the hardness of the classics." Keynes had a sense of the historical development of capitalism, an economy that had grown fragile and needed desperately to be patched up if it were to survive. "The whole elaborate structure of the metaphysical justification for profit was blown up when he pointed out that capital yields a return not because it is *productive* but because it is *scarce,"* Robinson maintained. Like Marx's *Capital,* the *General Theory* was an abomination to bourgeoisdom because of its disconcerting and outrageous proposition that, economically speaking, private virtues had become public vices. Keynes overcame the artificial barrier Jevons had erected between economic theory and practice. With Keynes having bridged mathematical economics and history, "Economics once more became Political Economy."[11]

Keynes declared, "I sympathize . . . with the pre-classical doctrine that everything is *produced* by *labor,* aided by what used to be called art and is now called technique, by material resources . . . and by the results of paid labor, embodied in assets." Keynes went so far as to regard labor, including the personal services of the entrepreneur, as "the sole factor of production." That explains why he took the unit of labor as "the sole physical unit which we require in any economic system, apart from units of money and of time." This concession to a political economy of labor accounts for his outrageous slurs targeting economic parasites. Rather than lower the interest and rent charged by the class of functionless investors and absentee proprietors, he called for their economic, if not physical, euthanasia—the "euthanasia of the cumulative oppressive power of the capitalist to exploit the scarcity-value of capital."[12]

However, most of Keynes's followers—known as neo-Keynesians because of their efforts to improve on this or that feature of his *General Theory*—chose to sidestep controversial political issues. For instance, a widely used neo-Keynesian textbook defines economics as "the study of how men and society *choose*, with or without the use of money, to employ *scarce* productive resources, which could have alternative uses, to produce various commodities over time and distribute them for consumption, now and in the future."[13] This definition by the Harvard economist Paul Samuelson makes implicit reference to the choice of means adapted to a given end, means that are economical in the sense of economizing time and energy. It is imperative, however, to economize time and energy not merely in the chase after narrowly economic objectives but also in pursuit of political goals.

Like Marshall and John Neville Keynes, the neo-Keynesians claim to have restored the connection between economics and politics. But by *political,* they mean simply matters pertaining to government and legislation. Such a definition unduly limits the scope of politics by reducing the enemy to a mere competitor. Unlike classical and Marxist political economy, neo-Keynesian economics does not target a class enemy. What would be the point, after Marx's devastating missiles against Mr. Moneybags? What would be the point of targeting a new class enemy—the class of professionals, the owners of expertise—unless professionals are to target themselves?

Unlike the pallid history of economics, political economy was from its birth in the eighteenth century a theoretical expression on the cultural front of the battle between the rising class of urban bourgeois and the waning class of feudal aristocrats in the countryside. At issue was whether profits or rents, capital or landed property, should have Goliath's share of the surplus. In contrast, mainstream economics stood above the class struggle and flattered itself for its objectivity.

The class struggle, however, has a habit of reviving on the cultural front whenever a new class rears its ugly head. In the nineteenth century, that class, in Marx's depiction, was the fighting proletariat, but Marx failed to mention that it was headed by an elite successful in mobilizing working stiffs. The founders of a revived political economy, Karl Marx and Frederick Engels were themselves members of that elite—the one a professional philosopher and doctor of juris-prudence, the other a manager of the British branch of the German textile firm of Ermen and Engels.

Since the 1960s, mainstream economics has come under increasingly heavy fire for its scholasticism, numerology, compartmentalization, mystification, and evasion of social reality. In contrast with an empirically and historically oriented investigation of how people really make their living, theoretical eco-nomics comes dangerously close to science fiction.

As Thomas Balogh summed up the irrelevance of mainstream economics, its weaknesses are due to three principal causes: first, a focus restricted to con-ventionally accepted economic relationships; second, a narrow interpretation of what constitutes economic relationships; and third, a reliance on methods of analysis suited only to conventional economic relationships. The retreat from reality began with model building and reliance on ideal types, based on premises so restrictive that economics lost its footing in the world. Because common sense was sacrificed for the sake of abstractions, Balogh concluded that the difficulties in using economic models to arrive at answers to macro-economic problems were virtually insuperable.[14]

Politics versus Civics

Both classical political economy and Keynes's revival of political economy were only moderately political. In stark contrast, Marx translated the "political" in political economy as class warfare—a struggle between friends and enemies. He redefined the political as a struggle for power in a more or less veiled civil war and political power as the "organized power of one class for oppressing another." Every class struggle is therefore a political struggle, including the everyday struggle of wage earners for their daily bread. But proletarians can-not successfully take on all their enemies at once. They are driven to unite with their fair-weather friend of the moment—the industrial capitalists—against a common enemy—the big landholders.[15]

"Who are our enemies? Who are our friends?" asked the great Mao. This question is of first importance politically, since "we must pay attention to uniting with our real friends in order to attack our real enemies." Marx could not have said it better. But this conception of the political is not uniquely Marxist. Carl Schmitt, who ran through the entire gamut of Germany's ma-jor political parties in his evolution from a near-Communist to a full-fledged Nazi, understood that "[t]he specifically political distinction . . . is the distinc-tion of *friend* and *enemy*." It is for politics what the distinction between good and evil is for ethics; what the distinction between beautiful and ugly is for aesthetics; and what the distinction between profitable and unprofitable is for economics. The enemy is not just a competitor or debating adversary; the enemy must be fought. If not marginalized or neutralized, the enemy must be annihilated. The political terms par excellence—friend, enemy, struggle— therefore derive their "significance from their relation to the real possibility of physical killing."[16]

Although political behavior culminates in killing, it suffices to challenge an enemy's vital interests for an act to become political. Cutthroat competition and price wars, expropriations and income redistribution through taxation, subsidies, and entitlements of various kinds all qualify as political because they infringe on another group's interests. Just as interparty and class cooperation belong to the realm of civics, so interparty and class antagonisms character- ize the field of politics. The class struggle between labor and capital, between management and labor, between the monied interests and the new class of professional workers is fundamentally political whether or not it escalates into civil war.

Not everything that is called political is, strictly speaking, political. Bipar- tisan politics is a glaring example of this confusion; techniques of conflict res- olution are another, as are all efforts at mediating disputes through some form of compromise. Diplomacy is a civic act even though it involves otherwise hostile powers.

In the United States, the civic society par excellence, politics are apt to be confused with civics. The common interest and the rights and duties of citi- zenship hardly square with the struggle for power, pelf, and privilege among adversaries. Conventional definitions of politics as the art and science of gov- ernment present a false picture of reality by blurring these differences. Unlike civics, a positive-sum game in which everyone is a winner, politics is a zero- sum game of winners and losers. Unlike civics, with its basis in a social con- tract and its focus on consensus, politics harbors the prospect of turning into a negative-sum game in which everybody loses. War is a classic example.

Reasoned discourse plays a minor role in politics. Politically, the credible arguments are anything but civil. They are the logically invalid ones: the *ar- gumentum baculinum* (argument of the cudgel) aimed at intimidating; the *argumentum ad crumenam* (argument to the purse) designed to buy allegiance; the *argumentum ad hominem* (argument to the person) appealing to preju- dice; and the *argumentum ad ignorantiam* (argument to ignorance) relying on deception.

Homo politicus cannot live without both dominators and dominated, vic- timizers and victimized. Domination and victimization take various forms, not the least of which is the privilege of superior wealth and income. The study of politics has for its subject matter class struggles over influence and the influential. Political economy is political in focusing on the winners, "who get the most of what there is to get," and on the losers, who get the least.[17]

Marxist political economy goes to the heart of this question. Marx's *Capital* is a critique of bourgeois political economy for failing to investigate the power relations of production, the corresponding process of exploitation, and the politics of working-class struggle. As Marx noted in volume 3 of *Capital*, it takes for its subject matter the "specific economic form in which unpaid surplus labor is pumped out of the direct producers."[18] Designed to unmask the civic appearance of human relations, Marxist political economy focuses on the historical modes of exploitation in the slave system, the feudal system, and the capitalist system.

Marx was among the first to stress the partisan significance of political economy in opposition to the civic content of economics. The three volumes of his so-called bible of the working class were intended to be *read politically*. It is therefore not surprising that, having completed the first volume, he called attention to, in his own words, "the *great contest* between the blind rule of the supply and demand laws which form the political economy of the [capitalist] middle class, and social production controlled by social foresight, which forms the political economy of the working class." The enactment of a bill instituting the ten-hour workday in 1848 was a great theoretical as well as practical victory, Marx added, because "it was the first time that in broad daylight the political economy of the middle class succumbed to the political economy of the working class."[19]

A Soviet manual presents the field of political economy as eminently political in focusing on class antagonisms arising from the way people earn their living. As a result, "there is not, and cannot be, a single political economy for all classes." Unlike academic economists, who try to present their research as having universal significance, "Marxists do not deny the class character, the partisanship of Marxist-Leninist political economy."[20] This refers to the questions addressed by Marxist political economists and is not meant to suggest that their investigations are less than scientific.

Heads, I Win; Tails, You Lose

Management has replaced capital as the main enemy of organized labor in the United States. This fundamental tenet of post-Marxist political economy is in keeping with labor's redefinition of the enemy as professional workers in supervisory positions rather than absentee proprietors. With the New Deal and the welfare state in reverse gear, labor's honeymoon with management is over. As a North Florida organizer for the National Union of Hospital and Health Care Employees (AFSCME) asserted to the author, "Management is inherently evil! If it keeps on union-busting, it will be dynamite all over again." Or, as his immediate boss, Jack Seddon, vice president of AFSCME and past director of field activities for the Professional Air Traffic Controllers Organization (PATCO), said in another private conversation, "Organized labor has its fair share of fighters. But what it needs is a general, faithful lieutenants, and an army."

With a new main enemy comes a new mode of producing and siphoning off the economic surplus, a mode that overshadows the capitalist mode. Up against the wall of big business, organized labor finds that professional people are calling the tune. The same situation exists in nonprofit corporations, in cooperatives, and in the public sector. We therefore hear a new voice fanning the flames of social discontent. It is the voice of the politically incorrect against political correctness, of the economically downsized, flexibly employed and underemployed, of intellectual misfits, Ph.D.'s in the wrong slots, professors without students, lawyers without clients—potential troublemakers peddling their grievances among working stiffs at the bottom of the wage pyramid. But this voice is lost on members of the academy.

As Marx noted in the preface to the second edition of *Capital*, the French and English bourgeoisie's assumption of political power sounded the death knell of scientific bourgeois political economy. Once the new rulers were above criticism, their ideas became the ruling ideas. As long as the aristocracy had enough clout to dispute the culture of the new business class, multiculturalism in political economy was the norm. But the empowered burghers soon established their own uniculture. As Marx put it, "It was thenceforth no longer a question, whether this theorem or that was true, but whether it was useful to capital or harmful, expedient or inexpedient, politically dangerous or not." In place of disinterested inquiry, the economics profession became rife with ideologues who uncritically assumed that liberal capitalism was the end of history.[21]

Now that the freedom-loving establishment has found a place for *Capital* in the canon, alongside other works by the great economists, Marxists have little to fear that they will not be heard. Although multiculturalism is once more the norm, it is again the turn of academicians to become prizefighters in defense of what is politically correct. As to how *their* unofficial censorship operates in the United States and throughout Western Europe, I offer the following illustration.

In 1987, the Polish philosopher and sociologist Leszek Novak, general editor of the series Poznan Studies in the Philosophy of the Sciences and the Humanities, commissioned me to put together a volume of invited essays to be tentatively entitled *Lordship and Tribute in the Information Society.* I sent out requests to a professional team working on the critical sociology of intellectuals, a research project sponsored by the International Sociological Association and its Committee on the Sociology of Science. I also contacted several internationally prominent political economists who I thought might be interested. As encouragement, I noted that the book was under contract and would be published in Amsterdam by Rodopi. The deadline was December 1988. The circular letter to potential contributors did not elicit the response I anticipated. A handful expressed an interest in lordship, but not a single soul could be persuaded to tackle the bottom-line matter of tribute. The projected volume consequently never materialized.

What had gone wrong? Such a big harvest, and so few intellectual workers. It was evident in the letters I received that my respondents resisted being classified with the beneficiaries of the economic surplus pumped out of the innocent and unsuspecting. Intellectuals showed compassion for the working stiff when it was in their economic interest to do so, but they now shared the driver's seat and had turned their backs on their former allies in the labor movement. A critical sociology of intellectuals had their support only if it steered clear of the thorny issue of their relationship with the underlying population. I was told that the labor question was being solved and that a more pressing problem—the hitherto unexplored and subtle forms of domination through intimidation—had taken its place. A flicker of the eyelids, the language of the body, the tone of voice, the choice of words—such were the matters I should have emphasized for the project to succeed.

In retrospect, they were right. What I proposed had to wait for the present study, a volume on post-Marxist political economy that went beyond their fields of competence. Upon rereading the circular letter after the plans for the volume had been trashed, I was struck by its adversarial tone. What follows is a glimpse of its contents:

> Among the deficiencies of Marx's analytical framework is its inability to answer the question: Who gets what, when, how? . . . Marx's framework focuses on capitalist accumulation and does not enable us to calculate the mass and rate of accumulation from other sources. By lumping together employee compensation for both manual and intellectual work, his framework indirectly provides an apology for noncapitalist exploitation in capitalist as well as postcapitalist societies. And it does so in *Capital*, where Marx assumes a constant rate of surplus value that makes any wages above the average appear as payment for increased productivity, as labor of a higher or more complicated kind that "creates in equal times proportionately higher values than unskilled labor." [Academicians claim they deserve not less but more pay, precisely because their work is of a higher kind.]

Hitherto, theoretical discussions of the rise of a meritocracy and the role of intellectual workers in the scientific-technical, managerial, information, or knowledge society have skirted this issue . . . without coming to grips with methods of calculating the noncapitalist surplus and with social science theories and ideologies relied on by intellectual workers to maximize their relative shares. [Some found this statement insulting.]

Intelligence is especially lacking on the extent to which the price of intellectual skills and services exceeds their cost of production. Ignorance prevails concerning the mass of surplus wages and salaries in a given private business, corporation, university, government, or national entity compared to entrepreneurial profits, dividends, interest, and rent from capital investments. University intellectuals are in a privileged position to report on how these mechanisms operate in their professions, but we have yet to hear from them on these sensitive issues. [On this score, I was told that I had targeted the wrong enemy.]

The concept of a "knowledge society" is sometimes used as an analytical category for Marx and Engels' "invading socialist society." Some use it to designate . . . the emergence of new social relations of production and domination involving supervisors and supervised instead of capitalists and wage-laborers. But whatever basic vocabulary is adopted, intellectual workers have their own mechanisms for pumping out and appropriating an economic surplus from the underlying population. [What self-respecting professional could agree with that?]

As an elite within the intellectual elite, the liberal arts-and-sciences intelligentsia has an inflated view not of its contribution to society, but of what society owes in return. Academicians regard as an absurdity and as a vulgar slur any insinuation that they might be getting something for nothing. But if it can be shown that intellectuals too share in the noncapitalist surplus . . . the question then becomes how and how much. [How ungrateful of me, after the sheltered life and leisure provided by academia, to snipe away at the university establishment!]

Such was the basic question toward the construction of a political economy and sociology of intellectual workers that I posed. My correspondents' speech-related strategies of lordship I took to be of secondary importance. Since I was concerning myself with a "dead issue," the intellectuals to whom I appealed turned a deaf ear. But post-Marxist political theory was a live dog; it was Marxist political economy that had grown senile.

When feudalism was dissolving, its enemies foresaw the advent of a new era ruled by the people, or Third Estate. The people turned out to be the bourgeoisie, the class of modern capitalists. Later, with the death agony of capitalism approaching, its enemies predicted the victory of the "working class." The outcome was another trick played on the unsuspecting when professionals took over the so-called Fourth Estate.

The class struggle between professional workers and ordinary workers is not simply a zero-sum game of "Winners take all, and the Devil take the hindmost." It is a game in which luck figures not at all. For professional workers, the outcome is predictable: "Heads, I win; tails, you lose."

2

the political economy of expertise

> If capital is embodied labor, one can talk of a labor theory of value. But a postindustrial society is characterized not by a labor theory but by a knowledge theory of value.
> —Daniel Bell, foreword to the 1976 edition of *The Coming of Post-Industrial Society* (1973)

> We are far enough advanced into the new post-capitalist society to [realize that] . . . the real, controlling resource and the absolutely decisive "factor of production" is now neither capital nor land nor labor. It is knowledge.
> —Peter Drucker, *Post-Capitalist Society* (1993)

With the advent of the Information Age, the study of expertise became an accepted part of the academic curriculum, whether as the theory of human capital, as the economics of education, or as a part of management theory. It testified to the ascendancy of professionals, to their economic and political preeminence in the postindustrial order. Since this leading class consists of experts, contemporary political economy is the political economy of expertise.

It may therefore come as a surprise that Marx's vaunted bible of the working class launched the first veiled political economy of expertise. Its subtitle, *A Critique of Political Economy,* underscores only its negative task of unmasking capitalist exploitation. Its positive task consists of explaining how ordinary labor and expertise are the source of all economic values. In Marx's ambiguous usage, *labor* covers all kinds of work—mental as well as manual.

What is expertise? In the spirit of Marx's magnum opus and his definition of capital, expertise is not simply professional skill. It is the power of education to command a surplus in excess of the average wage. To use Marx's idiom, expertise is a form of "self-expanding value" at the expense of working stiffs. Just as capital is not reducible to money, so expertise is something more than a professional education.

This is neither Marx's meaning nor the usual meaning of *expertise*. The Oxford English Dictionary defines it as advanced knowledge, training, or experience dealing exclusively with a particular subject or practice. Tied to a gainful occupation or career, this specialty becomes a profession. There is no indication that professionals pocket a surplus in excess of the cost of exercising special skills, much less that they get something for nothing. Unlike our definition of *expertise*, the conventional meaning sacrifices truth for respectability.

Corresponding to these two different meanings of *expertise*, there are two opposed political economies of expertise: one, a champion of professionals and professionalism; the other, a critique. The first version gained currency as a theory of the death of capitalism in the works of Karl Marx and Joseph Schumpeter and as a theory of the struggle for succession in the mainstream scenarios of Silvio Gesell and Thorstein Veblen. It came of age beginning with Adolf A. Berle Jr. and Gardiner Means's theory of the subordination of capital to management in the modern corporation and then as the theory of intellectual capital in the works of Johannes Alasco, Theodore Schultz, and Lester Thurow. The second version dates from the writings of Waclaw Machajski at the turn of the century, but it remained virtually unknown until revived by Max Nomad during the Great Depression. Within the ivy-covered halls of academe, Alvin Gouldner has been almost alone in recognizing the exploitative role of experts and expertise.

Through the filter of this ambivalent legacy, the following brief survey of the origin, growth, and maturation of the political economy of expertise helps explain the diminishing role of capitalists and the expanding role of professionals as decision makers in America's new economic order.

The Death of Capitalism

Talk of the death of capitalism presupposes an agreement concerning what is understood by capitalism. The single most influential definition is still that of Marx in volume 1 of *Capital:* "Capitalist production is not merely the production of commodities, it is essentially the production of surplus-value," that is, production for profit. To this, Marx added that under capitalism, the only laborer who is productive is the one who produces surplus value for the capitalist. What kind of laborer? The factory manager and engineer, not just the blue-collar worker. What kind of capitalist? Not the banker or the merchant but the industrial capitalist—the producer of commodities by means of wage labor—"the owner of the means of production and subsistence [who] meets in the market with the free laborer selling his labor-power."[1]

There are three kinds of capitalists for Marx: the owners of, respectively, industrial, commercial, and rentier capital. First place goes to the owners of industrial capital as managers of the process of production, the production of surplus value. In second place are the commercial capitalists who manage the exchange of commodities and the conversion of surplus value into profits shared with the industrial capitalists. Third place is reserved for the owners of rentier capital, so-called functionless capitalists absent from the process of production and exchange. By virtue of loaning money or land to functioning capitalists, they, too, share in the profits in the form of dividends, interest, and rent. But he insisted, "Industrial capital is the only mode of existence of capital in which not only the appropriation of surplus value . . . but simultaneously its creation is a function of capital."[2] Under the capitalist system, the other forms of capital are derivative.

The industrial capitalist is both the legal owner of the factory and the general manager in charge. Marx's definition of capitalism rules out, if not the early joint-stock company, at least its sequel—the modern corporation. Entrepreneurial functions may, of course, be delegated. But unless functionaries without capital are subordinated to a functioning capitalist, there is a loss of capitalist control; the modern corporation therefore fails to qualify as fully capitalist. "This is the abolition of the capitalist mode of production within the capitalist mode of production," Marx maintained. Consequently, joint-stock companies "should be viewed as transitional forms from the capitalist mode of production to the associated one."[3]

As Ralf Dahrendorf noted, transitional "joint-stock companies differ from capitalist enterprises in the structure of their leading positions." Originally combined in the position of the capitalist, the "roles of owner and manager . . . have been separated and distributed over two positions, those of stockholder and executive." For the purpose of analysis, one must "insist on the union of private ownership and factual control of the instruments of production as the distinguishing feature of a capitalist form of society"—that is, of capitalism in its pure state.[4]

Although a capitalist is anyone who lives off capital, for capitalism to exist the control of production must be in the hands of capitalists. That means they must be either owner-managers or stockholders with a controlling interest in the business and therefore in a position actively to determine policy. Otherwise, we have capitalist appropriation without capitalist production—a mixed economy rather than an exclusively capitalist one.

A mature capitalist system is neither nascent nor moribund. Nascent capitalism is an economic system in which commodity production is managed by capitalists, but the lion's share of appropriation takes the form of feudal and quasi-feudal dues or rents. Moribund capitalism is one in which commodity production has passed into the hands of professional employees, but capitalist appropriation still prevails. In sharp contrast to these half-emergent and half-alive capitalisms, mature capitalism is defined by both capitalist production and appropriation.

Unlike the clear-cut division between owners and employees, the delegation of managerial functions in the modern corporation obliterates almost to invisibility the dividing line between positions of domination and subjection. The professional staffs of engineers, chemists, physicists, lawyers, psychologists, and others, whose services have become an indispensable part of the corporation, are neither superordinates nor subordinates. They perform an auxiliary role as, in Dahrendorf's words, a "marginal part of the ruling class of the enterprise." Then, there is the far more numerous group of semiprofessional employees, few of whose positions are positions of subjection in the sense in which those of ordinary blue- and white-collar workers are. As bureaucrats with delegated responsibilities, they, too, "are members of the ruling class of industry and share its latent interests." Since this new class of professionals and semiprofessionals makes society markedly different from what it was in Marx's time, the resulting metamorphosis of capitalism can best be described as a social revolution.[5]

This is not how latest-stage capitalism was defined by Lenin and his epigones. In *Imperialism: The Highest Stage of Capitalism* (1917), Lenin depicted the system of modern corporations as a special stage of capitalism in which the separation of management from ownership is carried to the extreme—but under the rule of rentiers. It is "capitalism at that stage of development at which the dominance of monopolies and finance capital is established." Its characteristic feature is the merger of bank capital with industrial capital. It is monopoly capitalism without the entrepreneur but without the abolition of the capitalist system.[6] Lenin called it moribund capitalism—but it was not moribund as long as capitalists were in control.

That there is a fundamental difference between the Marxist and the Marxist-Leninist depictions of capitalism is evident from the Soviet *Manual of Political Economy*, originally published in 1959. Following Stalin's death in 1953, latest-stage capitalism was no longer defined as monopoly capitalism but as state monopoly capitalism, "the interlocking of private monopolies and the state." Under this system, the corporations make use of the state to strengthen their economic domination through the direct exercise of political power. Meanwhile, more and more enterprises are nationalized or come under state control. But nationalization is not socialization; it is not even "a step toward socialism." At least Marx's definition cannot be so stretched.[7]

Having defined capitalism as the domination of industrial capital, Marx turned to the main purpose of his magnum opus: "It is the ultimate aim of this work to lay bare the economic law of motion of modern society . . . viewed as a process of natural history." As Engels commented on the significance of this task, Marx's law of capitalist development leads to the conclusion that capitalism is doomed.[8]

What is this law of motion? What are its basic premises? Marx's law states that the increasing accumulation of capital corresponds to an increase of the inactive as well as the active army of labor. That means escalating permanent unemployment of a "surplus population, whose misery is in inverse ratio to its torment of labor." That capitalists end up feeding instead of being fed by this inactive army of labor testifies to their incompetence. "And here it becomes evident, that the bourgeoisie is unfit any longer to be the ruling class," Marx declared.[9]

Two fundamental premises undergird this conclusion. First, Marx contended, "[p]roduction of surplus-value is the absolute law of this mode of production . . . the rate of accumulation is the independent, not the dependent, variable." This means that capitalist accumulation excludes every rise in the price of labor that could seriously imperil capitalist exploitation. Second, "[r]elative diminution of the variable part of capital [occurs] simultaneously with the progress of accumulation and of the concentration that accompanies it." Such is the law of the progressive increase of constant capital, in proportion to the variable. The predictable result is that as labor becomes increasingly productive, there is a corresponding decrease in the demand for it.[10]

Marx divided capital into constant and variable. Constant capital consists of plant and equipment whose value is transferred piecemeal to their products without adding any new value. Variable capital consists of wage earners who add more value to the subject of their work than what they recover in wages. They alone are the source of self-expanding value whose monetary equivalent is profit. As Marx used the term, *exploitation* applies only to variable capital or to the process of pumping out surplus value.

In the third volume of *Capital*, Marx focused on the general law of motion that covers not just capitalist production but the process of capitalist production and circulation as a whole: the law of the falling rate of profit. The conditions of direct exploitation and those of profiting from it are not the same. The first act is to squeeze laborers for all they are worth; the second is to sell what they produce. "If this is not done, or done only in part, or only at prices below the prices of production, the laborer has indeed been exploited, but his exploitation is not realized as such for the capitalist." The first act is limited only by the productive powers of labor; the second is limited by the effective demand for labor's products that is restricted within more or less narrow limits.

Because of the unremitting tendency to accumulate, the market must be continually extended. "But the more productiveness develops," Marx observed, "the more it finds itself at variance with the narrow basis on which the conditions of consumption rest." We then have, simultaneously, an excess of capital and an excess population.[11]

Surplus capital means capital that cannot be profitably invested. Because it is a law of capitalist production that accumulation leads to a relative decrease of variable in relation to constant capital, according to Marx, the gradual growth of constant capital in relation to variable capital "must necessarily lead to *a gradual fall of the general rate of profit,* so long as the rate of surplus value, or the intensity of exploitation of labor by capital, remains the same."[12]

The rate of profit should not be confused with the rate of surplus value. The former is the ratio of surplus value to the sum of both variable and constant capital in circulation; the latter is the ratio of surplus value to variable capital exclusively. Since the rate of surplus value, or rate of exploitation, always exceeds the rate of profit, the rate of profit is only a partial index of the capitalist rip-off.

The overall result is that capitalists, as well as workers, become superfluous because their capital cannot find profitable outlets. To compensate for the falling rate of profit, capital must be invested in still more massive quantities, which, in Marx's words, "requires its centralization, i.e., the swallowing up of the small capitalists by the big." What is the end result? According to Marx, "This process would soon bring about the collapse of capitalist production if it were not for counteracting tendencies, which have a continuous decentralizing effect alongside the centripetal one."[13]

The most important factors countering the tendency of the rate of profit to fall are those tending to raise the rate of surplus value and the proportion of variable to constant capital. As enumerated by Marx, they include the increasing intensity of exploitation per working hour, the depression of wages below the value of labor power, the cheapening of the elements of constant capital through technological improvements and economies of scale, the opening of new lines of business that start out predominantly with living labor, the exchange of less labor for more through favorable terms of trade, and the higher rate of return on capital invested in countries where labor is comparatively cheap and capital is scarce.

These countertendencies, however, are insufficient to prevent the cyclical crises that by their periodical return threaten the existence of bourgeois society, Marx contended. Overproduction in the mad pursuit of profit generates its opposite. Bourgeois society then relapses into a state of momentary backwardness, as if a famine, a great flood, or a war of devastation had destroyed all means of subsistence. Industry comes to a halt. There is a slaughtering of values because "commodities on the market can complete their process of circulation and reproduction only through an immense contraction of their prices, hence through a depreciation of the capital which they represent." The general fall in prices paralyzes both production and the function of money as a means of payment. From too much production, there is too little—unemployed machinery at one pole and unemployed workers at the other. Since production is for the sake of profit, "a rift must continually emerge between the limited dimensions of consumption under capitalism and a production which forever tends to exceed this immanent barrier."[14] Herein lies the celebrated Marxist contradiction between the profit structure and the technical basis of capitalist production.

The rate rather than the mass of profit is the motive power of capitalist production, Marx asserted, so that "as soon as formation of capital were to fall into the hands of a few established big capitals, for which the mass of profit compensates for the falling rate of profit, the vital flame of production would be altogether extinguished." The entrepreneurial function tends to disappear as a result of the competition by which big capitalists outperform and underprice little ones. Stagnation is the ultimate result: "The *real barrier* of capitalist production is *capital itself.*"[15] The driving force of industrial progress both endangers and is endangered by the profit motive until one or the other has to give way.

A social revolution is therefore inevitable: first, because of the general law of capitalist accumulation that provokes rebellion in response to increasing exploitation and massive unemployment; second, because of the tendency of the rate of profit to fall, the proximate outcome of which is periodic depression and the final outcome of which is permanent stagnation. Marx summed up the final act of expropriating the capitalists: "Along with the constantly diminishing number of the magnates of capital . . . grows the mass of misery, oppression, slavery, degradation, exploitation; but with this too grows the revolt of the working class, a class always increasing in numbers, and disciplined, united, organized by the very process of . . . capitalist production." What the bourgeoisie produces, therefore, "are its own grave-diggers."[16]

Multisystem Failure or Metamorphosis?

Marx assumed that all capitalisms were equal and that they would all die of the same ailment. But an autopsy reveals that, as in the case of human beings who die from cancer, strokes, and complications of various kinds, capitalisms perish from a variety of single as well as multiple causes. Marx said that in giving birth to the proletariat, capitalism creates its own grave-diggers; instead, he might have said that it perishes from its erstwhile partners and dependent elites. While it is common knowledge that capitalism was robbed and finally killed in the Soviet Union and throughout Eastern Europe, it remains to be shown that it was robbed and killed by its partners in the United States. On each side of the Atlantic, neither Marx's general law nor a falling rate of profit, neither technical failure nor systemic breakdown, neither working-class immiserization nor revolt accounts for the eclipse of capitalism.

Marx's critique showed where capitalism was vulnerable. By itself, that was a major contribution. It was also a consequential one, since it provided the professional elites with an excuse for swindling, robbing, and killing their victim. However, it failed to highlight the leading causes of capitalism's eventual death. In the East, the cause of death was a major stroke by the professional elites—diagnosed as "galloping socialism"—before capitalism had a chance to develop and exhaust its potential for growth. In the West, capitalism died of gigantism, an abnormal growth leading to a structural metamorphosis and the delegation of entrepreneurial functions to the owners of expertise—diagnosed as "creeping socialism."

That capitalism was doomed owing to causes other than Marx's laws of motion or their contemporary equivalents—Keynes's theory of vanishing investment opportunity and mounting unemployment—was spelled out by Joseph Schumpeter, Keynes's principal rival for the starring role of premier political economist of the twentieth century. Unlike Marx, who focused on the economic and political factors basic to capitalism's self-destruction, Schumpeter focused on the "cultural complement of the capitalist economy," on its "socio-psychological *superstructure.*" Schumpeter believed that judgments about capitalist performance are irrelevant to the question of whether capitalism can survive, "[f]or mankind is not free to choose." Since most economic systems have disappeared before they had time to develop to their full potential, he discounted capitalism's singular success as evidence that the capitalist intermezzo was likely to be prolonged. Instead, its very success spells not continued life but death.[17]

First, it would die from the obsolescence of the entrepreneurial function. Since the methods of production have succeeded in satisfying so many wants of so many people, one may assume that they have reached a state of perfection that requires a minimum of further improvement. As Schumpeter put it, "There would be nothing [or very little] left for entrepreneurs to do"; they serve a social function "that is already losing importance and is bound to lose it at an accelerating rate in the future." Meanwhile, the adventure and romance of entrepreneurship has given way to technological innovation not by risk capital but by "teams of trained specialists who turn out what is required and make it work in predictable ways."[18]

Second, it would die from the destruction of the precapitalist framework that initially nourished capitalism, a capitalism that broke both the barriers to its progress and the flying buttresses that prevented its collapse. Besides removing institutional deadwood and the fetters on production imposed by feudal society, it also undermined its protecting strata. Protection was afforded by the postfeudal aristocracy that, in Schumpeter's words, "filled the offices of state, officered the army, devised policies . . . as a *classe dirigent.*" Besides taking account of bourgeois economic interests, the aristocratic element made itself the principal representative of the bourgeoisie politically. Although demoted to second place economically, it "continued to rule the roost *right to the end of the period of intact and vital capitalism.*"[19]

Third, it would die from the destruction of the institutional framework of capitalist society. Capitalism not only rooted out the lower strata of feudal society but also pulled the competitive rug out from under its own lower strata. The political structure of capitalism is profoundly altered by "the elimination of a host of small and medium-size firms, the owner-managers of which . . . count quantitatively at the polls and have a hold on what we may term the foreman class that no management of a large unit can ever have," Schumpeter asserted. As a result, the institutional support of bourgeois private property "wears away in a nation in which its most vital, most concrete, most meaningful types disappear from the moral horizon."[20]

Private property and free contracting—the institutional foundations of capitalism—have come to occupy a subordinate place in the world of big corporations dominated by salaried executives, managers, and submanagers. As for big and small stockholders, they barely resemble the capitalists of yore. "The capitalist process, by substituting a mere parcel of shares for the walls of and the machines in a factory, takes the life out of the idea of property," Schumpeter pointed out. Private economic activity withers away when one can no longer do as one pleases with one's own. Lacking this right, the bourgeois "loses the will to fight, economically, physically, politically, for his factory and his control over it, to die if necessary on its steps." As Schumpeter concluded in his discussion of this process of dissolution of the material substance of property, "Eventually there will be *nobody* left who really cares to stand for it— nobody within and nobody without the precincts of the big concerns."[21]

The predictable outcome of capitalism's crumbling walls is an "atmosphere of almost universal hostility to its own sacred order," according to Schumpeter. Those in the bourgeoisie discover to their amazement that their rational and critical frame of mind turns against them, "that the rationalist attitude does not stop at the credentials of kings and popes but goes on to attack private property and the whole scheme of bourgeois values." The bourgeois citadel thus becomes politically defenseless. Without extracapitalist props and extra-rational loyalties, it collapses from its own weight.[22] When poverty abounded and the instinct of private property flourished, the hostile elements in capitalist society could be subdued. But increasing affluence and leisure breed social unrest until hostility toward private ownership threatens its survival.

For hostility to produce a revolutionary situation, Schumpeter maintained, "it is necessary that there be groups in whose interest it is to work up and organize resentment, to nurse it, to voice it, and to lead it." The masses, the middle and lower strata of Marx's proletariat, can only follow or refuse to follow; they cannot lead a movement for overthrow. Their leaders, tantamount to a new social class, consist predominantly of intellectuals, defined by Schumpeter as those who wield the power of the spoken and the written word. Who are they? Mostly professionals. For "the members of *all* professions have the opportunity of becoming intellectuals; and many intellectuals take to some profession for a living."[23]

Intellectuals are the enemy within. The irony is that capitalism, as Marx was the first to perceive, produces its own executioners. Schumpeter added that unlike all other societies, "capitalism inevitably and by virtue of the very logic of its civilization creates, educates, and subsidizes a vested interest in social unrest." By presenting intellectuals with the printing press, and subsequently radio and television, capitalism transformed the intellectuals of the medieval period—mostly monks whose written performance was barely accessible outside the clergy—into the intellectuals of the modern world. Then, when their numbers exploded and their influence was felt everywhere, the bourgeoisie and its aristocratic partners proved incapable of bringing the new intellectuals to heel.[24]

The vigorous expansion of educational institutions in the later development of capitalism made capitalism's survival even more precarious. The supply of professionals beyond the demand gave rise to not only their unemployment but also their employment in substandard work at substandard wages and their outright unemployability in manual occupations for which they were psychologically unfit. Since their discontent bred resentment, it is not surprising that intellectuals made common cause with the budding labor movement. As Schumpeter put it, "Labor never craved intellectual leadership, but intellectuals invaded labor politics." They verbalized the movement and supplied a theory and strategy for class war that made workers aware of exploitation and prepared them for combating it.[25]

Capitalism is doomed not only because of the external enemies in its midst but also because of the psychological enemy within—the loss of will power, the failure of bourgeois motivation. Bourgeois morale is undermined by the success of capitalism. According to Schumpeter, the modern corporation, capitalism's final expression, "socializes the bourgeois mind; it relentlessly narrows the scope of capitalist motivation." Second, the resulting "Evaporation of Industrial Property" leads inexorably to the "Evaporation of Consumers' Property." The amenities of the bourgeois home are ceding ground to its burdens, while the objects of personal consumption turned out by the conveyor belt have reduced the cost of a bourgeois lifestyle such that the passion to accumulate is muffled and the "desirability of incomes beyond a certain level is reduced." Third, as soon as there is no longer a felt reason to save primarily for the family, we have a new kind of *homo oeconomicus* lacking the "capitalist ethics that enjoins working for the future irrespective of whether or not one is going to harvest the crop oneself." With the decline of the bourgeois family, the businessperson's time horizon shrinks and drifts into an antisaving frame of mind, until "the bourgeois order no longer makes any sense to the bourgeoisie itself."[26] The motive forces of capitalism thus die a natural as well as an artificial death.

To be sure, Schumpeter overstated his case. World War I and the Great Depression testify to the failures of late capitalism rather than to its successes. As we shall see, capitalism perished from causes barely considered by either Marx or Schumpeter. The separation of ownership from management in the modern corporation was a far weightier cause of capitalism's decline than either Marx's general laws of motion or Schumpeter's crumbling support structures. The scientific-technological revolution on the heels of World War II not only gave expertise an edge over capital but also propelled its owners into the driver's seat. As a result, professional workers in nonmanagerial roles have come to share decision-making powers with management.

The Struggle over Succession

In *Capital,* there is no struggle over succession. A homogeneous working class is destined to inherit the earth in the form of a classless society in which pay differentials have nothing to do with exploitation.[27] Marx's theoretical apparatus is unequipped to explain the appearance of a new exploiting class and the resulting class struggles under socialism. Most Marxists believe that socialist societies are classless. If classes and class antagonisms can be shown to persist under so-called actually existing socialism, then what is called socialism must really represent, according to their lights, not socialism but a new stage of capitalism.

Marxism's dilemma follows from Marx's premise that there are only "three big classes of modern society based on the capitalist mode of production"—landowners, wage laborers, and capitalists corresponding to the owners of the classical factors of production—land, labor, and capital.[28] Abolish private property in land and capital, and only wage laborers remain, but no longer as proletarians since there are no longer capitalists to exploit them.

To a critical observer, exploitation was not abolished in the Soviet Union or under any other form of actually existing socialism. Only private owners of the means of production were eliminated, that is, landowners and capitalists. If capitalism survived, it did so in the form of state rather than private ownership—state capitalism under the management of state bureaucrats—the state having become the collective exploiter and the bureaucrats its main beneficiaries. But capitalism *without* capitalists? That pill is too large for some critics to swallow.

The most credible escape from the horns of this Marxist dilemma is to posit a fourth great class, whose members are the owners of a fourth factor of production—expertise. We then have a class of experts as the private owners of specialized administrative, managerial, scientific, and technical skills in all walks of life—and a postcapitalist society.

Marx regarded expertise as compound labor, as multiplied simple labor, a derivative of simple labor rather than an independent variable in production.[29] His failure to distinguish a fourth great class predicated on the private ownership of expertise constitutes the single biggest stumbling block in Marxist political economy. For an understanding of class antagonisms in postcapitalist society, Marx's model had to be recast.

Several of his socialist precursors had already charted the way. "Gracchus" Babeuf, whose "Manifesto of the Plebeians" antedated Marx's *Communist Manifesto* by a full half-century, made a special point of underscoring the antagonism between brawn and brains, the labor of the body as opposed to that of the "small part of it that ruminates." Auguste Blanqui, who acquired more notoriety than Marx as the brains behind most of the communist conspiracies of the nineteenth century, defined wealth as the offspring of both intelligence, which he called the "soul" of humanity, and work, which he referred to as the "life" of humanity. Pierre-Joseph Proudhon, one of the founders of the cooperative movement, denounced property—including the privileged salaries of the owners of education—as theft.[30]

Like Marx, his precursors were professionals in one capacity or another; unlike Marx, they spoke with the voice of labor. On the one hand, they pinpointed the separation of brainpower from labor power and the subordination of the latter to the former. On the other hand, they were egalitarians, determined to level the privileges of the private owners of expertise. Marx turned this legacy on its head, making common cause with Saint-Simon and the Saint-Simonians in favor of a meritocracy that would ameliorate the condition of the poor.

Capital targets exploitation by capitalists and landowners only. All wage earners are assumed to share a common interest. Their cooperation through the division of labor results in what he calls a new power, that of the collective laborer, an additional source of profit for the capitalist, who pays for the value of a hundred independent labor powers but "does not pay for the combined labor-power of the hundred." All wage earners are therefore exploited collectively as well as individually. Although salaried managers, superintendents, and foremen do the capitalists' work for them, they are not the beneficiaries.[31]

Ironically, the failure of *Capital* to identify the owners of expertise as a fourth great class proved to be a practical asset, not just an intellectual liability. The professional class needed labor's support in its struggle to become the successor to the capitalists, and the best way of obtaining that support was to downplay the divergent interests of brains and brawn. Experts had a practical interest in deceiving both themselves and labor. Intellectual obfuscation contributed to practical clarification of the basic antagonism between bourgeois and proletarians.

Nonetheless, that Marx failed to envision a struggle over succession is a major defect in Marxist theory, one that his critics strove to overcome. Thorstein Veblen (1857–1929), Silvio Gesell (1862–1930), and Waclaw Machajski (1866–1926), born less than a decade apart and dying within half that many years of each other, were among the first of Marx's critics to investigate labor's principal rival, who from an ally in the struggle against the bourgeoisie metamorphosed into labor's enemy in the new economic order that replaced capitalism. Their major works appeared only two years apart: Veblen's *Theory of Business Enterprise* (1904), Machajski's *Intellectual Worker* (1905), and Gesell's *Natural Economic Order* (1906). Although they conceived of the struggle for succession differently, there is something to be said in favor of each.

The most farsighted and penetrating investigation of expertise was unquestionably that of Machajski. Although its foundations were laid by Michael Bakunin (1814–76), Marx's principal rival for control of the budding labor movement, the edifice was Machajski's own. Bakunin had pinpointed education as a fourth factor of production and its private ownership as the basis of a fourth great class—the class of scientists, engineers, and managers of the industrial system. As Bakunin envisioned it, the struggle for succession was between a Fourth Estate of professionals and a Fifth Estate of laboring people—the exploited underclass of peasants as well as wage earners. If the Marxists had their way, he argued, the outcome would be a republic of experts rather than equals.[32]

Machajski's contribution was to show that this fourth great class was destined to prevail in the immediate future, whatever the final outcome might be. Laboring people would therefore have to organize themselves independently of intellectual workers to defend their interests. Education, he argued, was a form of human capital, so that bourgeois civilization might be expected to outlast the death of capitalism: "Nineteenth-century socialism . . . destroys only *capitalist* exploitation . . . [it] by no means signifies the expropriation of the entire bourgeois society." The owners of human capital or expertise are bourgeois, not capitalists. The fleecing of human livestock survives expropriation of the capitalists because of the "high salaries paid to the intellectual workers."[33] A bourgeois society without capitalists would be the immediate outcome of the succession struggle, whether called state capitalism or state socialism.

The main defect of Machajski's scenario is the role he assigned to the state as the national exploiter, once the capitalists were expropriated. It would be through the state and only through the state that a redistribution of the national surplus would be made to the benefit of the professional class. Yet members of this class were already partial beneficiaries of this surplus under capitalism *without* state intervention. Why, then, did the state have to play the leading role after expropriating the capitalists? Except for the boondocks of modern civilization, Machajski's scenario has turned out to be mistaken, for the operation of the market mechanism suffices in raising salaries by redistributing the surplus formerly pocketed by people of property.

This recognition was one of Gesell's major contributions. In his scenario of the death of capitalism, only land would be nationalized. Capitalists living off interest and dividends would be expropriated by other, more subtle means. Interest and dividends are the prices charged for loan capital made possible through the scarcity of money—like scarce but unimproved land that cannot rot during the owner's lifetime. This gives money an unfair advantage in exchange for other commodities that *do* rot. Gesell therefore believed that money should be taxed at its source. Tax it at a rate equal to the average rate of depreciation of *other* commodities.

The taxation of money would suffice for what Keynes, under Gesell's influence, called the euthanasia of the rentier. Gesell envisioned the issue of new currencies that would retain their original value only when stamped with a weekly tax based on an officially determined rate of depreciation. He called it free money, money that rots like other commodities and therefore clears the way for interest-free loans—the counterpart of free land leased by the state for rents ultimately returned to the producers in the form of a wage fund.[34]

Just as the landed aristocracy is defined by the ownership of land, the capitalist is defined by the ownership of money. Both types exemplify Gesell's portrayal of the rentier. In contrast, workers are those living on the proceeds of their labor. Employers in the role of owner-managers are workers. What are called "profits, after deduction of the capital, interest, or rent usually contained in them, are . . . to be classed as yield of labor." Net profit derives not from ownership but from expertise. It is not a return for capital. The owner-manager does not buy labor power: "What he buys and sells is the product of labor."[35] The owner-manager is not an exploiter.

"The abolition of unearned income, of so-called surplus-value, also termed interest and rent," wrote Gesell, "is the immediate economic aim of any socialistic movement." However, the right to the collective proceeds of labor does not mean that socialists should trouble themselves about the high or low wages of individual workers. It suffices that "[n]o proceeds of labor must be surrendered to the capitalist as interest or rent."[36]

On the surface, there is no struggle for succession in Gesell's scenario. On this score, his theory resembles Marx's. But just as Marx envisaged the educated worker as the main beneficiary of the death of capitalism, Gesell envisaged a similar outcome. The spoils would be shared mainly by workers who perform the most highly qualified work because they are the "most securely withdrawn from the competition of the masses, and are therefore able to obtain the highest price for the product of their labor." Competition would decide who reaps the uppermost. "Industrious, capable, and efficient workers will, therefore, always secure larger proceeds of labor, proportionate to their higher efficiency," Gesell declared.[37] Note how this differs from Marx's scenario: the most capable workers include the most efficient owner-managers—*exploiters,* if Marx is right.

Like Marx's stumbling block, Gesell's mistake turned out to be a political asset. Through the intermediary of his main disciple, Gottfried Feder, it would be embodied in the 1920 program of German National Socialism. In effect, it contributed to eating the capitalist cake and having it too. As Keynes summed up Gesell's "third position" between capitalism and socialism, it aimed to establish "an anti-Marxian socialism, a reaction against *laissez-faire* built on theoretical foundations totally unlike those of Marx in being based on . . . an unfettering of competition instead of its abolition." To this description, he added his own belief borne out in practice: "the future will learn more from the spirit of Gesell than from that of Marx."[38]

Keynes was right—up to a point. Expert professionals and professional managers would replace the rentiers in the economically developed countries of the West. Only in the so-called Third World would the more extreme Marxist scenario prevail—although there, too, expertise would become the foundation of a new ruling class. Two roads would lead to socialism under two quite different conditions: extreme socialism for peoples suffering from extreme poverty and backwardness; and moderate socialism with survivals of capitalism for those living in the advanced metropolises.

Veblen's contribution to the successor problem was of a different kind. In the effort to cancel the traditional rights of ownership, he foresaw a struggle that pits scientifically trained professionals in industry against their fellow professionals who serve mainly pecuniary interests. On the one hand, he associated the expertise required of modern industry with the discipline of the machine and compared its bearers with "those industrial classes who are required to comprehend and guide the process, rather than . . . those who serve merely as mechanical auxiliaries of the machine process." On the other hand, there is a rival class of professionals, the "class of men [who] have taken over the work of purchase and sale and of husbanding a store of accumulated values." They, too, consist of salaried experts, except that their expertise is directed to making profit instead of manufacturing commodities. Consequently, they represent the past rather than the future of industrial society.[39]

These professional classes have less in common than their shared higher education would suggest, according to Veblen. There is an appreciable and widening difference between their modes of thought. For the pecuniary occupations, the ultimate court of appeal is "the natural-rights ground of property." In sharp contrast, "the classes engaged in the machine industry are habitually occupied with matters of causal sequence . . . which afford no guidance in questions of institutional right and wrong, or of conventional reason and consequence," Veblen wrote. Arguments in terms of material cause and effect therefore "cannot be met with arguments from conventional precedent or dialectically sufficient reason, and conversely."[40]

In Veblen's later formulation of this conflict of interests, these rival professional elites are designated respectively as the guardians of the vested interests and the general staff of industry. The first are the "lieutenants of the absentee owners." The second consist of "industrial experts," "skilled technologists," and "production engineers."[41]

These rival elites are defined by the ownership of two modes of expertise absent from the conventional trinity of land, labor, and capital. On the one hand, we have the pecuniary expertise of the "financial manager"; on the other, we have the technical "joint stock of knowledge derived from past experience."[42] Veblen makes them the basis of his two professional classes: the first paid salaries out of the profits of enterprise or the industry of others; the second out of the products of their own industry.

Veblen believed that no effective move aimed at the takeover of the modern corporation and the dispossession of its absentee owners could succeed "except on the initiative and under the direction of the country's technicians." If successful, this industrial directorate would, as a matter of course, abolish all rentier income. But it could not achieve this takeover alone; it would need both the understanding and the passive support of the underlying population, a "common understanding and a solidarity of sentiment between the technicians and the working force . . . in the greater underlying industries."[43]

The objective conditions required for succession were assuredly present, but the subjective conditions were absent. Veblen summarized the objective conditions under two headings: first, *waste* because of unemployment of material resources, equipment, and manpower, the needless multiplication of sales persons and shops, and the production of superfluities of all kinds; second, *obstruction* in the form of systematic "dislocation, sabotage, and duplication, due in part to business strategy, in part to businesslike ignorance of industrial requirements." As for the subjective conditions, the "technicians still are consistently loyal, with something more than a hired-man's loyalty, to the established order of commercial profit and absentee ownership," while the underlying population is uninformed on the state of things and "still in a frame of mind to tolerate no substantial abatement of absentee ownership." In the United States, the vested interests and their guardians had as yet nothing to fear.[44]

Veblen's two professional classes correspond to the two principal classes in Johannes Alasco's *Intellectual Capitalism* (1950): productive "P-men" and financial "F-men." Like Veblen, Alasco linked production specialists with the vanguard of the new order and financial experts with the rear guard: "As the P-men first of all belong to the factory, the F-men . . . belong to the executive offices." While P-men are dedicated to producing goods and services, F-men are concerned with gross sales and profits. Engineers, laboratory workers, and factory superintendents draw their salaries from what they create. Corporation officers, business managers, and top-ranking accountants also draw salaries, "but their salaries are, in fact, participation in the profits," according to Alasco.[45] F-men thus straddle the old order and the new, while P-men may be counted on to carry the new order to its final stages.

Unlike Veblen, Alasco believed that F-men, not just P-men, have an interest in displacing the absentee owners. As he depicts their separate efforts at takeover, "the P-men attempt to control industry through their knowledge of, and skill in, industrial operations," while the F-men attempt to control it "through their knowledge of, and skill in, financial operations." Thus "intellectual capitalism [Alasco's name for rule by the owners of intellectual capital] begins to take shape within the existing realm of the F-man, but is destined to become the realm of the P-man."[46] That is hardly the progressive role that Veblen assigned to F-men, but it is somewhat closer to the actual process of succession.

The distinction between P-men and F-men can be traced to Marx. Because of economies of scale, Marx's capitalist is obliged to delegate industrial responsibilities to professional managers who do the productive work of supervision and exploitation on the factory floor. The capitalist is also obliged to delegate commercial and financial responsibilities to unproductive profit-making specialists, to salespeople, clerks, and accountants, who perform the job of exploitation in the marketplace. Modern industry, Marx wrote, "makes science a productive force distinct from labor," but he failed to acknowledge that it also makes science an unproductive force. As for the private owners of this productive and unproductive expertise, they constitute "a superior class of workmen, some of them scientifically educated"—but a superior class *within* the class of wage earners, not a separate class.[47]

Was Marx unaware of the antagonism between intellectual and manual workers? On the contrary, he asserted, "An industrial army of workers under the command of a capitalist requires, like a real army, officers [managers] and sergeants [foremen and supervisors] who, while the work is being done, command in the name of the capitalist." Many of the original capitalists were also inventors, but the task of becoming scientifically educated was subsequently assigned to functionaries. Thus, as Marx quoted William Thompson, a socialist precursor, "The man of knowledge and the productive laborer come to be widely divided from each other, and knowledge, instead of remaining the handmaid of labor . . . has almost everywhere arrayed itself against labor."[48] That was for Marx the end of the matter, as he failed to develop this important insight.

It remained for Marx's critics not only to develop it but also to overdevelop it. The main objection to Veblen's and Alasco's scenarios is that they underestimated the common interests of P-men and F-men as salaried professional workers, while exaggerating their status as two separate and independent classes with different sources of income. P-men and F-men share the same defining feature of a professional class—the ownership of expertise, whether financial or industrial. Scientific and technical knowledge is only one example of expertise; financial and marketing know-how is another. The struggle for succession between P-men and F-men therefore needs to be reformulated as a struggle between rival sectors of one and the same professional class.

The Subordination of Capital to Expertise

Thus far I have considered only scenarios of the struggle for succession. I now turn to alternative depictions of the outcome, of the extent to which professionals have taken over decision-making powers.

Since Alfred Marshall's *Principles of Economics* (8th ed., 1920), it has become generally accepted that organization constitutes a fourth factor of production. By organization, Marshall understood management—the special knowledge associated with the orchestration and supervision of production on a large scale.[49] However, it remained for others to associate management with the emergence of a new social class that not only contested the rule of money but also subordinated it to the rule of expertise—initially in the name of management and then in the name of human capital.

In 1932, Adolf Berle Jr. and Gardiner C. Means published their seminal work, *The Modern Corporation and Private Property.* Authority in the modern corporation, they concluded on the basis of massive statistical data, had passed extensively from the owners of capital into the hands of salaried managers. Although their conclusion was initially disputed, some three decades later it had become virtually incontestable. Not only had stockholders become passive, but managers were pursuing objectives other than the mere maximization of profits. Relying on new data, Robert J. Larner published research in 1966 showing that in only 5 of the 200 largest nonfinancial corporations in the United States did an individual, family, or bloc of interests have majority control, while in 169 of them, professional managers clearly had the final say.[50]

The authors of the new paradigm did not rest on their laurels. A former member of President Franklin Roosevelt's brain trust during the early New Deal, Berle went on to publish *The 20th Century Capitalist Revolution* (1954), in which he described the shift from private capitalism to "corporate capitalism"—his term for the new economic order in the United States. The revolutions of the twentieth century were not exhausted, he argued, by the Communist, Socialist, and Fascist experiments. "The capitalist revolution in which the United States was the leader found apter, more efficient, and more flexible means [of concentrating economic power] through collectivizing capital in corporations," he declared.[51]

To this depiction of the new corporate or collective capitalism, he added in 1959 that it was tantamount to people's capitalism, by which he understood, paradoxically, a system of nonstatist socialism. Increasingly, "socialism and modern American capitalism are led by their evolution to converge," he observed. The struggle between the two systems "arises, not because of their structural incompatibility, but because their respective operators differ in their fundamental conceptions of the significance of . . . free choice."[52] In effect, the cold war was a contest over ideological issues, not economic ones.

As Berle noted in his study of American corporations undertaken at the Center for the Study of Democratic Institutions in Santa Barbara, California, the private property system had almost vanished from the scene: "Instead we have something which differs from the Russian or Socialist system mainly in its philosophical content." Capitalists had been replaced not only by managers of the big nonfinancial corporations but also by another set of managers in charge of mushrooming pension funds in the United States. These trust funds in the late 1950s totaled almost $31 billion, roughly half in the hands of insurance companies and the remainder in eight or nine New York banks. To keep up with inflation, the trust funds invest in equities. Having become major stockholders, they are "slowly 'chewing up' control of those corporations which offer the best means of equity investment."[53] Control over the economy had thus passed not just to nonfinancial managers but to financial managers as well.

The last vestige of stockholder control had slipped through the fingers of capitalists into the hands of pension trustees. Berle cites the example of the Sears, Roebuck Company, whose pension trust fund undertook to buy out the private stockholders in addition to the institutional ones. "As a result," Berle declared, "Sears, Roebuck is socializing itself *via* its own pension trust fund . . . and management is thus responsible to itself"—that is, the managers of the pension fund who control the stock but do not own it and the managers of the company in control of the business. Berle likened the result to "'socializing' property without a revolution."[54]

When Peter Drucker, a management consultant and professor of management, first pointed out that pension funds would become the prevailing mode of ownership in the twenty-first century, he called the new mode of ownership "pension fund socialism." Decades later, he called it pension fund capitalism but a capitalism "as different from any earlier form of capitalism as it is from anything any socialist ever envisaged as a socialist economy." Paradoxically, pension fund capitalism is not only "capitalism *sans* the capitalists" but also "capitalism without 'capital.'" That is because the money in the pension funds consists of deferred wages.[55]

Another name for this metamorphosis of American capitalism is David Bazelon's "Revolution of Non-Ownership." Two kinds of managers have taken over effective control of the corporation, he argued. "The smaller group is made up of the ruling strata of executives." As the politicians of the corporation, "their work is to adjust conflicts among individuals . . . and factions all the way down the line." "The larger group consists of people who are technically trained to do a specific kind of work, and actually do it"—for example, scientists, engineers, lawyers, accountants, advertising and marketing specialists, and personnel officers. Two trends are observable: first, the "increasing independence of the top organizational managers"; second, the "enhanced importance, prestige, and income of the technically trained group." Bazelon called them, respectively, the politicians and the intellectuals. He found both equally necessary to the operation of the enterprise, thereby disputing Veblen's thesis that the managers of the price system are entirely dispensable.[56]

Nonetheless, Veblen was on the right track, according to Bazelon. Veblen was among the first to perceive the chief contradiction in the new managerial society, the conflict of interests between the top political experts and the technical experts or professionals. In *The Paper Economy* (1959), Bazelon was already witnessing what seemed to him "a rather quiet and mostly polite 'revolt of the intellectuals.'" The intellectuals spearheading the revolution-within-the-managerial-revolution were not avant garde in the Greenwich Village or Left Bank sense of culturally advanced, highbrow, or alienated. They were professionals who used their education to generate incomes for themselves in corporate offices and on factory floors, not just in the groves of academe.[57]

This new class of intellectuals had so increased in size over the past few decades that, according to Bazelon, professionals were staffing the bureaucracies of the managerial society. Citing the basic figures assembled by the sociologist Daniel Bell, Bazelon noted that the number of nonproduction workers in manufacturing increased by 60 percent from 1947 to 1957, while the number of production workers remained roughly stationary; and that in the steel industry, to take but one instance, "when the union got a 19.4 cents an hour increase in 1957, the white collar non-union employees were given a 26.6 cents an hour increase—37% higher." This was the advent not of a new democratic society but of a new ruling class in the form of so-called middle management. The "'revolt of the intellectuals' consists in making a living—a good living . . . it is making what the new man has—education—as much as or even more important than what he doesn't have—property," Bazelon argued. Indeed, professionalization is the key to understanding the difference between what used to be described as American capitalism and what is currently called the new managerial order.[58]

A new class stands at the apex of American society. However, its members not only are united in their opposition to the rule of property but also are increasingly engaged in an intraclass struggle. The politicians are the brokers of the big changeover; "since they are charged with mediating between the New Class and the paper-rentiers," they move slowly. The intellectuals want to be managed less; they also want a faster and fuller development of the new managerial society. Bazelon predicted that this rising group of professionals "will eventually be as great a danger to the top ruling strata of the managerial order as the dispossessed workers were to the earlier age of capitalists." He thus identified the intellectuals with the vanguard of the managerial revolution and the politicians with the rear guard.[59]

What is it that makes the new class different from the old propertied class? The basis of the new order is technology, and that consists of headwork. "It is just brains"—a fourth factor of production distinct from labor and the factor responsible for managing the economy. Science, Bazelon argued, is replacing private, individually owned property with property owned by organizations and managed by specially trained people. It signifies the advent of a fully bureaucratized society of jobholders, from the highly paid executive down to the common laborer. In a fundamental sense, Bazelon claimed, both are proletarians. To that extent Marx was right. What he did not foresee, Bazelon noted, is that America's gift to the world would be "an increasingly comfortable proletarianization."[60]

Those Bazelon describes as the intellectuals of the new order correspond to John Kenneth Galbraith's chief discovery—the corporate technostructure. According to Galbraith, power in the business enterprise has passed not to the CEOs but to the organization under them. Group decision making by teams of specialists— professional workers who spend their time obtaining, assimilating, exchanging, and testing information—is the rule. Besides informal word-of-mouth discourse, there is the committee and its periodic meetings that increasingly take up the specialists' time. The need to coordinate their talents led Galbraith to redefine the corporation as a hierarchy of committees dedicated to pooling and testing information. The stereotypical organization chart of the business enterprise is misleading because power passes not only down from the pinnacle but also up from the professionals who assemble, assimilate, and assess vital information for the organization.[61]

Unless reviewed and acted on by a higher committee, group decisions "tend to be absolute." For Galbraith, this means that those at the top do not give orders anymore while those below passively execute them. Those below issue recommendations that serve as directives, while those above respond to and carry them out: "It is not the managers who decide. Effective power of decision is lodged deeply in the technical, planning, and other specialized staff." Increasingly, top management ratifies decisions made at lower levels.[62]

Galbraith concluded that "organized intelligence is the decisive factor of production." In the modern corporation, "the entrepreneur no longer exists as an individual person" because the managerial function has become a collective entity. The entrepreneurial group is fairly small and confined to the leading executives; the specialized staff is very large and "extends from the most senior officials of the corporation to where it meets, at the outer perimeter, the white and blue collar workers whose function is to conform more or less mechanically to instruction or routine." Such is the organized intelligence personified by those Bazelon calls the corporation's intellectuals—the brains of the enterprise.[63]

To Galbraith's account of the rise of the technostructure, Robert Reich added the changes in professional expertise with the shift from high-volume, standardized production to high-value, flexible production—a change corresponding to the shift from the era of management (1920–70) to the era of human capital (1980–present). A former professor of business and public policy at the John F. Kennedy School of Government at Harvard University, Reich served as secretary of labor during President Clinton's first term in office. His 1983 bestseller, *The Next American Frontier,* realistically depicted the latest advances of the new class once the professionally managed firm had become the standard form of modern business enterprise.

During the management era, the U.S. economy came to depend on the strength of large industrial enterprises producing long runs of standard goods. Thanks to business-government planning in response to the Great Depression, typically three or four giant firms set the agenda for industry-wide coordination in virtually every line of production. According to Reich, "The federal government had become both an agent and a silent partner of industry-wide corporate planning," thereby confirming post-Stalinist accounts of the U.S. economy as state monopoly capitalism, an interlocking of corporate and governmental agencies and personnel. The difference is that Soviet accounts assigned ultimate authority to finance capital, whereas Reich claimed that "professional managers maintained complete control."[64]

Such planning and coordination among firms in the same industry required expert knowledge of pending changes in supply and demand. "There was," according to Reich, initially "no organization and little professional expertise which pertained to whole sectors of the economy and to relationships among industries." Yet Schumpeter's prediction was being borne out: coordination reduced competitive pressure, especially in technical innovations. Unit costs continued to decline, but "there were few major breakthroughs, and industries were often slow to apply new technologies," Reich observed.[65] During the management era, economies of scale rather than new technologies became the rule—as in the Soviet Union before it collapsed in 1991.

World War II established the legitimacy of government management of public education, health, research, welfare, and labor relations. It also established the role of the government as general manager of the economy, responsible for the overall health of American business. New Deal planners, according to Reich, envisaged a system of industrial planning and coordination that would "manage profits along with investment and production and would give more authority to professional managers in government and labor." The federal government provided a substantial market for industry, while the Pentagon became industry's largest single purchaser. But the heyday of managerial authority eventually came to an end. "By the 1980s," in Reich's account, "the core industries of the management era—steel, automobiles, petro-chemicals, textiles, consumer electronics, electrical machinery, metal-forming machinery—were in trouble." Indeed, some of the giants of the past half-century—notably U.S. Steel, General Motors, International Harvester, and RCA—suffered sharply declining profits, much as Marx had predicted.[66]

America's relative decline, Reich contended, is a result of global competition. Although foreign trade did not figure significantly in the U.S. economy before 1970, by 1980 "19% of the goods Americans made were exported (up from 9% in 1970), and more than 22% of the goods Americans used were imported (up from 9% in 1970)." Even more telling, Reich pointed out that in 1980, "more than 70% of all the goods produced in the United States were actively competing with foreign-made goods."[67]

Newly developed nations with state-of-the-art technologies were doing a more profitable job in high-volume, standardized production than was the United States, with its higher wage rates. To meet this challenge, the industrialized countries, including the United States, began "shifting their industrial bases toward products and processes that require skilled labor . . . [as] a key barrier against low-wage competition." Whereas high-volume, standardized production may be launched anywhere, Reich observed, high-value production processes are feasible only in countries with large pools of expertise. "Industrialized countries," Reich noted, "are therefore moving into comparatively low-volume but high-quality, custom-made products like precision castings, specialty steel, special chemicals, process control and sensor devices, lasers, integrated circuits, aircraft engines, fiber-optic cables, and luxury automobiles."[68]

Reich summarized the significance of this shift to precision, custom-made, and technology-driven products: "Finance capital formation is becoming a less important determinant of a nation's well-being than human capital formation." The CEOs of the era of management, with their hierarchically subservient submanagers and overweening supervisors, are being replaced by "integrated teams of workers [who] identify and solve problems." In the era of human capital, the success of the new brainpower industries depends on quickly identifying and responding to opportunities in a rapidly changing global environment.[65]

Just as entrepreneurial functions were delegated during the era of management, so problem-solving functions are being delegated in the era of human capital. Teams of professional workers with only marginal supervisory responsibilities are replacing the former chain-of-command bureaucrats. As Reich concluded, the flexible-system enterprise means that Galbraith's technostructure is in the saddle.

Investing in Human Capital

Before World War II, the term *capital* referred almost exclusively to tangible, material things—nonhuman assets, whether money, commodities, or means of production used to make money. Initially limited to financial and commercial capital, in modern times it came to include productive or industrial capital. Only recently has its meaning become further broadened to include money invested in education.

In the case of usury, it was clear to virtually everyone that the banker got something for nothing, whether in the form of money or Shylock's pound of flesh. In the case of merchant's capital, it was clear that money was made by buying cheap and selling dear—inevitably, somebody was cheated. Then in the case of industrial capital, Marx revealed that employers exploited their workers without having to cheat them—a tour de force to which academic economists have as yet not given their stamp of approval. Nor are they likely to probe more deeply into the matter of human capital in the expectation that its owners get something for nothing.

Our story begins with the mysterious Johannes Alasco, who set the stage for the theories of human or intellectual capital that appeared with the flowering of the Information Age. His real name was Zbiegniew Domaniewski. The alias Alasco was adopted from his Polish countryman, the Calvinist reformer Johannes a Lasco (1499–1560), who regarded Martin Luther as an extremist. The only other details that help identify this elusive personage are his date of birth in 1905; his Canadian residence; his most important work, the aforementioned *Intellectual Capitalism;* and the two volumes appearing in 1970–71, *Cash-Flow Discounting and Technology* and *Benefit-Cost Analysis of Technology Prospects*—both self-published in Ottawa by a firm bearing the name Alasco. The high technical level of these later works suggests he was an economist or an accountant by profession.

Alasco's chief contribution was to show that government ownership is unnecessary to establish the rule of intellectual capitalists and that the privileged salaries of intellectual workers derive from their creative work. The intangible wealth of society comes from, in Alasco's words, "the joint efforts of highly paid specialists . . . engineers, research workers, business executives, lawyers." If the abolition of exploitation requires the expropriation of the owners of such intangible assets as stocks and bonds, then "their capital should be appropriated by the intellectual workers who have created it."[70]

By "capital" Alasco meant not just material things that are productive of other material things: "Capital is anything which can be defined in terms of legal ownership and may become a source of income." Capital values are no longer mainly what they were in the nineteenth century—the product of manual labor. The great change in the significance of capital is that business profits are "now in the main realized through investment in ventures representing . . . accumulated knowledge and experience."[71]

Alasco expected "the owners of knowledge, i.e., the professional intelligentsia . . . to continue the ventures of their predecessors, the owners of industrial equipment." He believed that this new class would be just as restless and ambitious as the old in seeking opportunities for the profitable use of its particular capital. "It will attempt to revolutionize the Western world for this sole purpose: its own personal profit"—in the form of privileged salaries.[72]

The major conflict of the twentieth century, according to Alasco, is not a struggle between bourgeois and proletarians; it is a struggle between the class of stockholders and the class of professionals. At issue are two competing forms of capitalism: finance capitalism, in which money is the controlling asset; and intellectual capitalism, in which knowledge is the decisive asset. The monied interest is bent not on saving and reinvesting but on consuming the fruits of the past. The contemporary conflict over economic expansion has thus brought to the fore a new class of intellectual capitalists who, unlike the stockholders, are not exploiters but are motivated by a passion for building.[73]

Alasco's work acknowledged the influence of Machajski, as did Alvin Gouldner's *Future of Intellectuals and the Rise of the New Class* (1979). Gouldner called the intangible property of those possessing a higher education "cultural capital," a stock of capital distinct from monied capital. Following Machajski, he likened the new class to a "cultural bourgeoisie which appropriates privately the advantages of an historically and collectively produced cultural capital." But unlike Alasco, he identified the common denominator of this new capital as the acquisition of "something for nothing." All capital is therefore exploitative.[74]

"Anything is capital," said Gouldner, that "serves as the basis of enforceable claims to the private appropriation of incomes legitimated for their contribution to the production of economic valuables or wealth." Because legitimated, capital is not used to extort wealth: "Capital is neither theft nor extortion but acknowledges the norm of *reciprocity* [something for something], claiming that it is *entitled* to what it gets because of what it has contributed." Gouldner admitted that this definition is ideological and self-serving for members of the old class and the new. Capital, he argued, "has access to incomes not because it necessarily increases productivity or wealth, but simply because its income claims are socially enforceable and culturally recognized."[75]

The revolution of the twentieth century consists of what, then? In the first world of capitalism, the old class of monied property keeps the new class in harness. "Socialism," Gouldner contended, "is the final removal of that limit . . . a way of extending the New Class's cultural capital." Although the defining feature of socialism is simply the elimination of monied capital, its inevitable consequence is to pave the way for cultural capital. However, state socialism is only the antechamber to the new society. "Under capitalism they [members of the new class] are limited by property; under state socialism, by the Party and its requirements of ideological certification."[76]

That the new class had yet to become the ruling class in the Soviet Union and China may come as a surprise. If not the new class, then who was in control? Gouldner's answer was the party bureaucrats. The split between management and ownership, between party officials and the technical intelligentsia, was no less evident under socialism than under capitalism. The bureaucratic organization common to both systems was controlled by an uneasy coalition of government officials and experts of the new class, in which bureaucrats had the final word. Power in the Soviet Union rested with the party bureaucrats. They controlled the behavior of those outside the ruling party as well as those inside it. Under state socialism, Gouldner declared, "the real choices are between the new technical intelligentsia and the old line bureaucrats."[77]

Gouldner excluded party bureaucrats from membership in the new class because their rule was grounded on legal authority and the use of force, in contrast to the intellectual workers' culture of critical discourse.[78] But did they constitute a separate class? That is the Achilles' heel of Gouldner's overly intellectualized depiction of the new class. It is as though he defined it in his own university professor image—too narrowly to encompass the relevant data.

At the opposite extreme, Gouldner relied on an elastic definition of capital too general to pass muster. Legal ownership of a source of income applies equally to other forms of privilege in other social formations besides capitalism. In Gouldner's usage—and Alasco's too—*capital* is loose enough to include slaves and unimproved land as well as expertise.

The concept of capitalism emerged in modern times in connection with the owners of means of production operating with hired hands. The theorists of intellectual and cultural capitalism have transformed it from a historically specific category into one applicable to all civilized modes of production. Both Gouldner and Alasco extended its meaning backward as well as forward in time, so that it covered "Feudal Capitalism," in which land is the controlling asset, as well as "Intellectual Capitalism," in which expertise is the controlling asset.[79]

A basic source of Gouldner's ideas was the discussion launched by Theodore Schultz's presidential address to the American Economic Association in 1960 and Schultz's discussion of human capital in *The Economic Value of Education* (1963). However, Gouldner disputed Schultz's claim that higher incomes associated with higher education may be explained by the higher productivity of the more educated. Increased years of schooling are dictated not only by job requirements, Gouldner argued, but also by competing professional groups intent on raising the standards of their profession, establishing a monopoly, and upgrading their salaries in a "war of each against all for wealth, prestige, and power." While conceding that some professions contribute more than others to the collective interest, he faulted Schultz for failing to recognize that professional standards mask the struggle of special interests for special privileges.[80]

Schultz's *Investing in People: The Economics of Population Quality* (1981) further developed some of his initial theses.[81] Since the Nobel prize–winning economist has done more than anyone to make the theory of human capital respectable in academic circles, let us see what he said in defense of his main contention that the best private as well as public investment is education.

"Differences in the productivity of soils do not explain why people are poor in long-settled parts of the world," Schultz pointed out. What accounts for such poverty is the failure to modernize. "An integral part of the modernization of the economies of high- and low-income countries is *the decline in the economic importance of farmland and a rise in that of human capital—skills and knowledge*," Schultz wrote. Advances in education and in the several sciences have improved the quality of the labor force; they have also raised the rate of return on investment.[82]

Schultz's data in support of the public benefits of modernization through education are indisputable. The weekly wage of unskilled workers in the United States in 1815 was equivalent to the price of two bushels of wheat; in 1890, it had risen to nine bushels and by 1970 to ninety-six bushels. Although the decline in the price of wheat by 50 percent between 1900 and 1970 must also be considered, Schultz contended that the "rise in the value of human time is, in large part, a consequence of the formation of new kinds of human capital in response to economic incentives."[83]

The data on real wages and salaries in the United States from 1900 to 1970 suggest that when due allowance is made for the cost of education, the real earnings of professional people are "determined in the long run by normal wages, that is, by what the labor market pays for the services of the rank and file of labor." By the real earnings of professional workers, Schultz meant "the sum of normal wages and the additional compensation that is required to have made their education worthwhile." Besides direct outlays for tuition, books, and laboratory fees, he included in the cost of a higher education the earnings foregone during its acquisition.[84] Although such an opportunity cost is not a monetary expense but an opportunity lost, Schultz's inflated cost of professional expertise suggests that the corresponding salaries must also be inflated to make the acquisition of human capital feasible.

Schultz's data on changes in real hourly wages for different categories of workers between 1900 and 1970 support the following observations: first, a large increase in the real hourly compensation of both unskilled and highly educated workers; second, an absolute increase in wage differentials sufficient to compensate for the rising cost of education; third, a similar increase in the value of human time in such comparable countries as the United Kingdom, France, Germany, and Sweden; and fourth, the presumption that "in high-income countries the rate at which human capital increases exceeds that of nonhuman capital."[85]

This presumption was borne out by Simon Kuznets's studies of economic growth in the United States and Western Europe. His conclusions indicated a large increase in the contribution of intangible human assets to national income and a corresponding decline in the share contributed by tangible assets after World War II. As Schultz noted, by 1970, approximately three-fourths of national income in the United States consisted of employee compensation, while the remaining fourth was classified as proprietors' income, rental income, net interest, and corporate profits. Considering the additional time devoted to the management of these property assets, he estimated that "the aggregate contribution of human agents in 1970 . . . was fully four-fifths of the value of the production accounted for in the national income."[86]

Schultz's data indicate that between 1900 and 1970 the U.S. work force was markedly upgraded in quality. In 1900, the ratio of workers with an elementary school education to those with a college degree was 2:1. In 1970, it was 1:1.5. Over the same period, the cost of an elementary education rose a little more than twofold, while the cost of a bachelor's degree increased sixfold. Compared with the stock of business capital between 1930 and 1970, the educational stock in the work force increased more than threefold. Although by 1970 the educational stock had yet to catch up with the business stock, it soared from 37 percent of business capital in 1930 to 75 percent in 1970.[87] The rise in the American standard of living during this period may be attributed to this increase.

But is education the best *private* investment? Are the escalating costs of a university education more than compensated by higher salaries? Schultz took for granted that private investment in human capital is no less worthwhile than public investment. Lester Thurow, an MIT professor of economics and the ideologue of the Democratic party's neoliberal wing, contested this assumption: "The risks that this investment will not pay off are enormous." If one considers the cost in money and the length of time before the payoffs occur, he explained, "it is highly unlikely that an educational investment will pay off for the individual."[88]

As partial evidence for this claim, Thurow cited the following data. First, in the mid-1990s, some 26 percent of white males with bachelor degrees earned less than the median high school graduate during their peak earning years of forty-five to fifty-four years of age—hence the probability that one out of four persons with college degrees will be losers instead of winners. Second, since productivity gains are more likely to show up as falling prices than as rising wages because of the fracturing of the post–World War II social contract between labor and management, "the gains go not to those making skill investments but to those buying the cheaper products made with those better skills." Third, because a government bond is a better investment, no capitalist-motivated mother and father can be expected to invest in a college education for their children. Fourth, the marked difference in median wages between white males with and without a college education in the mid-1990s—some $14,000—means that some get a big payoff from education but that others do not. Fifth, private investments in education are narrowly concentrated among those with large incomes, which results in a very unequal skill distribution. Sixth, knowledge workers are increasingly "fired when not needed and have their real wages reduced when alternative cheaper supplies are found."[89]

Human capital, according to Thurow, differs from physical capital inasmuch as its owners are not capitalists and the investments in knowledge required to generate new brainpower industries are mainly public instead of private. "No country has ever become even semiliterate without a publicly financed compulsory education system," he pointed out, yet that violates every principle of capitalism because it means giving away something that could be sold.[90]

The irony is that knowledge is termed "human capital" when a hard-nosed capitalist would seldom make such an investment. One may wonder what becomes of capitalism when capitalist enterprises do not own the human capital of their employees. Although Thurow identified the era of brainpower with the dominance of human capital, the capital that is human bears little resemblance to that owned by capitalists.[91]

What is the future of capitalism when brainpower becomes the controlling asset? Thurow's answer is that capitalism has no future without the public sector to make investments that the capitalists do not make. Just as socialism will not work without private incentives, capitalism will not work without public intervention. Capitalism can survive only in a mixed economy. Prior to the Information Age when capitalists were in command, capitalism was the senior partner in the mix. But with the owners of human capital at the helm, capitalism has been demoted to the role of junior partner.[92]

Contrary to Schumpeter, Thurow denied that capitalism has a tendency to self-destruct: "Stagnation, not collapse, is the danger." To its intrinsic problems—instability, rising inequality, a lumpen proletariat—Thurow added "capitalism's growing dependence upon human capital and man-made brainpower industries." These are the industries of the future with a competitive edge. New technology is placing expertise in the driver's seat just when an obsolete ideology of instant gratification is wrecking capitalism's ability to make long-term social investments in education, research, and infrastructure. To survive, therefore, capitalism "will have to undergo a profound metamorphosis," Thurow contended.[93]

A profound metamorphosis implies a radical change in substance. "Capitalism gave decision-making power to the owners of [physical] capital precisely because they controlled the key ingredient in the new system—the power source,"[94] Thurow observed, but those in command during the era of brainpower are not capitalists. They are the owners of *expertise*. So why call the new order capitalist? Virtually every social system is a mixed economy, and in each case, the proper name for it is that of the dominant partner in the mix.

The same criticism can be made of Thomas Stewart's *Intellectual Capital: The New Wealth of Organizations* (1997). By *intellectual capital,* Stewart meant the knowledge a company has that gives it a competitive edge: "*Intellectual capital is intellectual material—knowledge, information, intellectual property, experience—that can be put to use to create wealth.*" It is, simply put, "collective brainpower," the "economy's primary raw material and its most important product."[95] But is *collective* brainpower capitalist or socialist?

In a section entitled "The Rising Price of Brains," Stewart explained that, because knowledge or information is the greatest source of economic values in the Information Age, "educated people command a greater pay premium than they used to." Since the end of the 1970s, "only one group of U.S. men has made gains in real weekly earnings: college graduates." But instead of explaining this phenomenon as the result of a power struggle, Stewart made it exclusively a function of those graduates' superior productivity—as if intellectual workers had no say in the matter and the Invisible Hand alone were responsible.[96]

The typical generator of wealth in the new society is a hired mind, not a hired hand. *"Routine, low-skill work . . . does not generate or employ human capital for the organization,"* Stewart wrote. But this dividing line between high-quality and low-quality jobs is not presented as a class division. There is no exploitation in Stewart's social accounting: the surpluses generated by superior knowledge redound to its owners' benefit. "If intellectual capital is a tree . . . then human beings are the sap . . . that makes it grow," he asserted.[97] However, that intellectual workers create more wealth than others does not mean they are entitled to more wealth—that is a moral, not an economic imperative.

Marx assigned to labor the task of swallowing up expertise. Today, non-Marxist political economists go to the other extreme of swallowing it in the name of human or intellectual capital. Both parties make the same mistake in not recognizing expertise as an independent, fourth factor of production having the same status as land, labor, and capital. The main difference is that the theory of *intellectual capital* acknowledges the existence of a new class corresponding to the ownership of intellectual capital, whereas the Marxist theory of *intellectual labor* denies that its owners constitute anything more than an upper stratum of the proletariat.

Salaried Apologetics

In its mainstream version, the political economy of expertise exhibits several weaknesses. The foregoing mistake is only one of them. Another is the failure to treat professional depictions of expertise as self-serving. As yet, only a handful of accounts define expertise as a social relation between those in command who get something for nothing and those under orders who get nothing for something—tantamount to a self-critique by mainstream political economists themselves.

In the real world, according to Paul Samuelson in the most widely used textbook on economics during the Information Age, "everyone knows that the vast majority of higher-paid jobs are also *more pleasant*."[98] That they are higher-paid therefore cannot be explained as compensation for either nervous strain or tiresome responsibility. Nor does the high cost of acquiring expertise account for more than a token addition to one's annual salary when amortized—like one's dwelling over its productive life. Ditto, the sacrifice of pay in the course of acquiring that expertise. Incentives used to induce people to incur such sacrifices likewise account for only a small fraction of their professional salaries.

So what is a credible explanation for the big salaries, as opposed to apologetics for them? Samuelson's explanation was that the market for expertise is characterized by monopolistic or imperfect competition.[99] The best jobs seldom compete with each other because crossovers involve prohibitive costs of time and energy in learning a new profession. The more the job qualifications rise, the harder it is to fill the job. Demand outruns supply at the apex of the knowledge society; the opposite condition prevails in the middle and bottom registers.

Yet Samuelson claimed that many differentials in pay "would still persist if there were no monopoly elements." Given the *qualitative* differences among wage earners, "why expect one man to receive the same competitive wage as another?" Bidding for human talent is like bidding for race horses. Every personnel officer "knows that people vary much in their abilities and contribution to a firm's dollar revenue." Samuelson therefore contended that "differences in the quality of various grades of labor are probably the most important cause of wage differences."[100]

So much for an economist's explanation of professional salaries. Let us see what a management expert has to say on the subject.

In *The New Society,* Peter Drucker acknowledged that "resentment against the big salaries of the top executives poisons the political and social relations within the plant, aggravates the difficulty of communication between management and employees, and reduces management's chance to be accepted as the government of the plant." Yet there is no dearth of salaried apologetics. Among them, Drucker listed the following: (1) big salaries are the reward for contributing to a firm's profitability—but they are paid whether a firm is profitable or not; (2) top managers must be paid enough to compensate them for the fortunes they could make in private business—but the qualifications for top management differ radically from those for a successful entrepreneur; (3) if the top salaries were fully distributed to all employees, they would add only a few dollars pay to each—but resentment against the top salaries is not economic but social; (4) the resented salary is unreal since income taxes negate it—then why pay it in the first place? Drucker therefore concluded that the "reasons usually given for these top salaries are, frankly, nonsense."[101]

Still another argument is that the executive's salary is a reward for past performance. Drucker thought this was a weak one because there is no yardstick for measuring performance other than the market and a firm's profitability—which depend on Lady Luck. Moreover, past performance is not that important to a firm's well-being; the "most important function of management," Drucker maintained, "is to adapt product, process, and organization to change; to foresee, to innovate."[102]

So why the high salaries? Seek the explanation in the *chain of command,* said Drucker. Authority becomes credible when expressed primarily by money income. When incomes are not staggered according to the hierarchical structure of the big enterprise, he said, the threat of insubordination looms. *Greed* is not the issue, *authority* is: "A foreman must receive more money than the man working under him; a superintendent more money than the foreman; a plant manager more than the superintendent; a divisional general manager more than the plant manager; and so on." The bottom step on this authoritarian ladder is still a middle-class income necessary to exalt the foreman over his lower-income subordinates. Drucker maintained that "since the steps must be fairly large, the top rung must be in the clouds."[103]

Drucker was mistaken. From the end of 1917 to 1927, the top Bolshevik authorities in Soviet industry received no more than the average wage. Non-party experts under their authority were paid substantially more. In April 1918, Lenin wrote, "Now we have to resort to the old bourgeois method and agree to pay a very high price for the 'services' of the top bourgeois experts"—to keep *them,* not their subordinates, from being "seditious." Why? Because, due to the social environment that contributed to their expertise, the specialists were "bourgeois" in their thinking and behavior.[104] It is therefore not a question of *authority;* it is a question of *greed.*

The Bolshevik system of paying bourgeois experts more than their (Bolshevik) superiors was eventually abandoned, not because of insubordination or the threat thereof on the part of the high-paid experts but because their superiors *demanded* equal treatment. Sheer greed in the name of incentives to higher productivity accounts for the abandonment of the earlier policy.

Still, Drucker did contribute toward unmasking the greedy. Profitability, he argued, is not a reliable measure of managerial performance: "In the first place, this yardstick measures total performance and does not measure the performance of divisions and executives within the corporation"; profitability does not measure leadership. Nor does it distinguish between "profits resulting from changes in the competitive position of the corporation, and profits due to fortuitous circumstances." Since market conditions operate independently of executive judgment, profitability is only partly under control. *In nuce,* it is "by no means easy to work out a system under which wage rates are objectively determined by productive efficacy"[105]—except in the case of piece rates, which of course do not apply to professionals.

In *The Concept of the Corporation* (1946), Drucker was under the spell of the platitudes that he later excoriated as nonsense. He was then a hired consultant to General Motors Corporation, with which his book is concerned. He did a commendable job of pleasing his employer in such terms as these: "Since it is, after all, management whose efforts are usually alone responsible for any increase in productive efficiency, profits certainly deserve a major share." Furthermore, "we want to make it worthwhile for management and owners to exert themselves and to risk their capital as well as their efforts."[106] More recently, however, Drucker has argued that in the teamwork required in a great corporation, management alone is usually not responsible for productivity increases.[107]

In view of Drucker's critique and considering the extramonetary rewards for management, why reward the top professionals with more than the average wage? Why pay them more, when there are plenty of budding geniuses who can be recruited for the top positions? Does it not suffice that one is a celebrity? There are plenty of professionals who would be willing to pay, instead of being paid, for the honor of ruling General Motors Corporation.

3

the legitimizing myth

> The political life of the masses and the cohesion of society
> demand the acceptance of myths. A scientific attitude toward
> society does not permit belief in the truth of the myths. . . . In
> short, the leaders, if they themselves are scientific, must lie.
> —James Burnham, *The Machiavellians* (1943)

> Marxism, in its original form (like Christianity), had the ap-
> peal of the cause of the underdog. As with Christianity, the
> wheel of time has brought it to be a creed for top dogs.
> —Joan Robinson, *Economic Philosophy* (1962)

Preferential treatment of expertise is not without its apologists. Just as capitalism presents itself to the public as a virtual Eden of freedom, equality, and human rights, so does postcapitalist society, with its apotheosis of human brainpower. To the doctrine of free and equal exchange justifying the profits of Mr. Moneybags has been added the formula of equal pay for equal work, legitimizing the above-average salary of Mr. Professional. This formula and its socialist equivalent—from each according to his ability, to each according to his work—effectively mask the exchange of something for nothing in America's new economic order.

As Marx argued in *Capital,* it does not suffice to prove that equivalents exchange for equivalents to rule out the possibility of exploitation. The matching of burdens and benefits on the job can be interpreted in any way one wishes. Professional work is reputedly more burdensome, more stressful, and more difficult than ordinary labor. The consensus is that it is also more valuable to society. Ergo, equal pay for equal work implies that professionals should be paid more than other workers.

How much more? That is the question. The usual answer—as much as the market will bear. But is the market an impartial judge of persons and their performance? Is the price of labor determined exclusively by impersonal forces, or is it in part administered? Corresponding to the legitimizing formula of distribution under capitalism, "To each factor of production according to its net product," we have the new formula, "Equal pay for equal work." But work and labor in particular have yet to be thoroughly analyzed; until they are, this formula remains an empty bag.

Marx did as much as anyone to disseminate this slogan, but did he lie? As James Burnham observed, it is "hard to lie all the time in public but to keep privately an objective regard for the truth." To lie may also be ineffective when done with a lack of sincerity. "The tendency is for the deceivers to become self-deceived, to believe their own myths," Burnham noted.[1] If Marx lied, it was not from a deliberate effort to deceive others. The self-image of a freeloader and exploiter was foreign to him. That Marxism became a creed for top dogs may be attributed less to a hoax than to hypocrisy. Nonetheless, the big lie of Marxism is that professionals labor and, as wage earners, are exploited like ordinary laborers.

Marx's *Capital* targets the owners of physical capital but offers little comfort to the victims of human capital. As we shall see, it is an argument for professional exploitation, not just for the abolition of capitalist exploitation. Its vaunted labor theory of value assumes without proof that wage differentials correspond to differences in the productivity of intellectual and manual work. Marxist political economy is Janus-faced. As the first major contribution to the political economy of expertise, it is a critique of the political economy of capital in the name of a political economy of labor, but to the benefit of the owners of so-called human capital.

Because Marxist theory has become a major obstacle to understanding the new era of brainpower, a post-Marxist critique of Marx's political economy leads inevitably to the deconstruction of his concept of a working class and to the rejection of his major premises concerning the labor process. It also calls for the formulation of a caloric measure of work, the scaling of the human costs of industry, the matching of wages and standard hours of work, and the demystification of the "bottom line."

Deconstructing the "Working Class"

In the *Communist Manifesto*, Marx defined the working class as "a class of laborers, who live only so long as they find work, and who find work only so long as their labor increases capital." That is what defines the productive laborer under capitalism—the production of not just wealth but a surplus or profit for his employers. In his footnotes to the 1888 English edition, however, Engels broadened the original definition to cover other wage earners: "By proletariat [is meant] the class of modern wage-laborers who, having no means of production of their own, are reduced to selling their labor-power in order to live." Engels's definition included a special category of wage earners, salaried professionals who find work whether or not their labor increases capital.[2]

In volume 2 of *Capital,* Marx revised his earlier conception by including unproductive commercial workers in the proletariat. Although salespeople or accountants produce nothing, they reduce the capitalist's costs of circulation by one-fifth if they "receive daily the value of the product of eight working-hours, yet [function] ten." As Marx acknowledged in volume 3, labor power is the sole commodity that typically exchanges at its value, the only commodity whose price matches its cost—a cost that does not include the worker's unpaid labor, and a price unaffected by the capitalist's average rate of profit.[3]

It is only unskilled labor power in a competitive market that is unique in this respect. Skilled labor power is unique in quite another respect, for the discrepancy between its price and its cost of production typically exceeds the difference between the price and the cost of other commodities. Marx was mistaken: it is not true that "[w]ages . . . always imply the performance of a certain quantity of unpaid labor."[4] If the price of workers is high enough, they will not be exploited but will share in the surplus. So considered, equal pay for equal work is pure moonshine.

The work of skilled labor power is an exception to the rule. But suppose we break it up and consider its elements separately. Then the labor component may produce a surplus over and above its cost of production, while the skill component does not. It is the computer in workers' heads that is priced so far above its cost that professional workers, like their employers, get something for nothing.

To be sure, brainpower not only transfers the price of expertise to its products but also creates new products. All the major inventions, all the progress in technology we owe to it. Indirectly, it is the mainspring of our wealth. This is the sense in which Marx was right, that brainpower creates in equal time more wealth than simple labor power. However, most of its cost is borne by past generations. Consequently, for workers who sell their brainpower and for capitalists who employ it, the larger part of expertise is free. To be paid for it is to receive bonus pay.

Marx argued that skilled work produces not only more wealth than unskilled labor but also more profits for the capitalist. First, on the premise of a uniform rate of exploitation, he concluded that its higher cost shows it to be more productive. This argument is unconvincing, because there is no evidence of a uniform rate of exploitation of both skilled and unskilled workers. Marx begged the question by closing the door on the possibility that skilled work is worth more because it is paid more, not paid more because it is worth more.

Second, Marx insisted that skilled work is more intense than unskilled work—

if only because it requires a greater degree of concentration. Skilled work thus counts as the work of several unskilled workers. But between common laborers using their muscles and sedentary workers using their brains, surely the more plausible claim is that common laborers work harder than skilled workers. Brainwork does not fit Marx's description of it as multiplied simple labor.

Third, Marx claimed that the technological application of science is a productive force. Direct, living labor is thereby reduced to a subordinate role compared with scientific labor. As heavy industry based on modern technology expands, "the creation of real wealth depends less on . . . the quantity of labor utilized than on the power of mechanical agents"—it depends on scientific and technical workers who invent the machinery. It follows that, in Marx's words, "[t]he theft of others' labor time upon which wealth depends today seems to be a miserable basis compared with this newly developed foundation . . . subjected to the control of the general intellect."[5]

But does it follow from knowledge workers' above-average powers of producing use-values that they produce in equal time more surplus value than ordinary workers produce? If those superior powers are the cause of technological or organizational innovations that make possible surpluses above the average, then ordinary workers are also more productive than they would be without those innovations.

Marxist political economists claim that talent, expertise, and managerial ability get extra pay because of their superior productivity. If so, the socialist principle of payment according to work is also operative under capitalism. But how is one to measure the productivity of laboratory workers when piecework is not a criterion? Or the productivity of professional workers generally? Marx took too much for granted—namely, a knowledge concerning comparative outputs that only God possesses. "To each according to his work" is a perfect excuse for a new mode of exploitation concealed, like bourgeois exploitation, behind people's backs.

In teamwork, there must be workers who occupy the limelight and others who serve in the shadows—drudge people as well as innovators. In collective work, the outcome is a collective product in which all have participated equally *regardless of individual differences in productivity*. As Marx noted in his "Critique of the Gotha Programme," rewards proportional to work have nothing to do with personal merit since "one man is superior to another physically or mentally and so supplies more labor in the same time." Unequal natural endowments constitute what Marx called natural privileges.[6] As such, they are unearned.

Historical development has proven more adversarial than even Marx supposed it to be. As the Third Estate split into two great classes of bourgeois and proletarians, so Marx's working class split into professional workers and nonprofessional working stiffs, into antagonistic privileged and unprivileged members of the work force. There can be no solidarity in a class of wage earners that includes everyone from the janitor to the computer specialist and the CEO. Evidently, Marx's understanding of the working class did not surpass the Abbé Sieyès's grasp of the Third Estate. Nor has Marx's concept of the working class been without its critics.

Before the outbreak of World War I, the exrevolutionary syndicalist Robert Michels wrote that "within the *quatrième état* we see already the movements of the embryonic *cinquème état*." By the Fourth Estate, he meant the army of unskilled and semiskilled workers in menial employments; by the Fifth Estate, the better-paid, skilled workers organized in trade unions, together with the professional or "intellectual proletariat." These two estates constituted for Michels separate and antagonistic classes. Lenin, too, departed from Marxist usage by distinguishing a wage-earning intelligentsia distinct from the working class and a working class divided into a privileged upper stratum of "workers-turned-bourgeois, or the labor aristocracy," and a lower stratum constituting the "proletariat proper."[7]

On careful analysis, the so-called working class is a collection of classes, like the Third Estate. Those who typically labor with their bodies and work with their hands belong to one class; those who work mainly with their brains belong to another. Marshall distinguished the supply of hands without brains from the supply of brains that require other people's hands.[8] Why, then, include them in a single class?

In ordinary usage, *labor* is ambiguous. Broadly speaking, it means work; narrowly construed, it means toil. As toil, it is exertion involving pain or hardship, hence the implication of something to be avoided. It is also short on social recognition and material rewards. Since clerical work involves drudgery, not all labor is work mainly of the body. As for professional golfers and tennis stars who work with hands *and* bodies, not for nothing are they called "players"—the presumption being that they are not "laborers."

Whether the work process is considered analytically or historically, common to both approaches is the core problem of the mechanism of exploitation. The bottom line is the mass and rate of unpaid work that is mostly toil, travail, or drudgery. The modern laboring class is therefore to be understood as the class of exploited wage earners whose work is typically of the body and hands rather than the brain.

This is not how Marx defined it. By *labor,* he meant work for wages, exclusive of the work of independent artisans and peasants who own their means of production and have no master.[9] But by including professionals among wage laborers, he clearly did not mean that professionals toil, that their work is wearisome and grievous, painful and fatiguing, dull and irksome, or some combination of these.

D. H. Lawrence was more clear-sighted in distinguishing between repetitive *labor*—for which someone has to be paid—and creative *work*—which people would pay to engage in, if only they had the money:

> There is no point in work unless it absorbs you
> Like an absorbing game.
> If it doesn't absorb you, if it's never any fun,
> Don't do it.
> ("Work," *Pansies* [1929])

For Marx, "wage labor" signified workers hired by a capitalist or joint-stock company for the sake of profit, regardless of the kind of work—whether sedentary or strenuous, safe or hazardous, easy or difficult, interesting or dull, well-paid or ill-paid. Because it is dependent on another's will, all such work is alienated. Professional elites, however, are wage earners with a difference. Whatever their condition may have been in Marx's time, today they are rarely exploited—if they are, it is mainly as beginners. Nor are they typically alienated. Not a few of them describe their work as all-absorbing, which is ambiguous enough were it not for the lines from D. H. Lawrence.

Considering that what professionals do to earn a living is both less onerous and better paid than skilled or unskilled labor, it hardly fits the formula of equal pay for equal work. They offer, in opposition to that formula, a prime example of unequal pay for unequal work—more pay for less work.

The AFL-CIO excludes managerial and supervisory personnel from its organizing efforts. But what is one to include under the heading of supervisor? Should it be limited to those with direct responsibility for the work of others, or should it include professionally educated workers generally, those who indirectly determine what others do? The nontenured faculty at American universities in the lower ranks are at the mercy of their supervisors. Tenured faculty who indirectly supervise their performance count as management regardless of whether they occupy administrative positions. It is enough that the tenured are doing the watching and the nontenured are being watched.

What unites professional workers at the beginning of their career with factory operatives and common laborers is that they all reap only a fraction of what they sow. This is what wage labor has in common with slave labor in antiquity and with serf labor during the Middle Ages. Exploitation is their common denominator. As for professionals who are wage earners, they are *not* wage laborers.

Labor, the collective term for laborers, evokes the image of a taskmaster, whether slaveowner, landowner, or capitalist. For the purpose of this investigation, however, it may be used in a more restricted sense, as a shorthand expression for wage laborers. Even so, the term is still ambiguous because there are two different conditions of wage labor. One is defined by the social relations of production peculiar to capitalism; the other is defined by the productive relations of postcapitalist society.

We now see the rationale for a post-Marxist critique of expertise. Marxists are too generous to the new taskmasters, whether those included in the intelligentsia—educated members of the liberal professions unrelated to the process of accumulation—or in the upper stratum of the proletariat—trade union bureaucrats and the technical engineering and managerial elites. On close inspection, Marx's celebrated working class breaks down into working whips and working stiffs. Working whips manage and supervise, specialize, establish norms, advise, and show how things should be done; working stiffs perform the chores and do what they are told. Although all managers and supervisors are whips, not all whips are managers or supervisors. To qualify as a whip, it is enough to be a professional worker, a highly skilled technician or craftsperson, with lesser skilled helpers. Working stiffs are working inferiors; working whips are working superiors.

Among other things, a political economy of expertise is a theoretical response to the question of how labor is squeezed by its new taskmasters. By its anatomy of postcapitalist exploitation, it delegitimizes the myth of equal pay for equal work. Rather than a revelation of the secret of capitalist accumulation through surplus value, it is the disclosure of the secret of professional exploitation through surplus wages.

Just as *Capital* was the most powerful missile ever aimed at the head of the bourgeoisie, so post-Marxist political economy is the sharpest weapon for trimming the brains of the professional class. It, too, is an integral part of the class struggle in corporate America—the class struggle on the cultural front. The irony is that a post-Marxist critique of the Age of Information and the knowledge society is a political economy of expertise *of* and *by* experts, if not *for* experts—since only experts are qualified to unmask themselves.

What the Labor Process Is Not

Not for nothing did Bakunin and Machajski characterize Marxism as two-faced. Indeed, Marx's *Capital* shows a marked preference for workers who are not strictly laborers. *Capital* opens the door to the emancipation of working stiffs from capitalist exploitation and then slams the door shut on their emancipation from professional exploitation—in the name of equal pay for equal work.

Consider Marx's premises concerning the capitalist labor process: (1) only human beings labor; (2) labor power is a homogeneous factor of production; (3) skilled labor is more productive than unskilled labor; (4) the rate of exploitation of productive workers is uniform; (5) save for the wages of supervision, the wages of productive workers do not contain a hidden surplus under competitive conditions; (6) in the modern corporation, as in private business, the prevailing social relation is the relation between capitalists and wage laborers; and (7) the last mode of exploiting labor in the history of modern civilization is the capitalist mode. What follows is a post-Marxist critique of these premises.

First, for humanists like Marx, *man* is the measure of all things, and labor is measured in socially necessary or standard *man-hours*. It follows that nonhuman animals do not labor, that spiders and bees only *seem* to labor on their various productions. While acknowledging that horses and other draft animals contribute to the production of commodities, Marx considered draft animals as constant capital whose cost is amortized, like the cost of machines. That means draft animals are incapable of producing a surplus and can only recover what they cost.[10]

In his cavalier dismissal of animal labor, Marx disregarded the common plight that binds together humans and animals. On this score, Adam Smith's *Wealth of Nations* is more credible than Marx's *Capital*. Disregarding the initial cost of purchasing draft animals—like the slaves of antiquity—Smith likened laboring cattle to laboring servants: "The price or value of laboring cattle is a fixed capital in the same manner as that of the instruments of husbandry. Their maintenance is a circulating capital in the same manner as that of the laboring servants." Farmers thus make their profit by using their laboring cattle to produce a surplus—unlike their nonlaboring cattle that are "brought in and fattened, not for labor, but for sale."[11]

Second, labor power in Marx's usage conflates what analysis reveals to be two factors of production instead of one. Labor, as he defined it, consists of an expenditure of energy through the combined exercise of bodily and mental powers. But what defines mental activity is not only the amount of energy expended—negligible as compared to the amount expended in bodily activity—but also the amount saved because of a more efficient technology or management of scarce resources. Bakunin and the economist Alfred Marshall were right in singling out this difference between labor power and brainpower and in raising brainpower to the status of an independent factor of production to which Marx gave mainly lip service.[12]

On this score, too, *Capital* fails to meet the intellectual standard of veracity set by Smith in the *Wealth of Nations*. Smith likened an individual "educated at the expense of much labor and time" to "one of those expensive machines" before it is worn out, one that, "it must be expected, will replace the capital laid upon it." Brainpower is markedly different from labor power; it is more like a machine in the head. The expense of education is like a "capital fixed and realized, as it were, in his person," while the resulting expertise "may be considered in the same light as a machine . . . [which] repays that expense with a profit."[13] As constant capital, expertise is not a source of surplus value; therefore, it cannot be exploited.

Third, Marx claimed that skilled labor counts as simple labor intensified, as multiplied simple labor. He thus skirted the question of whether one hour of skilled labor really is multiplied, condensed, or intensified simple labor, whether its working hour is physiologically denser than that of unskilled labor. He meant that it is socially multiplied through the higher value assigned to it by custom and by the operation of supply and demand. It is a "social process that goes on behind the backs of the producers" that makes skilled labor count for more than unskilled.[14]

But is that all he meant? On the contrary, he took for granted that labor is the physiological expenditure of "a definite quantity of human muscle, nerve, brain, etc. . . . and these require to be restored." Skilled labor differs from simple labor in demanding a greater expenditure not of muscular energy but of nervous tissue and brain cells—and this "increased expenditure demands a larger income." Since the brain directs the work of both hands and body, it is "labor of a higher class."[15] Indeed, it is—work of a higher *social class*.

Not unlike a battery, the brain is a storehouse of knowledge and the work spent in acquiring it. To be sure, the energy required to activate a particular skill bears little resemblance to the amount expended in acquiring it. Brainwork is unlike bodily work in that an hour of it represents more work, even though more energy is expended in the same time by the common laborer. It takes years of learning to play the violin but only an hour to perform in Carnegie Hall. Yet all those years of practice are somehow condensed in that single hour. Skilled work for Marx therefore not only *counts* as simple labor multiplied; it *is* simple labor multiplied.

Fourth, a corollary of this mistaken premise is Marx's unwarranted assumption of a uniform rate of exploitation of those he calls productive workers. His assumption rests on the assumption of a freely functioning and competitive market in which all wage earners are paid according to their value, according to what they cost in standard man-hours. Thus, "if the labor of a goldsmith is better paid than that of a day-laborer, [it is because] the former's surplus-labor produces more surplus value than the latter's."[16] We have already established that this is a non sequitur.

The irony is that Marx acknowledged the role of differential rates of exploitation in the case of unproductive workers—those who produce no surplus. "We shall assume that he [the commercial worker] is a mere wage laborer, even one of the better paid," he stated. But if, through hiring the worker, the costs of circulation are reduced by one-fifth, from ten hours to eight, the average rate of exploitation in this case is reduced by three-fourths, from 100 percent to 25 percent. "A part of the variable capital must be laid out in the purchase of this labor-power . . . that creates neither produce nor value," he continued. *Variable* capital? Defined as capital that yields not just surplus labor but also surplus value, variable capital cannot include the wages of unproductive workers.[17]

Fifth, according to a widespread Marxist fallacy, the distributed surplus under capitalist conditions of production consists exclusively of income from property—mainly entrepreneurial profits, shareholders' dividends, interest on loan capital, and rents. But there is another form of surplus concealed in wages that even Marx recognized. Depending on a temporary increase in the demand for labor or a reduction in its supply, there is a rise in the rate of wages in excess of the cost of labor power. Marx called the resulting benefit to wage earners "surplus wages"—and rightly so.[18]

Marx acknowledged an additional source of surplus wages in the wages of supervision or management. "It is quite proper," he wrote, "to compel the wage-laborer to produce his own wages and also the wages of supervision as compensation for the labor of ruling and supervising him, or 'just compensation for the labor and talent employed in governing him.'" Managers are presented as personifications of the effort required for exploitation, which the capitalist can "shift to a manager for moderate pay"—moderate compared to the capitalist's profits. Managers are better paid than wage laborers but are nonetheless exploited—though even at moderate pay, their work of exploitation may yield a surplus for themselves.[19]

Marx further acknowledged a "swindle [that] develops in stock enterprises with respect to wages of management, in that boards of numerous managers, or directors, are placed above the actual director." While the wages of an English factory operative amounted to 5 shillings for a twelve-hour workday in the 1860s, the wages of supervision of these nominal directors were at least 21 shillings for each weekly meeting of some three or four hours, at most.[20] Herein, we have an implicit recognition of a professional mode of exploitation under capitalism.

What an anomaly. In acknowledging in the wages of supervision an excess in the price of labor power over its cost, Marx shared common ground with Bakunin's critique of the new slavemasters that would become the foundation of a theory of surplus wages in Machajski's *Intellectual Worker*. Made only in passing, it was an acknowledgment that should make us think twice about the germs of post-Marxist political economy hidden in the recesses of Marx's magnum opus.

Sixth, Marx assumed that in stock enterprises, as in private business, the fundamental social relation of production is between capital and labor. In fact, it is between salaried managers and their professional staffs, on the one hand, and the mass of ordinary laborers and office employees, on the other. It is a relation between executives and executants, between supervisors and supervised; it is a relation that has displaced the relation between propertied (owner-manager) and propertyless (working stiff). It is a relation between antagonistic classes of wage earners—one privileged, the other unprivileged—from which Marx's capitalists are excluded. High-paid wage earners live off the life-energy of low-paid laborers.

In this respect, the professional elites have less in common with the mass of productive workers than with members of Marx's unproductive class that produces no surplus for the capitalists, the "so-called 'higher grade' workers—such as state officials, military people, artists, doctors, priests, judges, lawyers . . . who appropriate to themselves a very great part of the 'material' wealth, partly through the sale of their 'immaterial' commodities and partly by forcibly [through state action] imposing the latter on other people." These elites are parasites on the actual producers—notwithstanding their propertyless status as wage earners.[21]

Finally, Marx was mistaken in assuming that the elements of a new society in the womb of the old point to the end of human exploitation. On the contrary, capitalism generates a new and different mode of surplus extraction that is eminently *professional*. The surplus is pocketed by a special category of wage earners as well as by capitalists, but Marx left us in the dark about the relative share of professionals in that surplus.

It is not enough to rethink or re-create Marxism when its conceptual apparatus is based on such shaky foundations. Neo-Marxists thus remain trapped within the body of a theory that was defective even during Marx's time and has since become still further falsified by events.[22]

A Caloric Measure of Work

The legitimizing myth of postcapitalist exploitation—equal pay for equal work—presupposes an effort to calculate the intensity of the working hour. Marx used piecework as a criterion.[23] Piecework, however, is a measure of physical productivity and only a highly intuitive index of the amount of physiological energy expended; it does not apply to professional work.

In Marx's time, the physiology of work and the chemistry of nutrition were in their infancy. A quantitative measure of work intensity had yet to be devised. With the development and use of ergometers, calorimeters, and gasometers, it became possible to measure human energy inputs and outputs with scientific precision.[24]

A more precise measure than piecework is given by the formula $W = L \times H$, where W is the intensity of work, L is the load lifted in kilograms or pounds, and H is the height the load is raised in meters or feet. Because the forms of energy are convertible, the intensity of work measured in kilogram-meters or foot-pounds can also be expressed in heat units or calories, one calorie being the energy required to raise the temperature of one kilogram of water ten degrees centigrade.

Since the law of the conservation of energy applies to the human body as well as machines, caloric output is equal to caloric input when the individual's weight is maintained over a period of time. Otherwise, a gain in weight implies an excess of caloric input, just as a loss of weight implies a deficiency of caloric intake. The daily caloric inputs required of workers in different occupations can be determined by measuring the amount and composition of food ingested.

As in other machines, the energy output of the human machine is equal to its input. But only part of its input is converted into mechanical work, the rest being dissipated as body heat. The efficiency of the human machine in converting energy into work is therefore less than 100 percent. Efficiency is measured by the ratio of work output to energy input in caloric units, the heat value of the mechanical energy delivered divided by the heat value of the food consumed per unit of time.[25]

To discover how much work a given amount of food can produce, the subject is made to pedal a bicycle or turn a crank like Pinocchio turned in drawing water, with the subject attached to an instrument called an ergometer. The heat given off by the body is measured by the oxygen consumption. One liter of oxygen used in burning food yields about five calories.[26] Oxygen consumption is measured with the help of an instrument called a gasometer tank, a bag with a closed air system, which the subjects carry on their backs. The amount of work done by the subject plus the amount of heat wasted or lost by the body in working are exactly equal to the energy contained in the food oxidized or burned during the working period.

Because of the heat lost in working, work is rarely more than 20 percent efficient. To survive, workers must make up for this deficit by employing other energy converters. Low-energy societies have relied on plants and animals as converters in addition to human power. In the course of evolution, such inorganic sources of energy as wind and water have been harnessed through the water wheel, windmill, and sailing ship to produce the needed energy surplus. Historically, the sailing ship was a high-energy converter, capable of producing a maximum of 250 times the energy required in operating it. Other high-energy converters, such as the hydroelectric turbine and diesel engine, also operate at a rate of efficiency greater than human labor.[27] Only with the help of plants, animals, and machines of various sorts, each of which operates at less than 100 percent efficiency, is a worker capable of producing commodities representing an hourly caloric output in excess of the person's consumption. In other words, only under human direction do these other forces of production make possible a caloric surplus.[28]

Scaling the Human Costs of Industry

The relevant consideration concerning equal pay for equal work is the energy differential during the work process. Taking the minimum hourly caloric expenditure for heavy work at around 480 calories, the energy differential between heavy and sedentary work is roughly 4.6:1.[29] In the case of extra-heavy work, the ratio would be somewhat higher, at about 5:1.

These ratios are corroborated by other studies. According to one estimate, sedentary occupations, such as office work, and most forms of brainwork involve the use of only small muscles, requiring about one-sixth of the calories expended by a common laborer in shoveling sand or cutting stone. According to another estimate, this fraction is closer to one-fifth, on the supposition that brainwork with the body relaxed requires little more effort than sitting at rest. In any event, physiologists agree that, over and above the caloric requirements for sitting at rest, the additional energy required for intense brainwork is about 4 calories per hour.[30]

It has been found that this extra energy can be obtained by eating one-half of a salted peanut or one oyster cracker. Quite literally, the additional energy required to perform the most taxing intellectual work does not amount to a bag of peanuts.[31]

To be sure, that coal miners expend five times the calories spent by office workers does not mean that they must consume five times as much food. At issue is the recovery of energy not just through food intake but also through the energy equivalent spent on durable goods. Otherwise, there will be no matching of burdens and benefits—no equal pay for equal work.

Contrary to much loose talk about the expenditure of nervous or mental energy, it has been found that maximum neural activity may increase the basal metabolism rate slightly less than twofold. Although during an eight-hour workday it is difficult to maintain a rate for heavy work of more than eight to ten times the basal metabolism rate, the differential between the most intense muscular work and the most intense mental activity is still about 5:1.[32]

The rate of recovery from intense brainwork is much faster than it is from intense muscular activity. The extent of fatigue experienced in brainwork is apparently muscular fatigue of the back muscles required to maintain a sitting or writing position. To this should be added fatigue of the hands, neck muscles, and facial and eye muscles in even the simplest forms of brainwork, such as reading, writing, and calculating.[33]

The question arises whether fatigue in different occupations is directly proportional to the intensity of work. Impairment or objective fatigue, not to be confused with a feeling of tiredness or boredom, may be defined as a physiologic loss of power to continue work at the previous pace.[34] Although subjective fatigue is related to such factors as motivation, monotony, recreational opportunities, and anxieties concerning work or domestic life, there is nothing to indicate that these factors are relevant to impairment and rates of recovery in different occupations. Nervous fatigue is not yet susceptible to quantitative measurement by ergographs and postexercise oxygen intake, but it results in muscular weariness and can be indirectly measured through muscular fatigue.

One outstanding difference between physical work and brainwork is that the amount of muscle tissue required in physical labor is such a comparatively large part of the total bodily weight that the energy expenditure is correspondingly greater. Even though the intensity of oxidation is comparatively high in brain tissue, only a very small part of the cerebral cortex is involved in brainwork. The total energy expended is therefore negligible compared with the energy requirements of muscular work. At the same time, there is reason to believe that brain impairment is no less incapacitating than muscular fatigue.[35]

The science of physiology is surely a better guide than psychology to understanding the work process. Caloric units are more informative than is Stanley Jevons's pleasure-pain calculus, with its positive and negative utiles. Maximizing pleasure and minimizing pain may be relevant to consumers, but it is irrelevant to producers who demand an equal amount of energy in return for energy rendered. In view of the differentials in intensity between sedentary, light, moderate, and heavy work, is there any point in resurrecting Marx's average man-hour? Since this average is a function of the rate of technical innovation and the diffusion of new technology, it will vary from time to time and in different places depending on the level of civilization. The Marxist man-hour is a flexible measuring rod, not a fixed one, precisely because it is an average representing continuously changing conditions of work. Consequently, there is a different standard for different countries and an international standard that also varies through time.[36] But which is more convenient, a shifting or a fixed measuring rod, like those of length and weight?

Marx believed he had discovered an exact measure of work intensity in piece wages, but he failed to notice its limitations. First, piece rates in one occupation are quantitatively incommensurable with piece rates in other occupations because of different materials and working conditions. It is impossible to obtain an average for a whole industry, much less an entire country. Second, even within a particular occupation, piece rates are an inexact measure of work intensity. A doubling of the number of pieces produced in a given time may or may not result in a doubling of the energy expended. Piece wages are also objectionable on humane grounds. Historically, they were responsible for the sweating system—a system of donkey's work.[37]

An objective assessment of work intensity calls for a caloric measuring rod. For the purpose of scaling, we take as our standard not the average man-hour but the lowest common denominator or basic hour of minimal work intensity, which would be the sedentary threshold of 105 calories per hour. The hourly expenditures of energy required in other kinds of work are multiples of this amount.

The various types of work can thus be classified into five principal categories, scaled according to the minimum and maximum numbers of calories hourly expended: sedentary (105–210), light (211–315), moderate (316–420), heavy (421–525), and very heavy (526 and more). Considering the lower limits of each, light work can be defined as double the intensity of sedentary work; moderate work as triple the intensity; heavy work as four times as intense; and very heavy work, five times as intense. To illustrate each briefly, the professions belong in the category of sedentary occupations; carpentry, metal work, and industrial painting belong in the category of light work bordering on moderate work; stone workers belong in the category of moderate bordering on heavy work; lumberjacks in the category of heavy work; and ditch diggers and longshoremen in the category of very heavy work.

These data represent not only the caloric expenditure in different occupations during an eight-hour workday but also the additional daily expenditure of energy during the remaining sixteen hours. The figure of 840 calories expended in sedentary work at 105 calories per hour by a man weighing 154 pounds—as in reading aloud or teaching students from a sitting position—constitutes only about one-third of his daily expenditures. On the supposition of another six hours sitting at rest or relaxing at 100 calories per hour, he will have spent 600 calories. Walking casually at 2.6 miles per hour to and from work, in shopping centers, and at home for two hours at 200 calories per hour amounts to 400 calories, leaving eight hours for sleep at 65 calories per hour for an additional 520 calories. The total calories spent by the teacher in this example thus comes to 2,360 calories per day.[38]

To the caloric profiles from his *Chemistry of Food and Nutrition*, Henry C. Sherman appends the U.S. National Research Council's revised daily dietary allowances for a male worker weighing 154 pounds. In its sampling of occupations, it recommends 2,400 calories per day for sedentary work, 3,000 calories for modest work, and 4,500 calories for heavy work.[39] Nutritional requirements thus also tell us how hard people work at different jobs.

An approximation of this standard is currently used by some industrial physiologists. According to one estimate, the daily minimum energy expended by a sedentary worker is approximately 2,400 calories. To this figure is then added, per hour of work, 50 calories for light work, 50 to 100 calories for moderate work, 100 to 200 calories for hard work, and more than 200 calories for very hard work.[40] On a daily basis, light work therefore represents an overall energy loss of roughly 2,800 calories; moderate work, 2,800 to 3,200 calories; heavy work, 3,200 to 4,000 calories; and very heavy work, over 4,000 calories.

What is important physiologically is the quantity of energy socially needed for the production of commodities. The intensity of work can be measured not in wage units or in energy converted into work but solely by the flow of total energy expended. This flow can be most conveniently measured by a standard hour representing the lowest common denominator of energy inputs and outputs required in the least taxing occupations, that is to say, sedentary work.

Matching Wages and Hours

The extension of the working day from the fifteenth century to the early nineteenth century involved a trade-off, a slackening of pace tantamount to a porous working hour. The intensification of work, in retaliation for the ten-hour workday bill enacted on May Day 1848, led in the opposite direction, toward a denser working hour. Whether the working hour was porous or dense, however, both wages and work loads continued to be unequal.

By a *porous hour,* Marx meant an hour of below-average intensity; by a *dense hour,* an hour of above-average intensity. The denser hour means increased expenditure of energy in a given time, heightened tension, and closer filling up of the pores "attainable only within the limits of the shortened working day." The "denser hour of the ten hours' working day" contains more expended energy than the "more porous hour of the twelve hours' working day." Marx called it "squeezing out more labor in a given time." It becomes possible either "by increasing the speed of the machines . . . [or] by giving the workman more machinery to tend."[41]

Although the production of more commodities in a given time counts as intensified work, it is really more intense only inasmuch as the working hour becomes denser. It *counts* as denser because of technological improvements. But it really *is* denser only through, in Marx's words, increased "expenditure of human brains, nerves, muscles" in a given time, whether the increase is due to the same amount of energy expended in less time or to more energy expended in the same time.[42]

In conformity with popular sentiment and custom, Marx assumed that work is more intense according to its difficulty, or the amount of brainpower required. This supposedly explains why, in a competitive market, brainworkers are paid more than manual workers. However, research in body chemistry shows that energy expenditure is greatest for physical work and least for brainwork. Thus, contrary to popular prejudice fostered by those with superior knowledge, equal pay for equal work requires that technical and professional workers be paid less, not more, than manual workers.

As Pinocchio learned the hard way, donkey's work ends at the bottom of the social pit with nothing to show for it. Faced with such an appalling future, Jack London swore never again to toil under such conditions: "All my days I have worked with my body, and according to the number of days I have worked, by just that much am I nearer to the bottom of the Pit. . . . God strike me dead if I do another day's hard work with my body more than I absolutely have to do!"[43] He, too, had learned that if workers are not to be exploited, those doing heavy or extra-heavy work must either be paid more than the average wage or have their work load reduced.

In matching wages and hours, the daily caloric expenditure of heavy workers must correspond to that for moderate work; otherwise, they must be paid more than the average wage. Take, for example, 367 calories as the average for moderate work in the range of 315 to 420 calories per hour. Then the per diem expenditure involved in moderate work in an eight-hour working day may be reckoned at 2,900 calories in round numbers. That is precisely the recommended daily dietary allowance in calories for males between the ages of nineteen and fifty-one weighing from 160 to 175 pounds. What is lost in working moderately is recovered through eating moderately, which is not to say that what is lost in working excessively is recovered through eating excessively.

Consider next the case of heavy work in the range of 420 to 525 calories per hour. Given a mean hourly expenditure of 472 calories, it may be injurious to a worker's health to demand more than 6.25 hours of work per day, also approximately 2,900 calories in round numbers. As for very heavy work at its lower threshold of 525 calories per hour, 5.50 hours of steady effort amounts to roughly the same daily expenditure. In the interest of saving such workers from overexhaustion, excessive wear and tear, and a premature death, their work loads would have to be reduced.

We see, then, that "equal pay for equal work" is a principle that cuts two ways. As interpreted by Marxists and mainstream economists, it is a license to pay professionals more than ordinary workers. However, a caloric measuring rod leads to the opposite conclusion, no longer a counterfeit of equal pay for equal work but the real matching of wages and hours. Although a justification of exploitation in postcapitalist societies, the legitimizing myth can be turned against itself. While its loose interpretation taxes credibility, its literal interpretation threatens the status quo.

"Equal pay for equal work" is not just an ethical issue; it is also an economic one. Unless compelled to, nobody will voluntarily accept less pay for more work, but virtually everyone will try to get something for nothing. Besides justifying more for less, "equal pay for equal work" is a least-cost principle, a safeguard against those who would reap what they have not sown. Matching wages and hours compels freeloaders, spongers, and other human parasites to work for what they get or otherwise do without. It both saves on consumption and encourages greater production.

Working stiffs do not ask for miracles. They want equal pay for equal work, equal benefits for equal burdens. There are several ways of matching up, some involving a caloric measuring rod, others less precise but more feasible yardsticks in view of other factors. First, as already indicated, the number of calories expended in a workday may be recovered with the monetary equivalent of a basket of goods representing the same expenditure. Second, by increasing the length of the workday for sedentary and light work and by reducing its length for heavy and extra-heavy work, the number of calories expended may be equalized for all jobs, thereby ensuring equal pay for all. Third, a workday of standard length may be required for everyone—again with equal pay for all—based on the premise that brains and brawn share equally in the final product and therefore have an equal claim to it regardless of the calories each expends. Fourth, the pleasantness and unpleasantness of different jobs may be gauged by the comparative demand for them, those in low demand being paid more per working hour than those in high demand. Fifth, the workday may be shortened for unpleasant jobs and lengthened for pleasant ones.[44]

Whatever else may be said for it, the higher education required of brainwork is irrelevant in determining equal work for equal pay. "Whenever they [workers] succeed in expressing themselves independently of the trade union bureaucracy," wrote Cornelius Castoriadis, an economist with the Organization for Economic Cooperation and Development (OECD), "working-class aspirations and demands increasingly are directed against . . . wage differentials." Not brainpower's superior productivity but only naked exploitation can account for differences in pay. According to Castoriadis, professional costs "spread out over a working lifetime would at most 'justify,' at the extremes of the wage spectrum, a differential of 2:1 (between sweepers and neurosurgeons)." As for productivity, he added, "it depends much less on bonuses and incentives and much more on the coercions exercised, on the one hand, by machines and supervisors and, on the other hand, by the discipline of production."[45]

"A fantastic opinion," wrote the French revolutionary "Gracchus" Babeuf, "leads people to attribute to the work-day of someone who makes a watch twenty times the value of that of someone who plows a field and grows wheat. The result is that the watchmaker is placed in a position whereby he acquires the patrimony of twenty plowers; he has therefore expropriated it." Watchmakers work with their hands and brains; plowers, with their arms and bodies. "It is only those who are intelligent," Babeuf pointed out, "who have fixed such a high price upon the conceptions of their brains, and if the physically strong had been able to keep up with them . . . they would no doubt have established the merit of the arm to be as great as that of the head, and the fatigue of the entire body would have been offered as sufficient compensation for the fatigue of the small part of it that ruminates."[46] Well said by the author of the *Manifesto of the Plebeians* in defense of equal pay for equal work.

The Bottom Line

But is there nothing to be said for established opinion? Indeed, there is. Money counts for more than calories. Power speaks louder than truth. The expenditure of energy has less to show for itself politically than the worker's contribution to the firm's bottom line.

The most consequential interpretation of the principle "to each according to his work" was the one advanced during the Soviet Union's struggle to catch up to and surpass the industrial economies in the West. Consider its case for paying knowledge workers more than working peons. The purpose of socialism, declared Stalin at his party's Seventeenth Congress (January 1934), is not only to abolish exploitation but also to ensure the abolition of poverty and privation. The Stakhanov movement became a model and the justification of unequal remuneration based on the amount of work—measured in outputs per units of time. "On August 31, 1935," Stalin proudly wrote, "[Alexei] Stakhanov hewed 102 tons of coal in one shift and thus fulfilled the standard output fourteen times over." He accomplished this feat because of his superior natural strength and innovative work procedures that showed he had learned to count not only the minutes but also the seconds.[47] "To each according to his work" came to mean that increased outputs would be matched by increased wages.

Under capitalism, work is productive if it increases capital and produces a profit for the capitalist. Under socialism, Stalin argued, work is productive if it benefits the masses. In view of the Soviet Union's backwardness, "to each according to his work" could only mean "to each according to his output."

In a heroic effort to overcome poverty and privation and to transform an agrarian society into a modern industrial power, Stalin launched the slogan "technique decides everything." In 1934, he followed it up with the slogan "cadres decide everything." Once state-of-the-art industries were established, the country faced an acute shortage of trained specialists capable of utilizing the new technology. A new Soviet intelligentsia of Red experts had to be created as the "main force in the management of our industries."[48] Experience had shown that even though it is impossible to determine each worker's output in a complex division of labor, technical innovation and organizational know-how were the keys to industrial progress. Material incentives were needed not only to raise a slumbering peasantry from its age-old lethargy but also to reward knowledge workers for acquiring and improving their expertise.

How else is one to understand Marx's implicit formula of distribution under the lower stage of communism generally known as socialism: "the individual producer receives back from society—after the deductions have been made [for social insurance, etc.]—exactly what he gives to it"? What does this principle imply, if not that inventors, engineers, technocrats, innovative managers, and supervisors will become the principal beneficiaries under a new economic order? But not just for their own benefit; for Marx, "to each according to his work" meant to each according to the individual's quantum of labor, the individual's hours of work, where those hours are of standard intensity.[49] In other words, equal wages for equal working times of equal intensity—provided that the norms peculiar to each occupation are fully met. We have seen, however, how his interpretation of matching wages and hours encourages professional workers to get something for nothing.

Nobody expects the competitive wage of a human being to be the same as that of a donkey. So why expect the medical profession to receive the same wages as manual work? It is the bottom line that accounts for the extraordinary differences between the salaries of professionals and the wages of ordinary workers. Nonetheless, human beings are not donkeys.

Although almost everyone agrees with the principle of equal pay for equal work, a class struggle is waged over how to interpret equal work. For Mr. Moneybags, it means an equal addition to a firm's profits. For Mr. Manager and Mr. Professional, it means an equal contribution of expert knowledge. For Mr. Drudge Forlyfe, Esq., it means an equal quantum of individual labor measured in hours of work.

As an impartial observer might perceive the lot of donkey workers, those who work hardest use their brawn, not their brains. But when it comes to political differences, who listens to impartial observers? In the political arena, artifice counts for more than science. Both the physiology of work and the science of nutrition support the manual worker's intuition that work is hard according to the amount of physical energy expended. But to this intuition, brainworkers counterpose their definition of work as hard in proportion to its difficulty—the amount of education required to solve complex problems. Like Marx, they claim that the quantity of work is proportional to its quality. Equal pay for equal work therefore means superior pay for intellectual workers.

Whose definitions are to prevail? That is the political question. In the conventional wisdom, the intensity of work is a function not of caloric expenditure but of brainwork. Precisely *that* is the consensus of experts. What matters is not the facts of the case but the interests at issue. The truth is, in George Gilder's words, "Equal pay for equal work is a principle that applies nowhere."[50] Political correctness and the definitions that count are those of the stronger party.

4

a new class structure

Why is it so often considered difficult to define the working class? . . . At what stage in the hierarchy does the skilled worker cease to belong to the proletariat?
—Raymond Aron, *The Opium of the Intellectuals* (1957)

Whatever the ruling class of post-capitalist society may be, it seems probable that it will tend to deny its own rule on account of its internal differentiation, which places every one of its members between two others.
—Ralf Dahrendorf, *Class and Class Conflict in Industrial Society* (1959)

If expertise amounts to a fourth factor of production and if it has become the controlling factor in the American economy, then we have arrived at the threshold of a new, postcapitalist knowledge society. Hence the fundamental question: Are Americans already living under a new social order? The political economy of expertise can provide an answer.

At issue is the fundamental question of political economy: Who exploits whom? Once that question is answered, one can proceed to the next one: Who gets Goliath's share of the surplus? If not private owners, then the new class of professionals. That means a new class structure, a veritable revolution in which professionals occupy the commanding heights, with capitalists as their junior instead of senior partners.

Once more, we need a yardstick. For masking exploitation, money is still the favorite device in both capitalist and postcapitalist societies. But we want to unmask it. Can a money unit of account serve our purpose?

A caloric measuring rod has only limited uses. Social accounting in standard man-hours can tell us who exploits whom in particular cases, but it cannot provide an accurate measure for the national economy. That is because the statistical abstracts rely exclusively on a monetary unit.

Lack of information concerning comparative costs in a man-hours calculus makes it nonoperational for most purposes, while the absence of caloric data in the statistical abstracts plagues the users of a caloric calculus. A money unit of account may therefore be generally relied on to provide the most data with the fewest headaches.

With its help, we can distinguish the cost from the price of brainpower, and the surplus wages pocketed by professionals from the surplus exacted by exploited workers in excess of their cost of subsistence. We can also determine the threshold below which wage earners are exploited and above which their fellow workers are exploiters—without any middle class between them. We can probe beneath the surface of cooperatives to their underlying reality where big fish thrive in little ponds, and we can face up to the reality that working stiffs belong no longer to a class for itself but rather to a class against itself.

Cost of Brainpower

Students enjoy a double privilege in the course of acquiring an education and developing their brainpower: they avoid drudgery and hard work, and their industrial exemption means that others pay for it. Expressed in the first person, the development of my expertise will cost me less than it costs others. Earnings from student employment will not cover my costs—certainly not the cost of a professional degree.

Like other capital investments, educational expenses enter into the cost of brainpower and are recovered through amortization, through being passed piecemeal onto their products. If a tractor costs $15,000 and serves for some fifteen years, at the end of which it has no salvage value, then each year $1,000 is recovered until at the end of the tractor's life its entire cost is recouped. Something similar might be said of the brainworker. "If," as Ronald Meek postulated, "p hours is his expected productive life, and t hours of surplus labor have been expended upon him and by him during the training period, then when he starts work each hour of his labor will count (for the purpose of estimating the value of the commodity he produces) as $(1 + t)/p$ hours of simple labor." In Paul Sweezy's example, suppose that his productive life is fifty years, some 100,000 hours, and that the equivalent of 50,000 hours of simple labor went into his training, "then each hour of his labor will count as one and one half hours of simple labor"—not 50 or 100 times but a modest 1.5 times.[1]

But pause a moment for reflection. Is it credible that half of a worker's life has been spent on his or her education? What kind of super-degree, super-Ph.D., costs that much? Is this not another instance of salaried apologetics?

How many standard work-hours are expended by a student in acquiring a college education? That would be over a period of four academic years or eight semesters of approximately thirteen weeks each, representing a total of 120 credit hours. But four years of only twenty-six weeks each of schooling boils down to two full-time years. A standard work-week of forty hours for fifty-two weeks comes to only 2,080 hours. That means that a bachelor's degree represents 4,160 hours of study. For a Ph.D., double the figure, making 8,320 hours, and for an M.D. add an additional 2,000 hours, for a total of 10,320. This ceiling figure is a far cry from the 50,000 hours cited in the foregoing illustration.

Intellectual workers would like to recover the cost of their education in one fell swoop or in several big doses, as soon as they begin working or shortly thereafter. But as with the cost of their services, so with the cost of their education—both are spread over a productive life.

Are student costs the only ones that go into earning a professional degree? That is a somewhat narrow vision of what constitutes a university. It overlooks not only the related work of the professorate but also the supportive work required to staff the library, keep records, type reports, assign classrooms, maintain buildings and grounds, operate the power plant, service the computer center, provide health care, and police the campus—work that is just as necessary to education as teaching is. The costs of this supportive work are not borne by students any more than instructional costs are. Why, then, should either set of costs enter into our calculation?

Inflated costs translate into inflated salaries—higher pay after graduation. Without material incentives, we are told, it is unlikely that professional jobs would be filled to the extent they presently are. Although professional work is cleaner, more pleasant, and more interesting than manual work, most professionals would rather stay home and do something else—were it not for the pay. Schooling itself is considered a chore. So why should anyone suffer through four years of grueling study and nerve-racking final exams without the promise of gold as an inducement?

So much for the conventional wisdom and concessions to it. But is it a fact that higher pay based on the number of years of schooling is socially necessary? No, it is not. There are negative as well as positive incentives. People can be compelled to study—or suffer the legal consequences. Elementary and secondary schooling occur without the goad of monetary incentives. What makes higher education an exception if not that it is currently voluntary?

Even if the conventional wisdom were true, it would not cancel the fact that professional workers get something for nothing—indirectly at the expense of others who make it possible. Nor do I have in mind the obvious instances in which new entrants to the professions perform on the same plane as their supervisors for one-fifth the pay. The universities are rife with such examples, from adjunct instructors who can never expect tenure to graduate teaching assistants at the minimum wage.

I have in mind what the typical student receives as subsidies for taking courses toward a professional degree—the per capita institutional expenditure in higher education at private and public colleges and universities. In 1993, for example, total expenditures were estimated at $182.7 billion for an enrollment of 14.3 million in round numbers. The per capita outlay was approximately $12,700 per annum—roughly the same figure for the years immediately preceding when enrollments as well as expenditures were lower.[2]

Putting aside the matter of student loans for those who do not earn their keep, compare this sum with what a student foregoes—the minimum wage for secondary school graduates. In 1993, the minimum wage was $8,500. But in an academic year of twenty-six weeks, the sum foregone would have been only half as much, some $4,250—roughly one-third of what a student received in exchange.

In a full cost-benefit analysis, the opportunity cost of a college education is offset by the opportunity benefit. Since for every year of college the sum of deferred wages comes to roughly one-third of school expenditures, the opportunity benefit of a higher education exceeds its opportunity cost by almost 200 percent. Far from being exploited as a result of working without pay, college students are getting something for nothing even before they start collecting their paychecks in the role of pampered professionals. To be sure, students have to pay for tuition, books, and laboratory fees. But only at private colleges will their opportunity costs plus these personal outlays match or exceed their opportunity benefits.

Consider what can be learned from applying a monetary unit of account. Florida State University's operating budget for the fiscal year June 1995 to June 1996 was $410.6 million. The tuition for some 24,000 undergraduates and another 6,000 or so graduate students came to $62.4 million—less than one-sixth of the operating costs. Tuition fell short even of the $121 million in instructional costs. A higher education therefore is largely a gift, one with seemingly magical properties as a source of income—for its beneficiaries, not its donors. Therein lies the rub and the rip-off. Since expertise is largely gratis, any claim to recover the costs of education from those who paid for it—costs hidden in the so-called value of expertise—is a legal equivalent of theft.

Such are the brass tacks in the unmasking of a legitimizing myth. But why have they escaped notice? In part, because political economists, no less than mathematical economists, are fearful of biting the hand that feeds them. Wage differentials are a political matter determined not only by impersonal economic forces, by supply and demand and the freezing and overheating of the economy, but also by limited access to certain occupations, public authority, wage and salary management, relative bargaining power, and class struggle.

The Victimizer Victimized

Among the paradoxes of the Information Age is that the owner of capital is bested by professional workers. The price of brainpower not only exceeds its cost but also is so escalated that its surplus goes to the seller, not to the buyer. In effect, Marx's "self-expanding value" yields a deficit rather than a surplus in exchange for expertise. In this case, which Marx never considered, Mr. Moneybags is exploited by Mr. Professional.

Marx confused wage labor with work-for-wages. Variable capital, as he conceived it, is capital used exclusively for producing a surplus through an exchange with wage earners. As matters turned out, however, it yields a deficit rather than a surplus in the case of professional work-for-wages. The capitalist vampire is thus no match for the professional shark.

Capital invested in the purchase of brainpower functions in a dual capacity. It is constant capital for the reasons already explained; the costs of education are recovered in the price of the product, but that price adds nothing to the capitalist's profit. It is variable capital inasmuch as what it yields to the capitalist diverges from its price; but unlike labor power, it creates no surplus—it only yields one to its employers.

Brainpower would not be bought were it not profitable to employ it. As Marx explained in volume 3 of *Capital,* under competitive conditions the averaging of the rate of profit means that equal capitals garner equal profits regardless of the number of laborers each employs. A competitive market for capital ensures that capital-intensive industries will not be losers in competition with labor-intensive ones. That means that the profits of capital-intensive industries are derived not only from their own workers but also from the exploitation of workers elsewhere. In Marx's words, "[A] capitalist who would not in his line of production employ any variable capital, and therefore any laborer . . . would nonetheless be as much interested in the exploitation of the working-class by capital, and would derive his profit quite as much from unpaid surplus-labor, as say, a capitalist who would employ only variable capital."[3]

Marx's *Capital* was meant to be read politically, but such a reading leaves one guessing about the accompanying process of professional exploitation. Nowhere does it tell working stiffs that their enemies consist of not only functioning capitalists and coupon-clippers but also fellow workers with college degrees. It never occurred to Marx that wage earners might rival capitalists in exploiting other wage earners and that surplus wages might rival profits as a source of tribute. For all its mistakes, *Capital* still offers the keenest anatomy on record of capital, capitalists, and capitalism, but its anatomy of exploitation applies only to the capitalist process of pumping out a surplus. A new theory is required to explain the professional surplus.

Surplus Wages and the Average Paycheck

Marxist political economy focuses on the leading role of capital and capitalists in modern society. In sharp contrast, the political economy of expertise stresses the key role of professionals. In turning from capitalist to postcapitalist exploitation, our perspective shifts from the appropriation of an economic surplus by capitalists to the appropriation of a surplus by workers who are not working stiffs. Since professionals have yet to acknowledge the existence of professional exploitation, there is no point in adopting their perspective in an attempt to describe it.

Let professional exploitation be defined as a privileged share of wages. Two key concepts define this privileged share: the average paycheck and a surplus wage. We know the meaning of an average paycheck. But what is a surplus wage?

The concept of surplus wages seldom figures in the writings of political economists. Among the few exceptions are E. Ray Canterbery and James K. Galbraith. For Canterbery, surplus consumption implies surplus income; supra-surplus consumption implies supra-surplus income in the form of wages as well as profits, dividends, interest, and rent. For Galbraith, "the idea of economic surplus keeps reappearing in economics, and for a reason"—it accrues not only to landowners and capitalists but also to wage earners as a quasi-rent for superior skills.[4]

Surplus wages is understood as the price of labor power and the price of brainpower in excess of their respective costs. But the annual cost of brainpower, of expertise prorated over a productive life, borders on insignificant, and the daily cost of maintaining it can be recovered in the price of four salted peanuts. A professional surplus is a privilege masquerading as a cost. The only real cost is that of expended energy, the basic cost of subsistence represented by the minimum wage.

Suppose the difference between surplus wages and the average share of surplus wages is positive, as in the case of the professions. Then professionals directly or indirectly exploit the labor of their fellow workers. But suppose the difference is negative, as in the case of working stiffs. Then wage earners are exploited, victims of professional exploitation, although they may be exploited by capitalists as well. Working stiffs thus come under attack from both sky and sea, bled by capitalist vampires and skinned by professional sharks.

A surplus wage is the excess over the minimum. Most wage earners are paid more than the minimum wage; they are priced at more than what they cost. Yet their share of surplus wages is not an index of exploitation. That index is the *average paycheck*—the minimum wage plus the average surplus. Whoever gets more gets more for less; whoever gets less gets less for more. The average paycheck is the dividing line between the victimizer and the victimized—as is the average surplus wage.

The average paycheck is an index of who is exploited and who is not. But isn't this definition loaded? To be sure, it is political, it conforms to the interests of the deprived, it comes from *down under*. However, its very questioning is also political and no less loaded—with a different set of class interests coming from *on high*.

Isn't any definition of exploitation at bottom a *moral* judgment, though? It is a moral judgment only when made on moral grounds—in the name of justice or fairness. It is a *political* judgment when made on grounds of power, and it is an *economic* judgment when made on grounds of cost. It is both economic and political in the case of post-Marxist political economy.

The claim that in teamwork each person's role is as indispensable as that of anybody else is not a moral judgment—it is a statement subject to public scrutiny and verification. It is no more moral than the professional's credo that expertise counts for more than work requiring less training, skill, and responsibility.

If one hour of expertise counts for more than one hour of simple labor, what happened to the democratic credo of "one man, one vote"? Wherever one chooses to spend it, a dollar bill counts only as one vote. Unequal pay therefore means that a busload of professionals can outvote almost any group of working stiffs.

If all workers recovered their cost of production plus an average share of the collective surplus, there would be no professional exploitation. But consider the cost of expertise compared with that of ordinary labor power. Although the cost of a professional degree is insignificant when prorated over a productive life, who can afford the initial cost of board, room, and tuition without borrowing or saving—the surplus mainly from a past history of exploitation, whether professional or capitalist? This surplus is a privilege that reproduces itself—hence the term *human capital* for investment in expertise.

David Bazelon defined the new class of owners of expertise as "that group of people gaining status and income through organizational position"—a position achieved mostly by virtue of education.[5] Knowledge alone does not enable members of the new class to command an above-average wage; it merely admits one into the company of the exalted. Organizational position is also necessary—the so-called bureaucratic factor. *Although the new mode of exploi-*

tation is essentially professional, the surplus from the ownership of expertise is also a bureaucratic surplus.

In the case of individuals, we can measure professional exploitation by invoking the so-called wage differential. Consider a CEO whose 1995 salary plus bonus was an immodest $850,000 and a working stiff paid the minimum wage of $4.25 an hour for a forty-hour week and a fifty-week year for an annual wage of $8,500. The CEO's pay is 100 times that of the ordinary worker. Are we to believe that the CEO's work is responsible for an output priced at 100 times that of the working stiff? Would this make the CEO's work *worth* 100 times as much?

There is no sure method of gauging managers' contributions to the final product compared with those of their subordinates. All that one can credibly say is that in teamwork each member's contribution is equally necessary—even though in talent and performance team players are demonstrably unequal.

Suppose that our CEO and working stiff are employed by a firm controlled by the descendants of robber barons owning a majority of the stock. Then, assuming teamwork and taking Marx's conservative estimate of a rate of capitalist surplus of 100 percent, the surplus from the productive application of both their labor powers would be $8,500—the same for each because they cost roughly the same. But the capitalists have to pay the CEO the extraordinary sum of $850,000. On balance, then, they do not exploit the CEO; they are exploited by the CEO. Although this indirect act of expropriation does not transform our CEO into a capitalist, what capitalist would not wish to change places with a top executive who does a better job of getting something for nothing?

In the *Communist Manifesto,* Marx assumed that the average price of wage labor was the minimum wage and that the minimum wage was roughly equal to the cost of subsistence. That was in 1848, but he made virtually the same assumption in *Capital* almost twenty years later. Times have changed. In 1995, the average price of wage labor was around $30,000; the minimum wage was $8,500.[6]

The Presumptive Middle Class

To eat or to be eaten—that is the question. Managers and their fellow sharks may remind one of the famous lines from *Hamlet*. Mistaking him for the king, Hamlet kills Polonius—a court bureaucrat—and dispatches him to hell. While the corpse begins to rot, the king searches the castle in vain for the missing one:

THE KING: Where is Polonius?

HAMLET: At supper! Not eating, but being eaten—by a politic worm.

Thanks to our rod for measuring professional exploitation, both positive and negative, we can detect the cut-off points between a new overclass of victimizers and a new underclass of victimized. We also perceive the outlines of a new class structure consisting of exploited workers with below-average paychecks opposite exploiting professionals with above-average paychecks. Are these the only classes peculiar to postcapitalist society? Or is there an intermediate class corresponding to the petty bourgeoisie under capitalism?

Evidently, there are wage earners who derive the bulk of their income from their own labors while siphoning off an above-average share of the surplus. Their average paycheck distinguishes them from the underclass at their lower boundary. What separates the underprivileged from the overprivileged sectors of the overclass? The minimum wage plus *twice the average surplus wage*—since those who receive more obtain the bulk of their surplus from other workers.

By these criteria, and given an average professional surplus of $21,500 and a basic wage of $8,500 in 1995, the boundary lines of these middle strata could be fixed at $30,000 at the lower limit and $51,500 at the upper. A registered nurse paid $28,000—within sight of the threshold but unable to cross it—would belong to the exploited underclass. A bus driver for Greyhound paid $40,000 would belong to the class of petty exploiters, those no longer exploited but still earning the bulk of their upkeep from their own labors. As for the professorate in 1995, only a minority at the best-endowed colleges and universities could boast of a salary in excess of the cut-off at $51,500; the bulk of them belonged to the underprivileged strata.

But do underprivileged strata constitute a middle class? That depends on the purpose of the classification. If the purpose is to determine the boundary between exploiting and exploited wage earners, then they make up the bottom tier of the overclass. Only if the purpose is to fix the boundary lines between persons with low, middle, and high incomes would middle strata constitute a separate class.

While this latter classification befits the interests of professionals concerned with reducing income differentials at the upper levels, the former is more befitting labor organizations. As the AFL-CIO Committee on the Evolution of Work predicted almost two decades ago, with robots and computers taking over functions in the factory and the office, a two-tier work force has emerged. As the committee described it, at the top are "executives, scientists and engineers, professionals, and managers, performing high-level, creative, high-paid full-time jobs." At the bottom are "low-paid workers performing relatively simple, low-skill, dull, routine, high-turnover jobs in a poor work environment." These constitute two classes between which there are "fewer and fewer permanent, well-paid, full-time, skilled, semi-skilled, and craft production and maintenance jobs which in the past offered hope and opportunity and upward mobility to workers who start in low-paid, entry-level jobs."[7]

One advantage of using the AFL-CIO's classification is that the statistical abstracts contain a paucity of data for estimating either the size or the relative share of the surplus absorbed by these middle strata. It is therefore difficult to fit them into a separate box. In any case, it suffices to distinguish a lower from an upper stratum of privileged workers. If the labor aristocracy is not an independent entity but rather the upper stratum of the class of exploited workers, then there are only two classes in postcapitalist society, each with an upper and lower tier. Otherwise, there would be a license for confusion by defining the labor aristocracy as a middle class, along with technicians—the graduates of technical, trade, and vocational schools—who may be found on both sides of the great divide with wages above and below the average.

Who, then, are the new slavemasters? In 1995, they included everybody earning wages in excess of $30,000—the bulk of the presumptive middle class. And who are the new abolitionists? Facing "the largest middle class in the history of America," in President Clinton's 1999 State of the Union words, they are apparently few in number; they are certainly hard to find.

The fact that in 1995 most high-grade technicians, supervisors, union organizers, teachers, social workers, and allied professionals had annual take-home salaries of less than $51,500 did not exempt them from getting something for nothing. Since the minimum wage was $8,500, a nurse supervisor or computer analyst earning $38,500 indirectly commanded the surplus labor of one minimum-wage peon at a minimum rate of exploitation of 100 percent. A chemist or biologist earning $47,000 would have been the virtual owner of two such peons, and a shop-floor supervisor at $55,500 of three wage slaves— indirectly, through the operation of the market.

Such is the reality overlooked by *Business Week,* the *New York Times,* and other mainstream publications that are currently shedding tears over the shrinking of the "middle class." In the light of the radical insecurity, flexible employment, and unemployment of professional and managerial cadres in middle-level positions, the question has been raised as to whether they, too, are exploited. However, one can be radically insecure because of uncertain and part-time employment and still be a part-time exploiter at rates in excess of the average hourly wage. That one's annual earnings fall below the average is not a factor in computing exploitation, unless the hourly wage is also depressed below the average. But the hourly wages of professionals on flexible time are typically above the mean.

Let us not waste tears on exploiters, however petty and insecure. Let us observe that those who by example counsel otherwise—self-styled liberals and defenders of the ordinary person—fail even to qualify as abolitionists on the issue of contemporary servitude. In view of the latent class war in the United

States, they are principled hypocrites, unprincipled opportunists, blind to the social question, ignorant of what is happening in the world, or indifferent to the lot of working stiffs.

Whether they hail from the industrial sector or from the financial sector, corporate yuppies are made of the same cloth. On Christmas Day 1997, I asked my oldest son, a thirty-four-year-old vice president of Chase Manhattan, if he was worth what he was paid or paid what he was worth. "I'm worth *more* than I'm paid!" was his reply. "What I bring to the bank through credit derivatives sold to the insurance companies is several times my annual salary-plus-bonus of $250,000." Two months later, he received an offer from Bank of America in San Francisco guaranteeing him half a million dollars annually for the next two years. Chase Manhattan entered into a bidding war, culminating with its offer of a whopping $900,000 per annum over the same period. Surely, the cost of his services had not changed in the meantime—it was only his price that had mushroomed. Since he never paid a dime for his education, his price amounted to roughly ninety times the cost to him of his brainpower—his subsistence at the new minimum wage

Business Week targets only the top dogs of the professional elites, the nearly seven hundred CEOs and other corporate executives whose individual short- and long-term compensation in 1996 exceeded $1 million per year. That the highest paid CEO pocketed over $100 million in salary plus bonus is evidence of an increasing wage differential that in 1996 had reached 10,000 to 1. Mr. Lawrence Coss of Green Tree Financial commanded an hourly wage of approximately $50,000; the minimum wage was $5 an hour. Instead of informing readers that Coss's one hour was the equivalent of five years of common labor or that he was the virtual owner of 10,000 head of human livestock, *Business Week* softened the blow by invoking averages. The average compensation of executive top dogs was therefore only 209 times that of factory employees.[8]

By flattening the income pyramid, *Business Week* gives the impression that middle strata typify the U.S. economy. But to typify is not to define. Nor is the issue simply a matter of scaling privileges. It is a question of who eats whom. Once more, Shakespeare on eating and being eaten (in *Pericles, Prince of Tyre*):

THIRD FISHERMAN: Why, I marvel how the fishes live in the sea!

FIRST FISHERMAN: Why, as men do a-land; the great ones eat up the little ones!

Big Fish in Little Ponds

Big fish in little ponds are no match for big ones in the open sea. As among fish, so among people. Professionals in modest enterprises are more likely to rank with little fish than with big ones. They are likely to flounder in a free-for-all on the open market—if they are not swallowed whole by their competitors.

In view of the foregoing, do professional workers in big and little ponds share the same economic interests? Do they belong to a uniform class of exploiters, or are big fish in little ponds not just eating but also eaten? The national picture is a compound of local differences between highly competitive superfirms and noncompetitive minifirms, while the average wage locally seldom conforms to the national average.

Professionals who become local exploiters do not thereby also become national bosses. Take, on the one hand, a cooperative in which the general manager earned less than the national average of $30,000 in 1995, while the average wage of its employees was only half the national one. In this firm, a professional earning more than $15,000 but less than the national average would be a local *exploiter* but nationally a member of the *exploited* class.

Consider, on the other hand, a leading corporation in which the CEO had a top salary-plus-bonus of $30,000,000 instead of $30,000 in 1995. In such a maxifirm, the average wage might be as much as twice the national average. Its employees earning less than $60,000 but more than $30,000 would belong to an *exploiting* class nationally but to the *exploited* work force in their own bailiwick.

In neither of these two cases is there a community of the exploited. In noncompetitive firms, professionals suffer under the same heel of exploitation as other workers do—but unequally. With more than a two-to-one advantage over their fellow workers in pay, they succeed in shifting the burden onto the backs of those least able to defend themselves. In competitive firms, those earning less than the local average also pass the burden onto others. But with more than a two-to-one advantage over their fellow professionals in noncompetitive firms, they belong to a different class.

These unequal conditions complicate the overall picture of class struggle in the United States. The contest between labor and the professions in firms in which professionals earn more than the national average coexists with another class struggle in which they earn less. Or, take professionals earning more than the national average but less than the average in a superfirm. Nationally, their interests are with the exploiters, whereas locally they find themselves in the same camp as labor. Professionals may therefore be in the awkward position of having to fight for their interests on two battlefronts simultaneously— and on opposite sides in each case.

Here we have an analogue of the old middle class—the penny capitalists, shopkeepers, or petty bourgeoisie in Marx's anatomy of exploitation. It is a class that is middle not only because its income is "in the middle" but also because it shares the defining attributes of both exploiting and exploited classes in the new class structure. Its members are in a unique position: either pocketing less than the average surplus nationally while pumping out more than the average surplus generated in their particular firm; or pocketing more than the national average while pumping out less than the local average.

Where, then, do their fundamental interests lie—with the victimizers or with the victimized? There is no overall answer to this question. In the case of the big corporation, whatever legitimizes their above-average salaries nationally is more in their economic interests than what legitimizes their below-average salaries locally. Evidently, their interests harmonize with those of the victimizers nationwide. In the case of noncompetitive firms, professionals and working stiffs are in the same boat. Their mutual interest is to reach for the oars and row to the safe shore of the national average.

Still, the overriding tendency is for professional workers in noncompetitive enterprises to complain that they are underpaid. By taking the same job elsewhere, they claim, they would be earning what they deserve. But it is not easy to shift to a different location, and there may be no job openings. Needless to say, labor can hope for little from those supervisors who, despite their complaints, are still privileged locally, if not nationally.

A New Look at Cooperatives

Where do cooperatives fit into this scheme of things? Initially, they were an adjunct of trade unions. While trade unions targeted the primary exploitation of wage earners as producers, cooperatives targeted their secondary exploitation as consumers. As the "Grand National Consolidated Trades Union Programme and Manifesto" (1834) of English workers explained, cooperatives were the "best means of . . . enabling the working classes to be *consumers* of the necessaries, conveniences, and luxuries of life, as well as the *producers* of them." They were the best means "to prevent the profits of their toil from going out of the circle of the productive classes into that of the unproductive classes."[9] But as sales expanded and co-ops began employing wage earners of their own, this is not what co-ops became.

Cooperatives, according to the countercultural New Left, are the ideal form of socialism: a decentralized, self-managed alternative to a command economy. This sanguine appraisal was in part shared by Marx. Cooperatives, he wrote, "represent within the old form [of society] the first sprouts of the new . . . the antithesis between capital and labor is overcome within them." For Engels, they represented a transition to socialism, while no less a revolutionary than Lenin claimed that cooperatives were "all that is necessary to build a complete socialist society."[10]

Are cooperatives really classless societies in miniature? Is there no class struggle between labor and expertise in these new business enterprises? Is there no festering resentment of the discounts to nonworking members? My interviews with co-op peons in Yugoslavia, Mozambique, Peru, Mexico, and Nicaragua, not to mention Canada and the United States, point to a negative answer to each of these questions.

Class conflict in cooperatives is not limited to the conflict between workers and management. It also includes the smoldering antagonism between management and boards of directors. Unlike the modern corporation whose directors are increasingly chosen from management, cooperatives typically exclude the management team from membership on the board. The general manager is under the thumb of rentiers with the lion's share of discounts, and the directors are beholden to blocs of shareholders who not only elect them but also ensure that the interests of shareholders are faithfully represented.

In *Labouring Men: Studies in the History of Labor* (1964), Eric Hobsbawm used the term *co-exploitation* for the fairly widespread phenomenon before World War I of "subcontracting exploitation and management."[11] Owner-entrepreneurs hired and paid managers and supervisors who in turn employed and paid their own workers. Similarly, co-op boards of directors hired a general manager who put together a management team while also acting as a subcontractor of labor. Initially, this practice included the private hire of helpers and assistants, although it no longer does.

The managerial revolution is no stranger to cooperatives, but it is at the expense of co-op workers rather than shareholders. The "owners'" increasing opposition to their "employees" having a voice in management or serving on the board of directors is a matter of record. Not only has the self-government of cooperatives long ceased to be the norm, but, as G. N. Ostergaard and A. H. Halsey pointed out, co-op democracy has increasingly become a facade behind which self-appointed oligarchies rule.[12]

To be sure, co-op managers are among the beneficiaries. Consider the overall picture in consumer co-ops. In 1995, the average salary of general managers was $20,277 in co-ops with annual sales under $900,000. In medium-size co-ops with sales ranging from $900,000 to $2,200,000, it was $29,531. In large stores with sales in excess of $2,200,000, it was $41,626.[13] Wherever the surpluses became larger, managers were given bigger salaries with the cooperation of their boards of directors.

Since most retail cooperatives are small or medium, general managers in

1995 typically pocketed less than the average wage of $30,000. Unlike top executives whose compensation exceeded $1 million each, the general managers of typical middle-size cooperatives with annual sales in the range of $1–2 million were lucky if their salaries exceeded the $30,000 mark. While the average wage in big corporations exceeded the national average, the average wage in the typical cooperative fell below it.

This disparity in local averages complicates the issue of who exploits whom. It tells us that the typical co-op is not competitive with most business firms and that most co-op managers are exploited through the operation of market forces beyond their control. Despite their professional skills and managerial roles, they are not members of the privileged class nationwide. Only locally, in their own stores, do they qualify as exploiters.

The International Cooperative Alliance—representing producer cooperatives, consumer and farm-supply cooperatives, marketing cooperatives, housing cooperatives, credit unions, electric and other service cooperatives—is generally recognized as the representative body of all cooperative societies throughout the globe. In September 1995, it published an amended "Statement of Cooperative Identity," the third restatement of its principles in 151 years: "A cooperative is an autonomous association of persons united voluntarily to meet their economic, social and cultural needs and aspirations through a jointly-owned and controlled enterprise."[14]

Is that the final word? If one is to believe co-op ideology, a cooperative is also a community of sharing and caring for its members, providing outreach and education in the philosophy of cooperativism to the larger community, while investing in employees through wages, benefits, and training for the sake of community. The buzz-word is *community*—exploitation is not an issue. What a world of difference between cooperatives with their relatively flat wage scales and corporations with their wage hierarchies and professional salaries running in the millions. But let us take a closer look at these incorporated societies that are supposedly so different from big business.

Is pooling all assets part of their definition? No, because a co-op differs from a commune in pooling only tangible assets, whether means of production or (in the case of buying clubs and consumer co-ops) finished products and services. Labor power and professional expertise remain private property.

Is self-management part of their definition? No, because most co-ops are run by professional managers. Co-op workers may be hired and fired at the manager's discretion, and only rarely do they vote on their own wages. The electoral machinery of voting for boards of directors is hardly an example of workers' self-management.

Is working in the co-op part of their definition? No, because members may consist of whoever contributes financially to the association in the form of a membership fee or equity.

Is nonprofit enterprise part of their definition? No, because co-ops need profits to expand their operations, to modernize, to provide higher wages and lower prices, and to reward members according to their equity.

Is the abolition of wage labor part of the definition? No, because co-ops frequently hire workers who are not members and are excluded from membership, while those who become working members retain their character as wage laborers despite the cover of formal ownership.

Is worker-ownership part of their definition? No, because workers who can be fired or laid off by management have no property rights other than in their own labor power.

Is fellowship through shared experience part of their definition? No, because the social relations between co-op peons and managers backed by professional staffs are antagonistic. Contrary to its ideologues, a co-op is not a classless society in miniature. Because benefits and burdens are unequal, beneath the veil of consensus building are festering hostilities that erupt periodically in open class struggles.

What then is a co-op? Except for nonbusiness co-ops, cooperatives are not only associations for pooling tangible assets and providing benefits inaccessible to individuals working independently. As employers of wage labor, they are the last refuge of professionals who, despite their benign intentions, manage to get something for nothing.

Disregarding utopian-socialist and anarcho-communist cooperatives that have barely made headway, there are two main kinds of cooperatives distinguished by the composition of their boards of directors. First, there are co-ops modeled on a nineteenth-century joint-stock partnership, whose directors consist wholly or mainly of nonwage member-owners who provide the equity, as in the United States. Second, there are those modeled on a fictitious conception of workers' self-management, whose directors consist of professionally trained member workers, as in the U.K., Spain, and Yugoslavia.[15]

The history of cooperatives in the United States is the story initially of labor's frustrated efforts to get out from under the heel of capitalist exploitation. Most of the original co-ops were driven to the wall by capitalist competition, while the later ones lost their ties to the labor movement. When co-ops expanded in sales, they stooped to hiring nonmember workers. As a result, the cooperative movement created, in Michael Bakunin's words, a "new class of workers who exploit and profit from the labor of their employees."[16]

Unbeknown to them, co-op peons are being sucked dry at both ends. Besides the member parasites, they have the management team on their backs. For the extent of managerial exploitation, one must calculate the average wage for co-op employees, but the obstacles to gathering the relevant data are enormous. Secrecy prevails; co-op workers are not privy to what transpires behind management's closed doors.

Like stockholders, the co-op's members are absentee proprietors; their discounts on purchases are equivalent to dividends. As rentiers, they care about as much for their working peons as they do for the plight of labor elsewhere. Unionization is fiercely resisted on the spurious grounds that co-op workers are part of the family. As for co-op workers, they have yet to hear, much less apply, what Keynes wrote concerning the euthanasia of the rentier. What they need to do, in line with the favorite IWW song, is to dump the membership off their backs.

Why are workers in American co-ops for the most part unorganized? I put this question to Jack Seddon, past president of the New York branch of the Professional Air Traffic Controllers Organization (PATCO)—before President Reagan broke the union in 1981. "The initiative must come from below," Seddon replied. "Sure, we'll organize a cooperative even if it has only three workers. But when we step in and start making trouble, they'd better not run and hide!" Unionization will not do away with wage labor, but it can provide protection with a collective contract. As shown by British cooperatives that were 85 percent unionized as long ago as the Great Depression, it can also make a difference in wages.[17]

Co-op workers are not taking their problems to the union local. "They haven't bled enough!" says Seddon. They relish their independence, and they distrust the labor bureaucrats who live off union dues. Like workers elsewhere, they are intimidated by their supervisors, fearful of losing their jobs and chances of promotion by taking an independent stand. With good reason—for the local food co-op has stooped to canceling the membership of at least one "labor agitator," calling the police when he supposedly disturbed the peace, and relying on police repression to bar him from trespassing, that is, shopping at the store.

It is typical of co-op workers to be hoodwinked by co-op ideology, the rhetoric of sharing and caring, and the apparent absence of a profit motive. Seddon wastes no time in demolishing the illusion that co-op workers are co-owners: "If they were really co-owners, they couldn't be fired."

There is still another feature of co-ops that is not generally known. Solvency is the express concern of co-op managers, but to judge from their behavior it is secondary to the concern of safeguarding their salaries. "The real boss is the customer," says the general manager, "and that means to expand sales." It also means piling up inventory—and that means spending more through additional borrowing. Meanwhile, increasing sales means more money in the till for professional salaries, business expenses, junkets, retreats, and additional discounts.

Management measures a co-op's success—and its own—in terms of sales, but it misleads co-op peons in claiming that more customers translate into higher wages. The *Cooperative Grocer* reports that basic wages increase as stores grow in size and in customers, but the *Natural Foods Merchandiser* reports the opposite. Merchandisers at the local food co-op give more credence to the *Natural Foods Merchandiser* survey. Consider its data on average hourly co-op wages in 1995: $6.76 in small stores; $5.93 in medium to large stores; and $5.83 in supermarkets.[18] Management's emphasis on sales may well disadvantage co-op peons, whose main concern is take-home pay.

Today, millions of Americans practice grass-roots democracy through the "ownership" and "control" of more than 23,000 cooperative businesses, including 11,000 employee-owned companies. Unlike its British cousin, with ties to the Labor party, or co-ops in the former Soviet Union and Yugoslavia—or Mozambique, for a more exotic example—the co-op movement in the United States is neither political nor labor-oriented. After all, Benjamin Franklin started the co-op movement with his mutual fire insurance company, and Teddy Roosevelt breathed new life into it with his national cooperative bank, the first of its kind.

What is the working stiff to make of a cooperative movement that boasts of being part of the mainstream—as American as apple pie? Most co-op members are passive, nonvoting, absentee owners with little interest in co-op affairs. In small and middle-size co-ops, a small minority of civic-minded activists effectively determines who will be elected to the board of directors. They are the ones who periodically attend the annual meeting to cast their votes. With the exception of absentee voting by these core members, rarely do absentee ballots make any difference to the outcome. The votes of owner-activists virtually ensure that a minority of owners will share control with management.

With the dissolution of the Soviet Union, the American Left has turned to cooperatives as a substitute wave of the future, although the much-touted cooperative movement is actually an invitation to reaction. While the big corporations represent a step forward in rule by and for members of the new class, cooperatives represent a step backward. That is because blocs of owner-members dominate the boards of directors, much as stockholders used to rule the corporations, and because discounts instead of professional salaries represent the biggest share of the surplus. Ironically, such reputedly socialist enterprises as the small and medium-size cooperatives represent not the vanguard but the rear guard of America's new economic order.[19]

Does this mean that working stiffs have no stake in co-ops and the cooperative movement? Not at all. Given their meager resources, cooperatives treat their workers better than do any other businesses. But the few concessions leave untouched the co-ops' sinister reality.

How cynical can one be? My reply is that cynicism is not just an attitude but also a philosophy—a philosophy *for* working stiffs, if not always *of* and *by* them.[20] As the philosophy best suited to defend their interests, it does more than expose the role of co-op managers and nonworking members. Just as important as unmasking labor's enemies is targeting false friends in its own camp—the cowardice and the foolishness of co-op workers. Labor has no more use for these potential scabs than it does for the Candides and Panglosses of the cooperative movement.

Although U.S. cooperatives keep sowing seeds of discontent, class struggle is dampened by the friendly relations among co-op members. Because of their business orientation, co-op managers and directors are downright hostile to any prospect of a collective contract that might cut into profits, although they do a first-rate job of covering up their hostility. When it comes to the bottom line, they are no different from managers and directors elsewhere—the self-serving liars and bullies in charge of U.S. corporations.

A Class against Itself

It is a sad commentary on present social reality that working stiffs are forging the new chains that bind them. Marxists believe there is an overabundance of victimization—but mainly of the capitalist vintage. Post-Marxists believe that workers are also exploited in postcapitalist societies. Some add that working stiffs are their own victimizers but that is hard for anyone to believe.

To be sure, working stiffs are not their own exploiters; if they were, they would also be the beneficiaries. Still, in supporting the principle "to each according to his work"—as determined freely by market forces—they are accomplices in their own exploitation. Every school child is taught that one is paid what one is worth and that with a college degree one is worth more than someone with only a high school education. Nobody obliges working stiffs to believe in a market ideology; but by believing in it, they uphold the system of expertise of which they are victims.

The most effective sanction of exploitation is a widely shared ideology eliciting the consent of the exploited. Such is the philosophy of the marketplace—

the principle of one dollar, one vote—and its political counterpart—one person, one vote. The irony is that these principles are at loggerheads because some have more dollars than others and therefore more votes. A free market means that those with the most dollars get the most. Everybody is free—to give *and* to receive.

Does this self-victimization through gift mean that workers are free to overcome their exploitation? Not at all, because the exploiters have the laws, the courts, and law-enforcers on their side. Still, working stiffs are free to trash the ideology that constrains them from joining together in self-protection. Astonishing as it may seem, however, they are governed less by solidarity than by petty egoisms. They are their own implacable enemies; their need to overcome exploitation collectively has yet to match their drive to pocket as much as they can individual'y.

In the *Communist Manifesto*, Marx distinguished two stages in the development of the proletariat as a class. During the first stage, wage earners direct their wrath against the instruments of production by smashing machinery to pieces and setting factories ablaze. Thus far, they lack political consciousness. Their political awakening must await further development when they become concentrated in large factories, recognize their common interests, begin to feel their united strength, and become organized. When workers come together to fight their class enemy, their struggle is political. What had initially been a class *in* itself is thus transformed into a class *for* itself.[21]

Marx failed to visualize a third stage when, after the displacement of the bourgeoisie as the ruling class, the proletariat would split into two antagonistic classes. The new professional class has since become a class for itself, but has the class of working stiffs reached the same level of awareness? On the contrary, from having been a class *for* itself, it has degenerated into a class *against* itself.

Henry Miller is one of the few Americans to have probed the surface of contemporary life. He was already well known for his message of sex instead of sacrifice when he challenged the great expectation of those who believe that working stiffs will inherit the earth. Over whose dead body? he asked. "The great bugaboo here in America is the 'dictatorship of the proletariat.' Looking at the rank and file . . . does any one honestly believe that these men will dictate the future of America? Can slaves become rulers overnight? These poor devils are begging to be led, and they are being led, but it's up a blind alley."[22]

Robert Tressell's *Ragged Trousered Philanthropists* is an anticapitalist novel, but it contains lessons on class politics. For Frank Owen, the novel's hero, social equality means that the mountains of wealth must be leveled and the valleys of want filled up. That goes beyond socialism to communism. However, working stiffs are taught that socialism would make life worse rather than better, while communism would mean total ruin. As Owen reflects on this social consensus, the system survives because "the majority are mostly fools; they not only agree to pass their lives in incessant slavery and want . . . but they say that it is quite right that they have to do so." They believe that the system is the best possible arrangement under the circumstances because they were told to believe it by their betters, by "those who were more educated and had plenty of time to study."[23]

They uphold the pecking order even among themselves. As one of Owen's fellow peons observes, "I can't see as it's right that a' inferior man should 'ave the same wages as me." Not just ignorance but self-complacence and apathy compounded by stupidity sustain the system. When the Borough Engineer's salary is raised to seventeen pounds a week, Owen calls it robbery. His fellow workers say that Owen would be glad to earn as much, apparently proving to their own satisfaction "that it was right for them to pay that amount to the Borough Engineer!"[24]

What was one to do in the face of such colossal imbecility, that of "starving, bootless, ragged, stupid wretches [who] fell down and worshiped the System"? There was little that anyone could do, for the workers deemed it safer to follow the prevailing wisdom than to rely on their own judgment. Worse still, they resented anyone among them who might tell them otherwise. "They did not know the causes of their poverty, they did not want to know. . . . All they desired was to be left alone so that they might continue to worship and follow those who took advantage of their simplicity." Like a flock of foolish sheep, they looked to a pack of ravening wolves for protection. Try to reason with them, to uplift them, and they turned against you. They were not only their own enemies but also the enemy their saviors would have to fight.[25]

The system has since changed; it can no longer credibly be called capitalist. However, the behavior of inferiors toward superiors is even more compliant than it was earlier. The differentiations among the exploited, the gradations among them, are so numerous and complex that it is not easy to see who exploits whom.

In the United States, the shift from old masters to new has barely changed the thinking of working stiffs. It is the general consensus that Americans are still living under capitalism; the shift itself has been barely perceived. Since the new relations of production are as yet unrecognized by most thinking people, what is one to expect from those unaccustomed to thinking about such important matters?

The public school system so supports the reign of expertise that the more education students receive, the less they know about what is going on. From kindergarten through grade twelve, social studies ensure that the new generation of social inferiors will learn cooperation, social responsibility, respect for our form of government, moral values, and the rights and duties of citizenship. Inferiors today consume more, and their trousers are seldom ragged; but these Robin Hoods in reverse are philanthropists nonetheless.

The charity practiced by these new working stiffs takes two principal forms. First, they agree to conditions of work that make it possible for superiors to exploit inferiors. Second, inferiors agree to a pecking order among themselves that benefits those in the upper ranks of the exploited. They are not coerced into doing so. Silvio Gesell's observation is as incisive as it is unfashionable: "Nothing prevents the workers in a factory, community, or trade union from pooling their wages and distributing the total amount according to the needs of the separate families. . . . No one prevents such communistic experiments: neither the State, nor the Church, nor the capitalists."[26] Nor, I should add, the new class of professional workers.

Most communist experiments have been dissolved by their leaders and by all whose work is above the average in pay. For the experiment to succeed, the most ambitious victims of exploitation would have to put their additional earnings into the wage fund as cheerfully as they put it into their wallets. But they are unlikely to do so should the results not meet their expectations of a better table, larger house, and more spacious garden. Communism in practice has almost always succumbed not to external factors but to "'inner enemies' consisting of the most efficient members of the community." As Gesell sums up the communist predicament, the larger the commune, the weaker is the impulse to work for its preservation: "An individual who works with one companion is less industrious than an individual who enjoys the fruit of his labor alone . . . if the whole human race is to share the proceeds of labor, everyone will say to himself: 'It does not matter how I work, for my work is but a drop in the ocean.' Work is then no longer impulse-driven; impulse must be replaced by some form of compulsion."[27]

The vain search for individual fulfillment, says the French novelist Louis-Ferdinand Céline, is the *bête noire* of communism. Working stiffs are so infected with invidious comparisons and the desire to get ahead that they do not care about those lagging behind. As Céline put it, the most militant worker, no matter how much he is exploited, "has about as much desire to share with his luckless brother worker as has the winner in the national lottery." The exploited are not ready for communism, and they are too depraved to appreciate it.[28]

In this respect, working stiffs resemble their exploiters. They, too, are predators, even if unsuccessful. They, too, are overcome by what theologians call original sin. As Céline told his Soviet hosts in 1936, "[T]he unique contribution of Christianity is that it acknowledges human beings to be the greatest scum on earth. But Marxists have the gall to dress up a turd and call it a caramel!"[29]

5

from professional power to professional pelf

[T]he unexplained increases in U.S. national income have been especially large in recent decades . . . the return to high school and to higher education has been about as large as the return to conventional forms of capital.
—Theodore Schultz, "Investment in Human Capital" (1961)

We find that in 1940 a total of 10,573,000 knowledge-producing workers were employed and earned a total of $15,120 million. . . . In 1958 there were 20,497,000 employed, earning $89,960 million.
—Fritz Machlup, *The Production and Distribution of Knowledge in the United States* (1962)

"The turning point in capitalist control over the economy," argued James Burnham in *The Managerial Revolution,* "was reached during the first world war." Since then, it has sunk continuously and in some areas has approached zero. Two kinds of control figure in his account: domination over the productive process and preferential treatment in distribution. For a new class to dominate, it is not enough that it occupy the driver's seat. It must also acquire the lion's share of the economic surplus. Together, these two kinds of control define the dominant or ruling class in society.[1]

We therefore need to ask the following questions. First, are capitalists still in a commanding position, and if not, why not? Second, are they still the principal beneficiaries of the economic surplus, and if not, who displaced them as members of a new ruling class?

Professionals' share of surplus wages is the Big Secret—the Great Unknown. With professionals in the saddle, talk about exploitation has become politically incorrect, a dead issue except for hangovers from the old order. Merit decides almost everything. But human livestock are still with us, and they are asking to be milked—if not by visible hands, then by the Invisible One.

How big is the professional surplus and the rip-off? To gauge their absolute size and to compare them with capital income, one needs to determine the ratio, first, of wages to profits; second, of surplus wages to profits; and third, of surplus wages in excess of the average paycheck to profits. Since the American economy is a showcase of the international economy, these data provide a clue to the global economy. Is it capitalist, or is it a new world order?

Professionals in the Driver's Seat

History shows that, in Burnham's words, "the most powerful (in terms of economic relations) will also be the wealthiest." But in Burnham's scenario, with the eruption of a new economic order challenging the old, power and income become unbalanced: "Those who receive the most preferential treatment in distribution (get the biggest relative share of the national income) have, in differing degrees in different nations and different sections of the economy, been losing control over access." Meanwhile, others who have gained control over access have yet to become its principal beneficiaries, although it is only a matter of time before the class in charge takes over the till.[2]

Burnham anticipated that the power-income balance would be restored during his lifetime, thereby heralding the doom of capitalism. But he lacked the conceptual tools for locating the threshold between the old and the new economic orders. Like his doctrinaire Marxist counterparts, he mistook state ownership of the major instruments of production for a necessary condition of control over the economy. Although Burnham correctly foresaw that a managerial elite would constitute a new ruling class, he mistakenly excluded other professional workers from membership in the new class.

Burnham made other mistakes. If one applies his criteria for distinguishing postcapitalist from capitalist society, then capitalism was *not*, as he claims it was, "dominant from the end of the Middle Ages until, let us say in order to fix a date, 1914." It took several centuries for the nascent capitalist sector to prevail over its feudal and landowning counterpart. Nor can one say with confidence that the Industrial Revolution, conventionally dated around 1776, was the threshold. Nor does anybody know when profits from capitalist agriculture and manufacturing in England caught up with rents from the ownership of land. Presumably, that had to wait until the first half of the nineteenth century when the Corn Laws came under fire and David Ricardo broke new ground by showing that the interest of the landlord is opposed to that of the consumer and manufacturer.[3]

While prematurely dating the consolidation of capitalism, Burnham prematurely dated its agony. Although professional managers may well have occupied the driver's seat during World War I, the capitalists' share of decision making has not "headed swiftly toward zero," much less their share of the national income. But then Burnham swung to the opposite pole by denying in the late 1970s that the end was even in sight.[4]

Burnham understated the evidence for a new order by excluding from his managerial class not only most professionals but also a high percentage of managers. His new ruling class consists of managers linked to the technical process of production, to the exclusion of executives, financial agents, and marketing specialists. Managers of banks, commercial houses, insurance companies, credit unions, mutual funds, hospitals, schools, trade unions, and government agencies also qualify for inclusion along with their professional staffs, for they, too, share in decision making and in a privileged share of the economic surplus.

In any case, the protracted process of creeping into a new order hardly implies the abrupt departure of the old one. The two may coexist for several generations, even centuries. Nor is informal ownership of the means of production through de facto possession or access the defining feature of the new class. The ownership of expertise, a virtual fourth factor of production, sufficed for the professional class to become the principal decision maker after World War I, thereby paving the way for it to become the principal beneficiary of the surplus after World War II.

The salient error in Burnham's account is that he took, as a preliminary condition of managerial society, a shift in the locus of sovereignty from parliamentary and congressional bodies to government bureaus under the direct control of professional bureaucrats *and* managerial control of the state through a one-party monopoly.[5] It never occurred to him that the market might play an even more crucial role in the redistribution of income, to the benefit of his managerial elite.

By management control, Burnham understood control *not* by "the highest ranked and best paid of the company officials . . . [with] the functions of guiding the company toward a profit" but by "operating executives, production managers, plant superintendents and their associates."[6] That some CEOs receive the bulk of their income from their accumulated capital in stocks and bonds rather than from executive compensation is therefore irrelevant to his claim that managers are in the driver's seat. Top executives do not have access to the controlling mechanism and are not even the principal employers of labor under the new dispensation.

Burnham misjudged the role of professionals in nonmanagerial positions, and he underestimated the role of accountants, marketing specialists, and business managers concerned with profit making and the importance of the educated elites in general who play a leading role in the administration of the state, the knowledge industry, and the service sector. As Christopher Lasch observed, "[T]he new professionals share so many characteristics with the managers of industry that the professional elite must be regarded . . . as a branch of modern management."[7] Rather than two independent classes, those of managers and professionals, there is only one that includes Burnham's managers. The question is what to call it. As the most widely used term for knowledge worker, *professional class* is a more accurate designation than *managerial class* for the elites destined to replace the capitalists.

Unlike Adolf Berle Jr. and Gardiner Means, who excluded stockholder-dominated and family-owned enterprises from the category of management-controlled enterprises, Burnham included them. While he agreed with Berle's assessment—"The waning factor is the capitalist"—he questioned Berle's conclusion—"The capital is there; and so is capitalism."[8] On the contrary, Burnham described the United States in the early 1940s as having a transitional economy intermediate to capitalism and managerial society.

The American experience is sufficiently complex to cast doubt on Burnham's premises. Professionals have become the principal beneficiaries without expropriating the monied interests and ridding corporations of their financial magnates and boards of directors. As late as 1965, family-owned and stockholder-controlled corporations still occupied a conspicuous place on the American scene. Nonetheless, being family-owned or stockholder-controlled did not insulate them from the general trend away from capital income in favor of professional compensation. The data for enterprises among the top three hundred nonfinancial corporations show that dividend distributions as a percentage of both retained profits and the wage and salary bill were not appreciably different from distributions in management-controlled enterprises in Berle and Means's sense. Capitalist hegemony on boards of directors is no guarantee that ownership interests will prevail, since professional workers have been carrying off a privileged share of the loot.[9]

That Burnham's theory failed to keep abreast of the times has not prevented establishment economists from dismissing it as premature. Professional managers, we are told, have in the course of time become capitalists. In his study of fifty large manufacturing corporations, Wilbur G. Lewellen found that the proportion of top executive income based on stock-related rewards jumped from 5 percent of after-tax income in the 1940s to 46 percent by the late 1960s and that "by the early 1960s the after-tax income of chief executives that was derived from all forms of ownership of the company . . . was on an average $6^{1}/_{2}$ times higher than . . . compensation based on their management of the company." However, top executives are not managers in Burnham's sense.

Moreover, Lewellen arrived at these figures by stacking his cards—by restricting the meaning of managerial compensation to salaries and bonuses.[10]

Using a more credible conception of managerial compensation, Robert J. Larner arrived at the opposite conclusion: "control by management rather than by stockholders existed in more than 80% of the 200 largest nonfinancial corporations in 1963." As he distinguished managerial compensation from ownership compensation, it has four components: "(1) salary, (2) cash and stock bonuses, (3) corporate contributions to savings and stock purchase plans, and (4) the realized value of stock options."[11] By this quite different stacking of the cards, he lent support to Berle and Means's theory of power without property, a managerial revolution within American business.

But is a share of the profits for managerial services not a disguised form of capital? No, because capital income is a return for the *ownership* of capital, so that it is only *after* stocks-in-lieu-of-a-salary-raise begin yielding dividends that professionals receive additional compensation in the form of capital income. Suppose corporate managers sell their stock options above their original market price. Then, only the profit from their sale—the excess over their price as payment for managerial services—counts as capital income. Even if the managers are lucky, the 10 or 20 percent increase in their market price will represent only a small percentage of their total payments.

In support of an obsolete theory of capitalism, Marxist political economists so stretch the meaning of capital income that it includes executive and top managerial salaries. Only by this questionable device are there grounds for asserting, as Victor Perlo did, that the "identity of class interests as between managers and controlling stockholders" is such that "corporate managers are part of, as well as agents of, a ruling group, the financial oligarchy."[12]

A more credible scenario of how managerial takeover relates to preferential treatment in distribution is provided by theories of a knowledge society. According to John Kenneth Galbraith, the corporate technostructure—including professionals other than managers—takes control from the capitalists because of delegated authority that supplies information under conditions in which expertise is scarcer than capital. According to the management guru Peter Drucker, knowledge is a factor of production whose pelf and power similarly derive from its relative scarcity. For both writers, the role of the university in the production and distribution of knowledge is a central fact of the managerial revolution, crucial to understanding the new industrial society.[13]

At least Burnham was on the right track in summing up the conditions of a new order: first, capitalists are displaced from positions of influence; second, capitalists are no longer the principal beneficiaries of the economic surplus.

Although the transition to a new order does not hinge mainly on distribution, a change in the social relations of production in time results in redistribution. As Galbraith belatedly acknowledged, he had not given Burnham his due. He should have, because in the second edition of *The New Industrial State,* he admits that "[t]he managerial revolution—the assumption of power by top management—is conceded."[14]

What has not been conceded is the second condition, that the surplus wages of managers and other professionals have caught up to and surpassed the income of capitalists in the United States. By *capital income* is meant the distributed net returns to individuals from the ownership of capital, that is, private profit in the most general sense that includes dividends, interest, rent, and entrepreneurial income but excludes undistributed corporate profits. Although an undisclosed portion of proprietor's income takes the form of wages of owner-managers and an undisclosed portion of capital income is pocketed by wage earners who are not capitalists, we have chosen to err—if err we must—on the conservative side.

Are capitalists, then, still the primary beneficiaries? To answer this question, the following ratios need to be calculated: first, the W/P ratio, where W represents total wages and related employee compensation—not just current wages but such wage supplements as bonuses and social insurance paid by employers and deferred wages in the form of retirement income—and P represents capital income or the distribution of profit in its various forms; second, the S/P ratio, where S represents surplus wages in excess of the officially established cost of subsistence of professional as well as nonprofessional employees; third, the B/P ratio, where B represents the share in surplus wages in excess of the average paycheck—the professional pelf attributable to exploitation.

The Wage/Profit Ratio

In the history of socialist thought, the W/P ratio still survives as an indicator of the threshold to a new society. Although its legacy may be traced to Saint-Simon and the Saint-Simonians during the first part of the nineteenth century, its classic formulation is in Silvio Gesell's *Natural Economic Order.* "The abolition of unearned income, of so-called surplus-value, also termed interest and rent," he wrote in 1906, "is the immediate aim of every socialist movement." But nationalization of the means of production is not the only way to achieve it. Abolishing interest and rent by controlling the money supply and nationalizing the land are enough for private ownership to lose its capitalist character. Given free competition under conditions in which money and land are no longer monopolized, "every able technician will become an able manufacturer . . . [and] the manufacturer's profit must be reduced to the level of a technician's salary."[15] In this scenario, capitalists are defined as owners of money for which they receive interest, and landowners are the recipients of rent. Everyone else is a worker. Consequently, only plutocrats and landowners are exploiters.[16]

As we have seen, Keynes developed a kindred scenario leading to government control of the money supply that promised a gradual euthanasia of the rentier. Meanwhile, the Nazi experiment settled on a similar course under the influence of Gottfried Feder's *Manifesto against Usury and Interest Slavery*. In distant Argentina, President Juan Domingo Perón paid homage to Gesell's legacy by raising the W/P ratio to the point where wages matched capital income—the presumptive threshold to socialism.[17]

It was the socialism of fools—no socialism at all. Argentina's labor leaders were slow to wake up to the reality that crossing the W/P threshold was, first, difficult to achieve and even harder to maintain in an economically dependent country; second, little consolation in view of labor's considerably greater share in such comparable countries as Canada and Australia; and third, incapable of getting the slavemasters off their backs. They had only to look to the materialist colossus of the North, where the W/P threshold came within sight as early as 1919 at 93 percent and was successfully crossed at 137 percent the following year: the workers there were still enthralled under new bosses and old. In the United States, socialism had to wait for the W/P ratio to climb from 206 percent in 1933 to over 400 percent in 1970, where it remained for a decade—a record unmatched at the end of the millennium.[18] Socialism, yes, but hardly the promised land of socialist ideologues.

The Surplus Wage Threshold

Consider next the S/P ratio, which varies directly with the W/P ratio. As the difference between the price and the cost of the various grades of manpower, surplus wages are a function of three principal variables: first, annual wages (W); second, the annual cost of subsistence as measured by minimum wages for a given year (M); third, the per capita minimum wage per annum (m) and the number of workers in full-time equivalents (n). Thus,

$S = W - M$, where $M = mn$

But haven't I forgotten a fourth variable, the cost of training and education? Since its cost is bound to exceed what is necessary to subsistence, the corresponding skills and expertise can be purchased only with an already existing surplus. Will the modest surpluses pocketed by working stiffs suffice?

On the contrary, the bulk of educational expenses must be paid out of profits or professional pelf, out of unearned income, so that additional income acquired by means of it is largely gratuitous.

In effect, most of the skills and expertise in the world are the fruit of other people's labor. If a full work load is required for subsistence, then a college education, which necessitates additional hours of study and money for tuition, is beyond the reach of the vast majority of ordinary mortals. Since it becomes a superhuman task, somebody else has to foot the bill.

But suppose we give the devil its due. Calculated like the price of a computer, not in a machine but in the head, the prorated annual cost of highly qualified brainpower turns out to be statistically insignificant. Assuming that the cost of different skills is due almost wholly to differences in training costs, even some Marxists concede that brainpower functions as constant instead of variable capital.[19]

These obstacles to calculating the S/P ratio having been overcome, one can turn to the appropriate tables in the U.S. government's *Statistical Abstract* covering employment, the minimum wage, and employee compensation to determine if and when the bulk of the distributed surplus began taking the form of surplus wages instead of capital income.

During World War II and the decade immediately following, the average weekly work load exceeded the 40-hour norm but then slipped down to bottom out at 34.5 hours in 1990 and 1995. In 1945, it topped at 43.5 hours, slid down to 40.5 in 1950, and remained roughly steady in 1955 at 40.7. In 1960, however, it fell abruptly to 38.6 hours, held at 38.8 in 1965, but then glided downward to 37.1 hours in 1970, to 36.1 hours in 1975, to 35.3 hours in 1980, and to 34.9 hours in 1985.[20]

If allowances are made for these shifts downward that were only partly accounted for in *America's New Economic Order,* the postwar professional surplus exceeded capital income by the following margins. In 1950, the S/P ratio was 128 percent but surged to a whopping 186 percent in 1955. In 1960, it again leaped upward to 195 percent and remained roughly steady at 217 percent in 1965. In 1970, it climbed to 253 percent and then reached a new record-breaking 267 percent in 1975, until it dropped back to 255 percent in 1980. In 1985, it continued roughly steady at 252 percent and was again at 250 percent in 1990. In 1995, it broke the 1975 record by climbing to 272 percent.[21]

Contrary to my earlier readings of the data, the S/P ratio did not collapse during the 1980s.[22] Designed to revive the private sector, the politics of the Reagan administration did not accomplish its purpose. At most, the Reagan presidency placed a cap on the S/P ratio that kept it from rising. Whatever the explanation of the leveling off at 250 percent, the great irony is that the president gave free rein to the pursuit of profit without paring down the surplus concealed in wages. There was certainly no restoration of capitalism in the United States. Figures do not lie, even though statisticians do.

Professional Pelf

While the surplus wage threshold is basic to determining the respective shares of labor and professionals in surplus wages, the average paycheck defines the lower limit of professionals' pelf comparable to capital income or profit. To repeat, professionals and allied technical workers with a desk, office, or bureau are bureaucrats, even if they do not belong to the management team. The term *professional* is broad enough to include all supervisory workers who are knowledge workers. There is a hierarchy of competence that includes in descending order the semiprofessional, the quasi-professional, and the professionaloid. Besides those with doctoral, master's, and bachelor's degrees, there are certified workers from community colleges and technical institutes of various kinds—all with some degree of professionalism. Otherwise, what distinguishes them from nonprofessionals is a wage or salary above the average—the spoils of office—the surplus that may be defined as professional.

There are three basic factors for determining the amount of professional pelf: first, the proportion of brainworkers or educated workers to the total work force; second, the average paycheck as a condition of calculating surplus wages in excess of the average; third, the surplus between the minimum wage and the average paycheck.

In our definition of professional pelf, B varies directly with S. How large, then, does the S/P ratio have to be for the B/P ratio to exceed unity? How large does the professionals' share in exploitation have to be for professional pelf to exceed capital income? The answers to these two questions will tell us whether brainworkers have surpassed capitalists in exploitation.

Turning to the tables on national income, we discover that the threshold to a new order first came into view when the S/P ratio rose from 186 percent in 1955 to 195 percent in 1960. Employee compensation (W) in 1960 was $295 billion with capital income (P) at $86 billion. There were 65.8 million wage earners working an average of 38.6 hours per week. The full-time equivalent (n) for a forty-hour week and a fifty-week year was therefore 63.5 million. The minimum wage (m) was $2,000 annually. Basic wages (mn) came to $127 billion; surplus wages ($W - mn$) amounted to $168 billion. If professional pelf (B) was at least as much as the surplus between the minimum wage and the average paycheck (D), professionals would have pocketed some $84 billion, only $2 billion short of the $86 billion in capital income.[23]

Let the S/P ratio serve as a rough index of the B/P ratio. If the huge increase in brainpower in the work force since World War II is taken into consideration, the B/P ratio may first have cleared 100 percent when the S/P ratio reached 200 percent—as it did in the years after 1960.

This index has three arguments in its favor. First, proprietors' income is a mixed bag that includes wages in addition to profits for owner-managers. Second, another part of capital income consists of token returns from savings deposits, municipal bonds, and stock owned by ordinary workers and the more-than-token returns to managers and other professionals. Consequently, when the S/P ratio reaches parity at 100 percent, the ratio of surplus wages to *capitalist* income must exceed this figure. Third, all of professionals' pelf qualifies as professional income. It follows that the ratio of professional pelf to *capitalist* income is always greater than the B/P ratio.

In 1970, for example, the privileged categories of workers—classified as managerial, professional, technical, craft, and kindred workers—consisted of 29.6 million in a work force of 78.6 million—about 40 percent. That same year, approximately the same 40 percent earned more than the average wage of $7,537. The minimum wage was then $3,200.[24] Although several million workers earned no surplus at all and most of their fellow workers earned only token amounts, it is an open question whether the professional pelf of the 40 percent exceeded the nonpelf surplus of the 60 percent. For lack of the relevant data and to proceed with the calculations, let us suppose that the B/D ratio was approximately 100 percent.

By 1970, the S/P ratio reached a record-breaking 253 percent. What, then, was the corresponding B/P ratio if B and D were roughly equal? In 1970, there were 78.7 million wage earners working an average of 37.1 hours per week. The full-time equivalent (n) for a 40-hour week came to 73 million. The minimum wage (m) was $3,200, and basic wages ($mn$) some $233.6 billion. Employee compensation (W) stood at $612 billion, resulting in surplus wages ($W - mn$) of $378.4 billion. On the supposition that professional pelf (B) was 100 percent of the nonpelf surplus (D), B was $189.2 billion. Since capital income (P) was $149.8 billion, the B/P ratio topped capital income by a healthy margin of almost $40 billion.[25]

The Bureau of the Census's 1982–83 *Statistical Abstract* shows a full-time equivalent work force of 79.1 million in 1980, employee compensation of $1,599 billion, minimum wages of $490 billion, a wage surplus of $1,109 billion, and capital income of $395 billion. If professional pelf were only half of the wage surplus, it would have been $554.5 billion. Although the S/P ratio remained more or less constant at 255 percent, the wage surplus and the corresponding professional pelf continued to rise, the latter topping capital income by almost $160 billion.

How did matters stand a decade later? In 1990, total employment surged to 118.8 million wage earners working an average of 34.5 hours per week. The full-time equivalent was 102.4 million. The minimum wage was $7,375, and the minimum or basic wages nationally totaled some $755 billion. Employee compensation was $3,353 billion, with capital income around $1,041 billion.[26] Surplus wages came to $2,598 billion, so if half consisted of professional pelf, the latter would have amounted to $1,299 billion. On the foregoing premise and notwithstanding the Reagan presidency, the B/P ratio kept surging ahead by a margin of $258 billion.

In 1995, total employment barely rose to 119.3 million, while the average work week remained steady at 34.5 hours. The full-time equivalent was only 102.6 million, but the minimum wage had risen to $8,500; hence, basic wages increased from $755 billion in 1990 to $872 billion in 1995. Employee compensation was $4,209 billion, with capital income at $1,229 billion.[27] Surplus wages amounted to $3,337 billion. Assuming a B/D ratio of 100 percent, professional pelf would have peaked at $1,668 billion—a record-breaking increase over capital income of $439 billion.

Overall, professionals' share of the surplus has moved steadily upward— indeed, at a rate exceeding the increase in capital income.[28] There are multiple explanations of this phenomenon. First, the share of wages relative to capital income has risen. Second, the wage surplus has increased relative to capital income. Third, the median wage for professional workers has risen proportionate to increases in the minimum wage. Fourth, the upper limit on professional wages has mushroomed almost beyond belief. Fifth, the number of professional workers has grown relative to that of ordinary workers. Sixth, the professional pelf has increased relative to labor's share of the surplus. Seventh, the professional surplus has risen compared with labor's share, although its actual size is still the Great Unknown.

I have suggested that we take the S/P ratio as an index of the B/P ratio. On the premise of a B/D ratio of 100 percent, the B/P ratio must exceed unity when S/P passes the 200 percent mark. This threshold was first crossed with a substantial margin in 1970 when the S/P ratio reached 253 percent. Since this ratio has remained consistently around the 250 percent mark since 1970, it is safe to conclude that the Great Society inaugurated by President Lyndon Johnson was the dividing line, the turning point between America's old order and a new one.[29]

Although the Information Age preceded by a decade the advent of President Johnson's Great Society, it was the harbinger of a postcapitalist society. The technological revolution represented by the invention of the silicon chip in 1958–59—with its fabulous powers of memory and calculation and its electronic circuitry in a miniaturized space too small to see—made computers cheaper and faster until they became ubiquitous in corporate decision making. On the one hand, the flow of reliable information so strengthened the hand of top management that it began skipping over the company's middle-rung bureaucracy.[30] On the other hand, the bypassing and downsizing of middle management brought about an increasing demand for professional knowledge in other capacities. Overall, the salaries of professional workers in the 1960s went up the escalator instead of the stairs, and in the 1970s they took to the elevator. Consequently, a strong case can be made for dating the transition to our brave new world not with the budding but with the flowering of the Information Age. By then, President Johnson's Great Society had begun to bear fruit.

The 1980s and 1990s present a somewhat confusing picture. While the S/P ratio remained stable throughout the Reagan and Bush administrations, rentier income soared and a small number of households became amazingly rich. The growth in employee compensation failed to keep pace with the growth of capital income. The W/P ratio fell from 405 percent in 1980 to 322 percent in 1990, and it barely recovered during President Clinton's first term, to 342 percent in 1995 due in part to a significant boost in the minimum wage. The Reagan presidency kept it down. Only labor's share suffered disproportionately. The share of professional workers continued its upward climb.

Postcapitalist society made its debut during the late 1960s and early 1970s, so that neither mainstream nor Marxist political economy any longer applies. Yet the Marxist prophecy has been realized. Marxist political economy aspires to become obsolete. As Abraham Guillén put it, "The day in which the historical and economic conditions that gave birth to it no longer exist, it will cease to explain its world."[31] Although the transition to a new order took place in unexpected ways, behind closed doors, and with surprising results, Marxists still have reason to celebrate. The capitalist juggernaut is no longer in control, a new order has dawned, and their beloved proletariat has become its principal beneficiary—albeit a proletariat of exploiters instead of exploited.

Preferential Treatment in Distribution

We have to consider two questions that are likely to be confused. First, how big is the professional rip-off? Second, what is the professional share of surplus wages? Thus far we have arrived only at a calculated guess in response to the first question.

Unlike the capitalist rip-off, the professional surplus consists of two quite different parts: the pelf in excess of the average wage and the professional share of surplus wages below the average but in excess of the minimum wage. Answering the first question leads to a comparison of the relative shares in exploitation of property holders and professionals; answering the second question leads to a comparison of their relative shares in the total surplus. As we shall see, a definitive answer to the first question depends on answering the second.

To estimate the extent of preferential treatment in distribution, we need a measuring rod other than the one used to measure professional exploitation. Professional pelf (B) extends only upward from the average paycheck. The professional share in surplus wages (S) extends not only upward but also downward to the minimum wage. Let Q stand for this additional component in the professional share, and let L represent labor's share of the surplus so that the nonpelf surplus $D = L + Q$. Then

$$S = (B + Q) + L$$

From this formula, we can derive the formulas covering both professional exploitation of the labor force (B) and the professional share of surplus wages ($B + Q$). The formula for professional or bureaucratic exploitation is therefore

$$B = S - (L + Q)$$

This formula is fundamental in comparing the exploitation of labor by professionals, on the one hand, and by capitalists, on the other. So conceived, B is the perfect analogue of P, representing profits. By comparing the size of B and P, we can determine which class is the bigger exploiter. The B/P ratio can also tell us if and when capitalist society was overtaken by postcapitalism.

The formula for the professional share of surplus wages provides a measure of the professional surplus vis-à-vis capital income. Thus

$$B + Q = S - L$$

This formula has the advantage of including the entire professional share in the surplus—even though its Q portion may be earned. To determine who gets the largest chunk of the surplus is no less vital than to ask who gets something for nothing. The former rather than the latter provides the guideline to preferential treatment in distribution.

Table 527 in the 1996 *Statistical Abstract* contains all the data needed for our purpose. Based on federal adjusted gross income (AGI) tax returns by source of income and income level, it greatly simplifies the task of ferreting out the data relevant to preferential treatment. Thanks to table 527, the Great Unknown becomes the Great Known—if only for the targeted year 1993.

At issue is the division of the total surplus between professionals and proprietors of real and surrogate wealth—that is, the ratio of the professional surplus to capital income. This ratio $(B + Q)/P$—the measure of preferential treatment in distribution—may be determined on the basis of the following information in the 1993 tax returns:

1. total wages: $2,723,086 million
2. minimum-wage threshold between the first tax bracket (under $10,000) and the second tax bracket ($10,000–$19,999): $10,000.
3. number of professional tax returns: 41,854,000
4. number of labor returns between the average and minimum cutoffs: 33,961,000
5. wages under the minimum-wage threshold: $49,348 million
6. average-wage threshold between the third tax bracket ($20,000–$29,999) and fourth tax bracket ($30,000–$39,999): $30,000.

The legislated minimum wage in 1993 was $8,500 for a forty-hour week and a fifty-week year. The minimum-wage threshold for tax purposes was thus $1,500 above the minimum wage. Recalling our formula $S = W - M$, let us begin by calculating the subsistence cost of the 1993 work force on the basis of this inflated figure.

Given that $M = mn$, where $m = $10,000$ and $n = 41,854,000 + 33,961,000$, the cost of the work force paid the minimum wage or more came to $758,150 million. Add to this figure the $49,348 million representing wages under the $10,000 threshold. Therefore $M = $807,498$ million. Subtract this figure from $W = $2,723,086$ million to get the sum of surplus wages: $S = $1,915,588$ million.

The professional surplus $(B + Q)$ is the sum of professional salaries in the top tax brackets, four through seven, less the subsistence cost of professional brainpower—that is, less the cost of $418,540 million. Salaries in the fourth bracket ($30,000–$39,999) came to $360,875 million; in the fifth bracket ($40,000–$49,999), the total was $337,999 million; in the sixth bracket ($50,000–$99,999), it was $915,569 million; and in the seventh bracket ($100,000 and up), it was $532,218 million, for a total sum of $2,146,661 million. Thus, $B + Q = $1,728,121$ million.

We are now positioned to calculate B and Q separately as a condition of comparing the B/P ratio with the $(B + Q)/P$ ratio. Let us first calculate Q, the product of 41,854,000 professional tax returns and the approximately $20,000 per capita professional surplus below the average paycheck. Therefore $Q = $837,080$ million. Subtracting this sum from $B + Q$, we get $B = $891,041 million.

In 1993, capital income or profits (P) came to $659,678 million. (This sum excludes from the tax returns AGI pensions and annuities, a mixed bag of deferred wages and deferred profits—alike indeterminate.) Therefore, comparing professional with capitalist pelf, B/P came to 135 percent. That is a fairly healthy margin to the advantage of professionals. But compare it with professionals' preferential treatment in distribution: (B + Q)/P = 262 percent. If we look back from 1993, the threshold to postcapitalist society was no doubt crossed two or three decades earlier—if not during President Johnson's Great Society, then in the 1970s.

We can now dispense with our calculated guess in the preceding section—that is, that professional pelf compared with the nonpelf share of the surplus was roughly 100 percent. (The 1993 data indicate it was 87 percent.) We can now calculate L because of the values assigned to S and to $B + Q$ in our basic formula:

$$L = S - (B + Q)$$

Since S = \$1,915,588 million and $(B + Q)$ = \$1,728,121 million, L = \$187,467 million. In 1993, B was \$891,041 million. Consequently, the B/L ratio was approximately 475 percent. As for the (B + Q)/L ratio, it was almost twice that amount—a whopping 921 percent.

These ratios further corroborate the thesis that the threshold to postcapitalist society was crossed as early as the Vietnam War—a war not between capitalism and socialism but between two very different socialist powers.

Socialist regimes differ over how the surplus is divided, not just between professionals and proprietors but also between expertise and labor (B + Q/L) and between capital and labor (P/L). Although professionals have replaced capitalists in both power and pelf, there are significant differences in preferential treatment in distribution between a society in which labor ranks as professionals' main ally and one in which capital plays that role. At stake is whether capital's share exceeds labor's share of the surplus or conversely.

Class struggle continues under conditions of actually existing socialism, if not for the primary share of the surplus, at least for the secondary share. Who occupies second place makes a huge difference to organized labor and the surviving capitalists. Their relative shares underscore two main types of postcapitalist society: fascist socialism, in which the P/S ratio exceeds the L/S ratio; and communist socialism, in which the L/S ratio tops the P/S ratio. The cold war and the Korean War were fought in part over this underlying question; the same question subtended the Nazi-Soviet confrontation during World War II.

Globalization: Capitalist or Postcapitalist?

Is there a new world order corresponding to America's new economic order? Globalization, we are told, spells the end of U.S. hegemony—at least economically. Multinational and transnational institutions, along with a new transnational elite, have supposedly established their own global economic and political hegemonies. American, European, and Japanese corporations rather than their domestic economies are defined as the principal actors. The interpenetration of national capitals is held responsible for the transformation of multinational corporations into today's transnationals, merging markets, and free trade associations, while the regional breakdown of the world into core and periphery is losing its relevance. Such are the ingredients and such is the scenario of a new world order in the making.

But is globalization capitalist, as it is almost universally depicted? Did the collapse of the Soviet Union in 1991 spell not only the end of the cold war but also the end of actually existing socialism? Or has the American model proven to be a more dynamic version of postcapitalist society? The cold war was supposedly a struggle between capitalism and socialism. It began as such, but that was hardly how it ended.

Let us briefly consider the case for and against the prevailing perception of the global economy. "We are now in a new epoch, the fourth one in the history of capitalism," declaims Roger Burbach in a lead article in the quarterly newsletter of the Union for Radical Political Economics. First came the Age of Discovery and Conquest of the New World (ca. 1500–1600); then the rise of the bourgeoisie, the Industrial Revolution, and the forging of the nation-state (ca. 1600–1900); next, the emergence of the modern corporation, imperialism, and a socialist alternative to capitalism between the two world wars (ca. 1900–1970); and finally, the onset of "globalization, highlighted technologically by the microchip and the computer—the Information Age, if you will—and politically by the collapse of twentieth century socialism." Among the milestones or markers of this fourth epoch, Burbach lists the ending of the Bretton Woods currency agreements, when the United States went off the gold standard in 1971; the formation of the Trilateral Commission in the mid-1970s; and the Cancun Summit in Mexico in 1982, when the major powers began imposing neoliberal adjustment programs on the Third World. There you have the latest fashion among radical think tanks in the United States— a rethinking of classical Marxism in line with the rethinking of former New Deal liberals.[32]

Why rethinking? First, because of the break with Marxism's relentless pursuit of economic development at any price, its rush to modernization that, according to Burbach, ultimately failed to bury capitalism. Second, because of the break with Marxism's focus on a working class that is today fragmented and can no longer be credibly regarded as the sole or even primary agent of radical social change. Third, because of the break with Marxism's strategy for winning the battle of democracy, a strategy increasingly irrelevant in a corrupt democracy tied to the big money and corporate interests.[33]

But is the new world order capitalist? If America's new order is postcapitalist, the globalization of corporate America is unlikely to be anything less than a magnified version of America's postcapitalist order. Because the principal players are not private but quasi-public enterprises, the transnationals resemble enterprises with state participation in generating wage surpluses in excess of the returns from capital investment.

Theoretically, this means that the S/P and B/P ratios of the transnationals tend to exceed the ratios of the national economies in which owner-managed firms still have a role. Some three decades ago, before the contours of a new world order were being drawn, the ratios of surplus wages to profits in some of America's top corporations were several times the national ratios. In 1965, for example, the S/P national ratio was roughly 2:1, whereas in my sampling of corporations, even with family-controlled boards of directors, the ratio varied from 6:1 (Allied Chemical) to as high as 27:1 (Chrysler).[34]

Further research would be required to arrive at overall figures for America's corporate sector, but for any given year the corporate ratio would still be several times the national ratio. This means that the degree of socialization in America's share of the global economy is bound to exceed the degree at home. That is because the national ratios are dragged down by the private sector.

Most political economists, whether Marxist or mainstream, have yet to envision the hegemonic role, first, of a socialist sector in the United States without benefit of socialists; second, of a capitalist sector without benefit of capitalism. A double paradox, but not to be taken lightly.

At issue is what defines socialism and capitalism. Is state, municipal, and cooperative ownership of the means of production crucial to the definition of socialism, or is it the mode of pumping out and appropriating the surplus? The latter is fundamental; the former is derivative. As Marx put it, "The specific economic form in which unpaid surplus-labor is pumped out of direct producers, determines the relationship of rulers and ruled, as it grows directly out of production itself."[35] It was only on the erroneous premise that there are only three factors of production (land, labor, and capital) that he concluded that socialism requires not only the abolition of bourgeois private property but also its collectivization. We have seen that neither of these conditions is necessary. Because of the private ownership of expertise, all that is necessary is that knowledge workers pump out a surplus concealed in wages that exceeds the capitalists' share.

As for the accumulation of capital without capitalism, it may be found at both the dawn and the dusk of capitalist production. For Marx, the precapitalist forms of capital are trading or merchant's capital and its close relative, interest-bearing or usurer's capital. Why precapitalist? Because they appeared under modes of production antedating the rise of industrial capital and the specifically capitalist mode of pumping out a surplus. As Marx wrote, "The independent and predominant development of capital as merchant's capital is tantamount to the non-subjection of production to capital." As for interest-bearing capital, it "belongs with its twin brother, merchant's capital, to the antediluvian forms of capital, which long precede the capitalist mode of production."[36]

Although islands of capitalist production appeared as early as the sixteenth century, the emergence of capitalism could not have occurred prior to the Industrial Revolution in the last quarter of the eighteenth century, when the bourgeoisie, having ceased to be predominantly commercial and financial, became predominantly industrial. How long it took for capitalism to prevail is evident from the class struggle between bourgeois and proletarians, in Engels's words, "a struggle which, apart from England, existed in 1848 only in Paris and, at most, in a few big industrial centers."[37] As for the eclipse of capitalism in the advanced industrial countries—at least in the United States—it may be dated from the third quarter of the twentieth century, when America's new economic order caught up to and surpassed, without burying, the old.

Although Marx failed in his assessment of the new mode of production— the prospect of socialism without socialists never occurred to him—he fully understood the history of capitalists without capitalism. But do Marx's epigones understand this history? Their present efforts to peg the global economy as capitalist miss the mark. Instead of focusing on industrial capital, they stress the role of finance capital in the global market, the fact that "over one trillion dollars a day is traded or moved in international currency markets"—as if finance capital were the principal motor behind the process of globalization.[38]

On different grounds, experts in high-tech finance in the spectronic (speculative-electronic) or casino economy claim that global leadership rests with the paper economy. McKinsey and Co., for example, estimated that of the $800 billion or so traded every day in the world's currency markets in the early 1990s, at most $25 billion involved global exchanges in actual commodities—a volume of trade in paper over thirty times greater than the trade in real wealth. Financial leadership is also claimed for America's domestic economy. According to Kevin Phillips, "Each month, several dozen huge domestic financial firms and exchanges . . . electronically trade a total sum in currencies, futures, derivative instruments, stocks, and bonds that exceeds the entire annual gross national product of the United States!" In the 1990s, purely financial transactions by American firms had swollen to an annual volume "thirty or forty times greater than the dollar turnover of the 'real economy.' "[39]

These figures are impressive; they are also misleading. Although trading profits at Wall Street investment banks and securities houses in 1992 reached the staggering figure of $16.3 billion, the profits of corporations as distinct from capitalist income in the same year came to $401.4 billion—almost twenty-five times as much.[40]

Global trading in currencies and securities redistributes already existing surpluses instead of creating new ones. The size of such transactions is no indication of their economic importance. The emerging world order is spearheaded not by the global financial network but by a few hundred imperial corporations, many of which are wealthier than most sovereign nations. As Richard Barnet and John Cavanagh pointed out, "Ford's economy is larger than Saudi Arabia's and Norway's. Philip Morris's annual sales exceed New Zealand's gross domestic product." Note well the examples; they are not banks or brokerage houses. The global economy consists of global production and marketing with financial backing. Industrial corporations, not banks, lie at the core of the global economy. Summing up their extensive research on globalization, Barnet and Cavanagh concluded that "a few hundred business enterprises control the human energy, capital, and technology that are making it happen. They are the midwives of the new world economy."[41] Their prime beneficiaries are professionals, not capitalists.

Technology transfers, not transfers of currency or securities, define what these authors call the "Global Workplace," the "Global Shopping Mall," and the "Global Cultural Bazaar." The driving force behind them can be traced to three hundred corporate giants in the United States, Japan, and five European countries (Germany, France, Switzerland, the Netherlands, and the United Kingdom). "The combined assets of these top 300 firms now make up roughly a quarter of the productive assets of the world," Barnet and Cavanagh wrote in 1994. The "Global Financial Network" is mainly icing on the cake.[42] Since distributed profits are no longer a match for professional pelf in these corporations, one can only conclude that both the U.S. economy and its share of the global economy are no longer capitalist but are part of a postcapitalist world order.

Professional Pelf and Financialization

When capitalists are pushed out of manufacturing, where do they go? They move into the financial sectors, into banking, into trading on the bond and stock exchanges. What Phillips called "financialization" is the specific form of finance capital after manufacturing industries begin to decline and nations pass their zenith as "aggressive societies of entrepreneurs, tinkerers, and engineers."[43]

But is the bulk of financialization capitalist? Is there no casino economy under socialism corresponding to the one under capitalism—as in the former Yugoslavia and today's China? Profits from buying cheap and selling dear occur under both systems.

Gambling and speculating in currencies, commodities, equity, credit, and interest rates are not a monopoly of capitalists. It all depends on the players. If they are private owners and entrepreneurs, they are capitalists; if they are public or quasi-public corporations, their gambling and speculating are post-capitalist once the B/P ratio exceeds unity.

The same reasoning that pertains to nonfinancial institutions applies to financial ones. If at General Motors professionals' share of surplus wages exceeds distributed profits, the corporation is only secondarily a capitalist one. In financial corporations, surplus wages are a deduction from gross interest and from profits in trading currencies and securities—it does *not* follow that they are a form of capital revenue. If the financial engineers at Chase Manhattan and Merrill Lynch pocket a professional surplus in excess of the distributed profits, it is hardly credible to characterize that surplus as capitalist.

The concept of finance capital is central to most analyses of the paper economy. In keeping with the conventional wisdom, they take for granted that the paper economy is the capitalist sector par excellence. On the contrary, the so-called securities industry is even more socialized than is manufacturing.

In 1993, the ratio of employee compensation to pretax net profits in manufacturing was 5:1. The number of employees in the industry came to 18.2 million, with a per capita or average wage of $31,500—slightly higher than the national average. In the securities industry, the ratio was 3:1, owing to only 450,000 employees and not quite 7 million in the paper economy as a whole. But the startling fact is that the professionalized character of trading in securities and the high risk factor raised the average compensation of employees to $90,000—a professional surplus unmatched in manufacturing. Since the total professional surplus was $27 billion and pretax net profits were $13 billion in round figures, professional workers were pocketing twice the amount of surplus that the industry was delivering in the form of capital income.[44]

That was during a good year for profits. By comparison with a bad year, the results are truly astonishing. In 1990, for example, the ratio of employee compensation ($23 billion) to pretax net profits ($790 million) was 29:1 in the securities industry. The number of employees was 411,000, with a per capita or average wage of $56,000.[45] Since the national average was roughly $30,000, the per capita surplus from milking subordinate staff in financial instruments came to $26,000—a grand total of $10.7 billion. Consequently, the ratio of the professional surplus to pretax net profits was a whopping 13:1. From these figures, one can readily see who were the winners and who the losers. Professional workers came out ahead; capitalists trailed behind in both "good" years and "bad."

Phillips has described corporate America as a two-tier economy—a capitalist real economy at the base and a capitalist paper economy at the summit.[46] Predicated exclusively on a spatial metaphor, his model is unrealistic. The fundamental distinction is between an older capitalist economy—the private sector *sensu strictu*—and America's postcapitalist economy—the quasi-public sector of semiautonomous corporations. Although there is a real and a paper economy corresponding to each, it would be difficult to find a paper economy at the commanding heights of either one. In either case, professional pelf exceeds capital income.

The media and academic think tanks associate the increasing role of international finance capital with a new world order—global capitalism. However, the global economy is not as neoliberals depict it, a haven of free trade beyond the control of national governments. Nor are the high-tech and mathematical-wizard features of financial capital uniquely capitalist. What, then, are the real germs of a gradually emerging global economy? They are the same germs that dominate America's domestic economy—the quasi-public corporate sector.[47] As in the United States, so in the world; not capital, but expertise is the controlling factor in the real economy—and in the paper one.

There is nothing capitalistic per se about free trade or profits from foreign operations. The capitalist surplus in the global economy consists mainly of interest, dividends, and capital gains extracted by institutional investors across national boundaries. Repatriated profits from direct investments qualify as capital income only if the predominant relation of exploitation involves rights of ownership rather than expertise. Transnational buying cheap and selling dear—whether of commodities, currencies, or securities—do not define an economic system. They are a capitalist function of postcapitalist as well as capitalist enterprises.

What are the boundaries of the global economy? Do they enclose only the corporations' transnational activities? On the contrary, they encompass the sum total of the corporations' operations. At issue is not whether the bulk of the revenue from global transactions counts as rentier income or profits from trading but whether the net returns of the global giants consist mainly of capital income or wage surpluses. If the latter, then the global economy is postcapitalist—a corporate economy on a world scale based on expertise.

Globally, not only does capitalism play second fiddle to economies of expertise, but the latter feed off the former. Such is the inverted substance of Marxist theories of imperialism, which envision a socialist Third World in-the-making under conditions of frightful exploitation by the capitalist First World. Instead, what we find is a postcapitalist First World in the role of exploiter of a capitalist Third World.[48]

In the preface to volume 1 of *Capital,* Marx wrote, "The country that is more developed industrially only shows, to the less developed, the image of its own future." Whether the United States is that flagship, Marx's statement applies mainly to the leading nations of the First World—the United States, those in the European Union, and Japan. It is a safe guess that in this select group, capital income is the loser and professional pelf the winner.

Objection and Reply

I am aware that the calculations of the professional pelf and of preferential treatment in distribution will be found objectionable by most of those who read this book. Its conclusions run counter to the ingrained prejudices and beliefs about the United States shared by middle-of-the-road liberals, die-hard conservatives, and right-wing extremists as well as by Marxists representing both the Old and the New Left. The book's predecessor, *America's New Economic Order,* had more than its share of hostile criticism. But to be grossly misrepresented or cavalierly dismissed says nothing about the evidence at hand.

The controversial character of this work hinges on the calculations of a surplus wage—what remains after allowing for the cost of subsistence. But is subsistence faithfully reflected in the minimum wage? The main objection to taking the legislated minimum as a measure of subsistence is that it is a fringe wage, paid mostly to secondary workers in high-turnover jobs—women, minorities, teenagers—and rarely supports, it is said, a full-time head of household. Since minimum-wage earners are eligible for a variety of nonwage supplements, such as Medicaid, food stamps, legal aid, and sometimes public housing, it may seem reasonable to figure the monetary equivalent of these items into the subsistence wage packet.

One should not minimize the extent of income-maintenance supplements to low-wage earners, especially those in part-time jobs. As Frances Fox Piven and Richard A. Cloward pointed out, "Taken in the aggregate, all cash and 'in-kind' benefits (food, health care, and housing subsidies) account for an average annual equivalent of $2,500 for each person who would otherwise fall below the poverty line." That was in 1980–81. Since almost half of the income of the bottom 20 percent of the population took the form of social welfare benefits, the poorest people in the United States were "as much dependent on the government for their subsistence" as they were on the labor market.[49]

Does this mean that individual wage earners cannot subsist on the minimum wage? No, it does not. Workers who do not qualify for outright cash subsidies subsist even though the minimum wage falls below the standard of decency.

Although minimum-wage earners have a vested interest in inflating their subsistence package, employers do not. It is in the interest of both proprietors and professional workers to keep subsistence wages low, to provide nonmonetary supplements out of general taxes rather than to raise minimum wages that would indirectly cut into their personal incomes. The irony is that the minimum wage is a double-edged sword. Unlike nonmonetary supplements to the subsistence package, it does not minimize the dimensions of the purely monetary rip-off.

Potential critics assume what amounts to a cultural prejudice, that the legislated minimum does not suffice for subsistence. But *whose* subsistence? Their own imagined one or what is in fact possible to live on? How does one explain, for example, that millions of Americans subsist at levels considerably below the minimum wage, often without government handouts? One should beware of confusing physical subsistence with customary subsistence, with what the poor *should* be paid on moral, humane, or so-called reasonable grounds.

What do average Americans know about subsistence? Are air-conditioning, hot and cold running water, and meat and dairy products on a daily basis necessary to survival? Think of Bangladesh, Mozambique, and Haiti; ask how their populations survive at one-half or one-fourth of the American minimum. Professional economists and social scientists generally block out huge segments of reality when they confuse the subsistence minimum with a standard of decency. That professional workers cannot imagine living on the minimum wage tells us nothing about how working stiffs survive at even lower levels of poverty.

But suppose we adopt a different measuring rod, the sole alternative in general use—the poverty index. Unrelated individuals are classified as being above or below the poverty level based on the poverty index devised by the Social Security Administration in 1964 and revised by Federal Interagency committees in 1969 and 1980. The poverty index relies solely on money income and does not include noncash benefits for low-income persons in the form of government or public relief. Based on the Department of Agriculture's Economy Food Plan, it reflects the supposed consumption requirements of different-sized families and unrelated individuals. The poverty threshold is updated annually to reflect changes in the Consumer Price Index. Thus the question at issue is the extent to which the minimum wage corresponds to the poverty threshold.

Compare, for example, changes in the minimum wage from 1980 to 1994 and changes in the poverty threshold for unrelated individuals. In 1980, the minimum annual wage for a forty-hour week and a fifty-week year was $6,200; the poverty threshold was $4,190. In 1987, the legislated minimum was $6,700; the poverty threshold was $5,778. In 1989, the legislated minimum remained steady at $6,700; the poverty threshold almost caught up to it, at $6,310. In 1991, the legislated minimum rose to $8,275; the poverty threshold lagged behind at $6,932. In 1994, the legislated minimum stood at $8,500; the poverty threshold still fell behind, at $7,547.

If the poverty threshold for unrelated individuals represents the minimum required for subsistence, the legislated minimum must include more than a subsistence wage. Indeed, the minimum wage may support more than one person. In 1980, the minimum wage was $6,200, while the poverty threshold for two persons was $5,363 and for three persons $6,565. How many persons can subsist on two minimum wages? In 1980, the combined minimum wages for two persons could have supported six persons whose poverty threshold was $11,269, leaving more than $1,100 to spare.[50]

Contrary to critics, if anything is to be faulted about the legislated minimum as a measure of subsistence, it is not because it is too low. It is so far above the official subsistence level that it amply covers the prorated costs of a higher education that my calculations deliberately excluded.

The minimum wage at full-time hours is more than a legal gimmick. It is a physiological and socially necessary minimum, albeit more generous than the poverty threshold. In any event, there are only these two yardsticks for measuring subsistence that have any appreciable public support. Any other yardstick is vulnerable to the charge of being arbitrary, subjective, and idiosyncratic.

But suppose a standard of decency becomes the measuring rod—somewhere between the average and the minimum wage. Would it change significantly the outcome of our calculations? In the formula $B = S - (L + Q)$, not a whit. That is because B is a function of not the minimum wage but the average wage. The total surplus would be less, but so would labor's share and also professionals' share short of the professional pelf. The reductions in S, L, and Q notwithstanding, B would remain constant. The only change would be in calculating preferential treatment in distribution. The reduction in the surpluses below the average wage would not alter our dating of America's new economic order.

6

a republic of experts

Communism, Fascism, Nazism, and the New Deal now appear to be . . . just one revolution and just one significant *ism:* socialism.
—Lawrence Dennis, *The Dynamics of War and Revolution* (1940)

Intellectuals usually express their general outlook through their way of looking at knowledge. Is it privately owned or publicly owned?
—Mao Tse-tung, *A Critique of Soviet Economics* (1977)

Just as the decisive factor of labor explains the preeminence of slave-owners in ancient society and the vital role of land explains domination by a landed aristocracy during the medieval period, so the controlling factor of capital accounts for the rule of modern businesspeople and the key role of expertise defines the new ruling class. If labor, land, and capital were the sole factors, there would be solid grounds for believing that capitalists represent the final mode of production and the highest form of civilization. Corresponding to a fourth factor of production, however, is a fourth governing class—the professional owners of expertise.

A new economic and political order accompanies the rule of this new class. The thorny question is how to characterize it. James Burnham, in his influential *Managerial Revolution,* acknowledged only three possibilities: the survival of capitalism; its replacement by socialism; or a third historical alternative, neither capitalist nor socialist.[1]

Burnham so stacked his cards that the third option became the only credible one. Capitalism, he believed, rested on the private ownership of tangible assets, thereby excluding corporate control through the separation of management from ownership; socialism relied on a democratic and classless society, not merely on the expropriation of the capitalists.[2] So defined, capitalism bordered on obsolescence, while socialism belonged to an indefinite future; the former was in its death throes, and the latter had the earmarks of a communist utopia. As for the other candidates for depicting the new order—Russian communism, German nazism, and the American New Deal—these supposedly exemplified his third historical alternative or the transition thereto.

But is it the most credible scenario, and is the theory of a managerial revolution its most credible version? Burnham's definitions have come under criticism for being idiosyncratic. Once his cards are unstacked, a case can be made for corporate capitalism without control by capitalists and for creeping socialism without benefit of a socialist or communist party at the helm.

How do these rival scenarios stand up under scrutiny? The case for a corporate, managerial, bureaucratic, postindustrial, informational, or intellectual capitalism turns out on analysis to be an argument for either a transitional economy or socialism under a different name. The literature on socialism includes not just centralized, planned economies but also transitional economies, a market socialism without state ownership and a fascist socialism with only state control. Whereas a maximal definition rules out the depiction of America's new order as socialist, a minimal definition makes not only socialism but also a dictatorship of the proletariat credible—even in the United States.

As a shorthand for describing the essential features of a republic of expertise, some names contain more accurate information than others. This observation applies not only to the core terms, *capitalism* and *socialism,* but also to their qualifying adjectives—such as *managerial, bureaucratic, fascist, and postindustrial.* What follows is a critical assessment of these different depictions of the new order as seen through the eyes of their principal representatives.

Neither Capitalism nor Socialism

Burnham was not the first to develop what Cornelius Castoriadis called the "Third Historical Solution"—the alternative to both capitalism and socialism. That honor belongs to the dapper but mysterious Italian Bruno Rizzi (1901–77), shoe salesman and author of one of the most controversial books of the twentieth century. His *Bureaucratization of the World* (1939) distinguished three modes of production and corresponding political societies: (1) capitalism, resting on the class of owners of the means of production; (2) socialism, having its social base in the class of exploited workers; and (3) bureaucratic collectivism, corresponding to a "new exploiting class . . . [owning] a form of property transitional between private and socialist property." As the collective property of the bureaucracy in control of Soviet society, the new economic order was thus appropriately named.[3]

The rise of this new class of clerks—more accurately described as bureaucrats or professionals—was depicted by Rizzi as more than a uniquely Russian phenomenon. By bureaucrats, Rizzi understood not just political commissars but also technicians, specialists, trade union and party functionaries, company managers, independent professionals, and military officers. Wage and salary differentials were the visible result of the surplus extracted from the workers they managed. Although the Soviet Union was the most advanced outpost of the new society, Nazi Germany and Fascist Italy had already moved in its direction, while the American New Deal was said to harbor within its professional bureaucracies the same spreading germs of totalitarianism.[4]

Like Rizzi, Burnham believed that the new world order would be both an *exploiting* economy and a *progressive* one, with a greater per capita output of material goods and a higher standard of living than under capitalism. Because of the striking resemblance of their works, Burnham was widely accused of plagiarism. However, published in France in the wake of the Soviet-Nazi Non-Aggression Pact in August 1939, Rizzi's book was almost immediately banned, impounded, and pulped. Burnham had only indirect knowledge of its contents because of Trotsky's polemic "The USSR in War" (September 1939), based on the lone copy mailed to and extensively criticized by Trotsky. It is noteworthy that Rizzi's characterization of the new class included not just the managerial stratum of professional workers in charge of production but also financial managers—indeed, the entire professional elite.[5]

Max Shachtman, Burnham's collaborator in splitting the American Trotskyist party, followed Burnham in recognizing a third historical alternative. However, he pinpointed party bureaucrats rather than corporate managers as the chief agents and beneficiaries of the new order. Like Rizzi, he called the successor to capitalism "bureaucratic collectivism," but he disputed the thesis that nazism and fascism, much less the New Deal, were ruled or about to be ruled by any class other than the bourgeoisie. Shachtman maintained the Stalinist bureaucracy was *unique:* "it is not a bourgeois bureaucracy and not a proletarian bureaucracy, but . . . a new and *reactionary* exploitive class."[6]

Thinking along the same lines as Shachtman, Cornelius Castoriadis broke with the Trotskyist Fourth International over Trotsky's depiction of the Soviet Union as a degenerate workers' state. It was not just degenerate, he argued, but it had become the breeding ground of a new species of exploiters. Following Shachtman, he described the new society as bureaucratic and reactionary—as a bureaucratic form of barbarism. But he believed that bureaucratic society was not peculiar to the Soviet Union and that the label bureaucratic collectivism was misleading. "Bureaucratic property is neither individual nor collective," he wrote in 1947. "It is a form of private property since it exists only for the bureaucracy . . . a private form of property exploited in common by a class" and only to that extent collective.[7]

The scenario for Castoriadis's Third Historical Solution derived from Trotsky's critique of the theory of bureaucratic collectivism. Although Trotsky faulted it for being premature, he was not so sure about its future. Should the proletariat not emerge from World War II as the master of society, he predicted, there would occur a relapse into barbarism and the "foundering of all hope for a socialist revolution."[8] As we shall see, Castoriadis abandoned this glum scenario for that of bureaucratic capitalism—the characterization of the new society as postbourgeois but not postcapitalist—with socialism as its possible successor.

Like these precursors, Milovan Djilas characterized the new order in the Soviet Union as rule by a new class—the title of his 1957 book. His analysis of the Communist system led him to the following conclusions: first, socialism or rule by the working class was not a present reality anywhere but was nonetheless inevitable; second, Soviet society strongly resembled a system of state capitalism, total state capitalism; third, the Soviet order was not to be confused with either a socialist or a capitalist one but considered a special type of new social system.

Unlike Burnham, for whom the new class was headed by industrial czars in charge of the productive apparatus, Djilas identified its brains with a party oligarchy. "In view of the significance of ownership for its power—and also of the fruits of ownership—the party bureaucracy cannot renounce the extension of its ownership even over small-scale production," he asserted. Consequently, what appeared to be common ownership was really rule by this new class of owners and exploiters.[9]

Historically, Djilas's new class was unique in having crystallized *after* rather than *before* attaining political power. Its roots were implanted by a Marxist-Leninist party intent on establishing socialism—but that was not the outcome. "The party makes the class," he observed, but then the new class grew stronger until it no longer needed a party to sustain it. Such was the "inescapable fact of every Communist party in power." Speak of prescience; the party collapsed when it became more of an impediment than an asset to the new class in further developing the economy as a power base.[10]

The major pitfall of Djilas's depiction was that his new class was not a universal class but was peculiar to countries in which a Communist party ruled. "To divest Communists of their ownership rights," he declared, "would be to abolish them as a class." Since ownership of the state was a defining condition of the new class, it followed that the managerial revolution in the West was not the harbinger of a new class, much less of a new society.[11]

Capitalist Perestroika

Burnham posited as part of his scenario of managerial society a transitional economy or halfway station on the road from capitalism to managerialism, but his successors were not convinced that capitalism was doomed. In the wake of World War II and the widespread adoption of Keynesian economic controls for preventing a second Great Depression, capitalism was almost universally believed to have recovered. In view of the information revolution sparked by the war, a new order was imminent. It was therefore believed that, far from replacing capitalism, this new historical alternative would enter into a symbiosis with it and restructure capitalism in line with the new technology of the Information Age.

Competing scenarios of this capitalist *perestroika* (restructuring) concurred with Burnham's scenario of a transitional society in that they combined management control of the means of production with capitalist control of the available surplus. They differed from Burnham mainly in questioning whether the shift to new decision makers would lead to income redistribution. Control in the hands of the professional elite was no guarantee that it would enjoy most of the benefits. Why not a balance of power instead of an untenable situation pregnant with instability? Instead of a full-fledged managerial revolution, Burnham's critics settled for the scenarios of "managerial capitalism," "postindustrial capitalism," "knowledge capitalism," "brainpower capitalism," and "informational capitalism"—to cite only the main contenders.

Consider Alfred D. Chandler Jr.'s case for managerial capitalism, *The Visible Hand: The Managerial Revolution in American Business* (1977). Chandler's tour de force was to show in historical detail where, when, how, and why power and property became divorced in the modern corporation. By the middle of the twentieth century, he concluded, managerial hierarchies were fully in control, and the managerial revolution in American business had been consummated.[12]

In broad brushstrokes, Chandler's history of the managerial revolution reduces to the following eight propositions: (1) the modern corporation replaced small privately owned enterprises when administrative coordination permitted increased productivity, lower costs, and higher profits than did coordination by the market mechanism; (2) such advantages depended on the creation of corporate managerial hierarchies; (3) these hierarchies appeared when the volume of production and distribution reached a point at which administrative coordination became more profitable than market coordination; (4) business enterprises controlled by managerial hierarchies outperformed other enterprises in permanence, power, and growth; (5) the work performed by these hierarchies became increasingly technical and professional; (6) as the volume of business increased and the work of managers became more professional, management became separated from ownership; (7) professional managers favored long-term stability and growth over profit maximization; and (8) when professionally managed enterprises came to dominate the major sectors of the economy, they transformed the economy as a whole. Notwithstanding his differences with Burnham over the question of the permanence of capitalism, Chandler acknowledged a revolution within American capitalism through the rise of a distinctive managerial class.[13]

What for Burnham was only a transitional economy leading to his third historical alternative was for Chandler the end product firmly fixed within the boundaries of a restructured capitalist economy. As an historian, he mainly described the stages through which modern capitalism has evolved: first, entrepreneurial individual or family capitalism based on private ownership of the means of production; second, corporate ownership dependent on outside sources of capital and shared control with representatives of banks and other financial institutions—so-called financial capitalism; and finally, managerial capitalism.[14]

Managerial, yes—but why the highest or last stage of capitalism? Because people of property continue to be the primary beneficiaries of the new order— hence the combined term *managerial capitalism*. Capitalism has been restructured, but it has not been overcome.

Chandler's data on the rise of managerial capitalism covered mainly the years from World War I to the mid-1950s. Prior to the mid-1950s, finance capitalism still held sway—a thesis shared with Soviet economists. In *Imperialism: The Highest Stage of Capitalism* (1917), Lenin called it a new kind of capitalism predicated on the separation of ownership from management as early as World War I. According to his data, some 90 percent of all brainwork in capitalist business activities was already being performed by salaried employees. Instead of being autonomous, they were dominated by a financial oligarchy of absentee proprietors or rentiers. Chandler would have agreed, since only with the advent of managerial capitalism after World War II did management become independent.[15]

In support of this thesis, Chandler cited data from Robert Larner's 1966 investigation of ownership and control in the two hundred largest nonfinancial corporations between 1929 and 1963.[16] Larner's data suggested that managerial capitalism did not become the dominant system in the United States until the mid-1960s. Larner's findings are questionable in two key respects: first, with the advent of President Johnson's Great Society, capitalists ceased to be the main beneficiary of the distributed surplus; second, the data supplied by

Berle and Means suggested that management was calling the tune as early as 1929—or at least by the outbreak of World War II.

The pièce de résistance of depictions of America's new order as a capitalist perestroika was a work that established the paradigm for those that followed: Daniel Bell's *Coming of Post-Industrial Society* (1973). Formulated after the new society had gotten underway, it had the advantage over its predecessors of describing as well as forecasting essential features of the new order.

After discussing the contributions of Rizzi, Burnham, Shachtman, and Djilas, Bell turned to the remarkable study by a research team of Czechoslovak sociologists as the foundation of his new theory—Radovan Richta's *Civilization at the Crossroads* (1968)—the English translation of a book first appearing in 1967. What Richta and his associates called the "scientific technological revolution" Bell depicted as a sociotechnical revolution in which intellectual technology displaced machine technology as the prelude to a postindustrial society. The term *postindustrial* was not his own but was coined by Richta and associates.[17]

Bell argued that unlike industrial technology, which was developed with the help of talented tinkerers who worked independently of the fundamental work in science, postindustrial technology is characterized by "*centrality of theoretical knowledge.*" Theoretical rather than practical knowledge underlies the "new science-based industries—computers, electronics, optics" and the new intellectual technology utilizing mathematical and economic techniques, modeling, simulation, systems analysis, and decision theory. Thus, the economics of goods, which responded to the problems of capital accumulation in industrial society, is today supplemented by the economics of information in response to the knowledge-oriented problems of postindustrial society.[18]

Unlike the major cleavage in industrial society between those who own the means of production and an undifferentiated proletariat, the essential division in postindustrial society is between "those who have the powers of decision and those who have not." What is surprising is that "post-industrial society does not 'succeed' capitalism or socialism, but, like bureaucratization, cuts across both," Bell declared. As late as 1973, capitalism was still dominant in the Western world, while socialist planning in the Soviet Union and Eastern Europe was largely an alternative route to industrialization rather than a successor to capitalism. Although both the United States and the Soviet Union were still predominantly industrial societies, Bell predicted that by the end of the century both would have to confront the privileges of the new technical elites.[19]

In depicting the new society as neither capitalist nor socialist, Bell did not posit a third historical alternative destined to replace both. Just as socialism and capitalism were creations of industrial society, so he anticipated that both would take on new dimensions instead of disappearing in the Information Age. Already, he noted, capitalism had been transformed into managerial capitalism and socialism into state socialism. But what is one to make of his caveat: state socialism is "actually state capitalism in which the maximization of production of each enterprise is the primary goal"?[20]

There are four black holes in this otherwise illuminating picture. First, the new class's rule over both production and distribution was not "coming" when Bell penned his magnum opus. It was already here—on both sides of the Iron Curtain. Second, the Information Age has ceased to be contemporaneous with managerial capitalism. On the contrary, the knowledge-interest prevails—capitalism has been superseded. Third, postindustrial society is not a rival system superseding socialism. It is the sociotechnical dimension of postcapitalist society. Fourth, exploitation is still an issue, though Bell's work gave the impression that it has somehow disappeared. A fundamental lacuna in Bell's treatment of labor conflict and the labor issue was his failure to critique what he called the "knowledge theory of value"—the political economy of expertise that has replaced Marx's defunct labor theory of value.[21] Had he done so, he might have discovered that exploitation lies at the heart of both postindustrial and industrial societies.

Bell was not alone in depicting the emerging knowledge society. Peter Drucker, the guru of management theory, was among the first to call attention to the new class structure based on knowledge and organization. As early as *The New Society* (1950), he cited evidence for a new worldwide economic order that was neither specifically capitalist nor socialist. Unlike Burnham, to whom he acknowledged an intellectual debt, he took for granted that socialism was the successor to capitalism but pointed to a third historical alternative as the successor to both.[22]

The key institution of the new society, Drucker argued, was the industrial enterprise, with its leadership centered in management rather than its nominal owners. On both sides of the Iron Curtain, the business enterprise was managed on the same principles: the avoidance of loss and the pursuit of profit as a yardstick or measure of performance.[23]

The divorce of ownership and control portended the end of both capitalism and socialism. "If 'control' were indeed based on ownership, a shift in the legal title from the 'capitalist' to the 'worker' would shift control from 'management' to the 'worker,'" Drucker argued. But the former shift had occurred without the latter happening: "The elimination of the 'alien' owner and the substitution of worker ownership does not result in a 'withering away of management'. . . . Though the profits go to the workers, the government of the enterprise is as little a government *for* the worker as it had been before."[24]

Under both socialism and capitalism, two new classes had effectively disfranchised both bourgeois and proletarians: the new ruling group of executives and union leaders and the new salaried middle class of trained, skilled, and educated workers.[25] These two classes were distinguished by the extent of their authority and the range of their salaries in the hierarchical organization of the enterprise. But was this difference in degree rather than in kind sufficient to distinguish them as separate classes?

In an epilogue to the 1962 edition of his book, Drucker called knowledge workers the most important class in the new society—the largest and fastest growing group of employees in the industrially developed nations. This new middle class of "technical and professional employees . . . owns the one essential resource of production: knowledge." But are not managers also professionals—at least the graduates of business schools—and are they not also knowledge workers? Should not Drucker have included both in the same class, "this group whose emergence really makes ours a 'new' society"?[26]

Drucker's *Post-Capitalist Society* (1993) developed the central thesis of his earlier work. The 1944 G.I. Bill of Rights, he noted, "signaled the shift to the knowledge society"—an event even more important than the invention of the computer. It gave every retiring veteran of World War II the money to attend university. Professionals mushroomed through the pores of the old society, replacing Marx's bourgeois and proletarians—the fundamental classes of capitalist society—with the fundamental "classes of post-capitalist society . . . knowledge workers and service workers."[27]

This new classification improved on his earlier distinction between a managerial ruling class and a professional middle class by acknowledging both to be members of a single class opposed to service workers. The difference between knowledge and service workers was defined in terms of supervision. In sharp contrast to service workers, "[k]nowledge employees cannot . . . be supervised," Drucker declared.[28]

Although Drucker depicted the knowledge society as "both a non-socialist and a post-capitalist society,"[29] the new society continued to exhibit both capitalist and socialist features. Outstanding were the enormous pools of money held by pension funds in the United States that "dwarf anything the greatest 'capitalist' of past times commanded." From his choice of idioms, he seemed unsure about what to call this striking phenomenon, whether "pension fund socialism," "pension fund capitalism," or "capitalism *sans* the capitalists."[30]

Because employees own the means of production through their pension funds, Drucker originally described the new society as pension fund socialism. *Post-Capitalist Society* was of a different mind. "Might 'employee capitalism,'" he asked, "be a better term?" The rule of capital in the knowledge society, he asserted, is "totally different in theory as well as in practice from that which capital had in 'capitalism.'"[31] Being of several minds, Drucker never faced up to the question of how the knowledge society can be *neither* capitalist *nor* socialist and also *both* capitalist and socialist.

In *The New Realities* (1989), Drucker described knowledge workers as neither exploited nor exploiters, as those who "individually are not capitalists but who collectively own the means of production through their pension funds."[32] A Soviet bureaucrat could not have said it better with respect to his own society. But was that the new reality on either side of the Iron Curtain? Or was the reality, après Rizzi, Burnham, Shachtman, Castoriadis, and Djilas, that professional workers in key positions were the new exploiters—not just the new masters?

Historically, the Soviet Union was the first society to have abolished capitalism, while serving as a preview of the knowledge society by replacing the old cleavage between bourgeois and proletarians with a new division between knowledge workers and service workers. This depiction runs counter to Drucker's more recent work, however: "Instead of capitalism being a transition stage on the socialist road, it now increasingly appears that socialism is a detour on the capitalist road."[33] It would seem more likely that if socialism succeeded capitalism, the knowledge society is its highest stage.

Like Drucker, Lester Thurow depicted the knowledge society as a restructured capitalism—with as many reservations. Physical capital is still necessary, but, according to Thurow, "brainpower and imagination, invention and the organization of new technologies are the key strategic ingredients."[34] The key ingredients define the knowledge society, not the physical capital that is still necessary.

"Capitalism," Thurow stated, "gave decision-making powers to the owners of capital precisely because they controlled the key ingredient in the new system—capital." But the generals of capitalism are no longer in command; they no longer control the vital power source. This led Thurow to pose the embarrassing question: "What does capitalism become when it cannot own the strategic sources of its own competitive advantage"—when brainpower replaces capital as the strategic asset of a new postcapitalist class?[35]

So formulated, Thurow begged the question and therefore the answer. Just as feudalism became obsolete when land ceased to be the decisive asset, so prima facie capitalism becomes a museum piece when its inanimate power source—mechanical energy—gives way to brainpower. But that is not how Thurow saw it. "Capitalism without ownable capital" survives, he contended, as a result of a conceptual trick, "by calling skills, education, and knowledge 'human capital.'"[36]

Thurow acknowledged that the shift from physical to human capital is tantamount to a social revolution that has the same magnitude as the shift from feudalism to capitalism. After all, 60 percent of the wealth of the United States now consists of human capital. The danger is not that capitalism will implode as socialism did. But "it will have to undergo a profound metamorphosis."[37] Is that not to acknowledge that the old system is in agony, if not already dead?

Following in Bell's footsteps, Manuel Castells's three-volume *Information Age* (1996) ranks as one of the most significant attempts since Burnham's *Managerial Revolution* to understand what is happening in the world. According to Castells, societies in the twentieth century are characterized along two axes: modes of production and modes of development. Among the former, he distinguished capitalism and statism; among the latter, he pointed to the continuing industrial and new informational revolutions. This classification makes possible distinctions among social systems beyond the ken of Marx's conceptual apparatus, such as industrial statism (collectivism in Bell's terms), industrial capitalism, and informational capitalism. (As yet there is no informational statism).[38]

Castells amended Bell's classic formulation of postindustrialism in three major respects. First, what distinguishes late industrial societies from incipient postindustrial ones is that the latter not only are knowledge-based but also restructure the economy around the principle of maximizing the knowledge basis of productivity while making knowledge a direct productive force "in a cumulative feedback loop between innovation and the uses of innovation." Second, Bell was mistaken in associating postindustrial society with the demise of manufacturing. On the contrary, recent data show that in the mid-1980s, some 50 percent of America's GNP came from value added by manufacturing firms and services directly linked to manufacturing. The term *postindustrial* is therefore misleading and should be replaced by the more accurate *informational* society. Third, it is a mistake to depict the growth of informational-rich occupations linked to the professions as the sole core of the new occupational structure. Alongside this trend is the growth of low-end, unskilled, service occupations, a substantial proportion of the informational society in absolute numbers. The result is a polarized, two-tier structure, where the "top and bottom increase their share at the expense of the middle." The republic of the learned elite thus has its nether side.[39]

Among the curiosities of Castells's work is its definition of *statism*—a grossly misleading dysphemism for actually existing socialism. *Capitalism* is defined as a system oriented toward profit maximization based on the private ownership and control of the means of production. In sharp contrast, *statism* is a mode of production oriented toward maximizing power rather than profit through "the military and ideological capacity of the political apparatus for imposing its goals." Castells defined its new ruling class as *apparatchiks,* the former Soviet term for bureaucratic power holders—a definition that holds also for the political, military, and corporate managers in the United States.[40]

The new order defined as informational or network capitalism dates, according to Castells's data, from roughly 1970—the threshold to cyberspace and the Internet revolution. The immediate predecessor to this "capitalist perestroika" (his term) was an industrial capitalism characterized by managerial hierarchies—that is, Chandler's managerial capitalism. By the mid-1990s, this informational-restructured capitalism was concentrated on an educated sector of the population under the age of forty, a twenty-million computer-literate elite—the privileged upper layer of a *new working class* growing exponentially. Structured around a network of financial flows, capital works globally as finance capital, said Castells. Such is the "concrete meaning of the articulation between the capitalist mode of production and the informational mode of development." It is Lenin's highest stage of capitalism—finance capitalism—restructured as an "electronically operated global casino."[41]

"Who are the capitalists?" Surprisingly, they are not just the legal owners of the means of production and rich corporate executives. In the United States, they consist of a "colorful array of traditional bankers, *nouveau riche* speculators, self-made geniuses-turned-entrepreneurs, global tycoons, and multinational managers." They also include the money-laundering mafia and the public corporations. But for Castells, there is no global class corresponding to them, only a "faceless collective capitalist, made up of financial flows operated by electronic networks . . . capitalism in its purest expression of the endless search for money by money through the production of commodities by commodities."[42]

The fundamental distinction is between capitalists *in* the informational/global economy and capitalists *specific* to it. The first constitute "the holders of property rights"—the increasingly predominant corporate shareholders in addition to individual entrepreneurs, owners of family businesses, and *"the managerial class* . . . the controllers of capital assets on behalf of shareholders . . . [and] managers of state-owned companies." The second consist of the players in search of higher profits in the stock, bond, and currency markets and in futures, options, and derivatives—through buying cheap and selling dear. Their financial and management networks constitute the collective capitalist, the *"nerve center of informational capitalism."* It is this faceless collective capitalist that typifies the new order, in which "capitalists are randomly incarnated, and the capitalist classes are appendixes to . . . the global flashes of computer screens."[43] Appendices, yes—but also to full-blooded, flesh-and-bones, computer-literate professionals who, pace Castells, are *not* capitalists except in rare instances.

Corresponding to this collective capitalist is the collective worker whose products are appropriated by the capitalists. Castells estimated the upper tier of this proletariat at about one-third of the employed population in Western Europe, Japan, Canada, and the United States. Education defines this superior group of managers, professionals, and technicians, these new producers of informational capitalism. Most of the remaining two-thirds belong to an inferior group, to the category of potentially machine-replaceable *generic labor*.

This polarization of the work force accounts for the fundamental cleavage in today's society. Although both groups are exploited, the educated elites are in a position to strike a privileged deal. Notwithstanding the persistence of powerful social conflicts enacted by organized labor, Castells concluded that "they are not the expression of class struggle but of interest groups' demands and/or of revolt against social injustice." On the one hand, there is no contradiction between the owners of informational expertise and the collective capitalist of global financial networks. On the other hand, the internal fragmentation of the work force between informational producers and generic labor means that labor can no longer count on defenders among people of expertise.[44]

There are three main objections to this scenario. First, by invoking the financial and managerial networks of a faceless capitalist as the ruling force in the Information Age, Castells underestimated the extent to which capitalist relations of production have been superseded by new relations of expertise not based on traditional forms of ownership. Second, the transformation he accurately depicted within the work force is not a cleavage internal to a so-called working class; it is a cleavage between antagonistic classes. Third, class struggle has not disappeared from view but rages anew as the struggle between labor and the new professional elites. To summarize, the word *capitalist* no longer fits a republic of experts in which employees have become the employers—a society that is capitalist only in name.

Socialism in the Name of Capitalism

Drucker and Thurow were not the first to note the metamorphosis of capitalism into something radically different. Paradoxically, some of the Marxist ideologues who preceded them also persisted in calling the new reality by the same name as the old. Thus, in refusing to give up the outworn label, they, too, salvaged the name without the substance.

If the term *capitalist* applied to quasi-public corporations seems fatuous, imagine what it must seem in application to public corporations—to state-owned enterprises and collective farms in the former Soviet Union and China. The irony is that Marxist political economists were the first to brand the economies of actually existing socialism as "capitalist." To give the devil its due, consider briefly the arguments in support of this perverse effort to salvage the capitalist label.

After flirting with the label "bureaucratic society," Castoriadis settled for "bureaucratic capitalism" as the best description of the social systems on both sides of the Iron Curtain. Bureaucratic capitalism was thus the successor to bourgeois capitalism.[45] Paradoxically, the capitalist class had ceased to be necessary to capitalism.

In retrospect, Castoriadis explained, it was the evolution of a system that mattered, an evolution that "led the traditional capitalism of the private business firm . . . to the contemporary capitalism of the bureaucratized enterprise, of regimentation, of 'planning,' and of the omnipresent State." But why trash his original label? Because the "objective outcome of this evolution has been a more efficient and more systematic organization for exploiting and enslaving the proletariat." Elements of capitalism remained and had become intensified. Wage labor had not been abolished, while capital had passed out of the hands of private owners into the possession of a "new boss class . . . disguised as directors, specialists, and technicians." The outcome of this replacement of bourgeois by bureaucratic rule was a revolution, but a revolution within capitalism. The Marxist class struggle between bourgeois and proletarians had thus passed into history, to be superseded by a post-Marxist struggle between directors and executants.[46]

It remained for another ex-Trotskyist, Tony Cliff, to revive and reestablish the theory of state capitalism as an alternative to theories of bureaucratic capitalism and collectivism. "What is specific to capitalism is accumulation for accumulation's sake," he wrote in an amended version to a book first distributed in duplicated form in 1948, published in 1955, and republished in 1974 as *State Capitalism in Russia*. "The more that part of the surplus value devoted to accumulation increases as against that part consumed, the more purely does capitalism reveal itself." Since a shortage of goods, a dismally low level of consumption, and relative overaccumulation practically defined the Soviet system, "the *Russian bureaucracy*, 'owning' as it does the state and controlling the process of accumulation, *is the personification of capital in its purest form*," Cliff declared.[47]

According to Cliff, to describe the system of rule by a bureaucratic class in Russia as managerial society or bureaucratic collectivism fell short of the mark because it ignored a vital fact: "the bureaucracy fulfills the tasks of the capitalists . . . [which] makes it the purest expression of this class." Although distinct from the capitalist class, the Soviet bureaucracy was "the nearest to its historical essence . . . *the truest personification of the historical mission of this class.*" It follows that capitalist relations of production in Russia were more advanced that those in the United States and that two different variants of state capitalism needed to be distinguished: America's "State monopoly capitalism" in opposition to the Soviets' "Bureaucratic State Capitalism."[48]

In formulating this theory, Cliff turned to Marx's *Capital* for support, mainly to chapter 24 of volume 1, where Marx defined the capitalist as personified capital fanatically bent on making value expand itself. That was the historical function of capitalism, accumulation for accumulation's sake. But, in Marx's words, "As capitalist production, accumulation, and wealth become developed, the capitalist ceases to be the mere incarnation of capital." Unlike the original capitalist who branded individual consumption as "'abstinence' from accumulating," the nonpuritanical successor looks upon accumulation as "'abstinence' from pleasure."[49] Who, then, represented the mission of capitalism and the personification of capital in the twentieth century? Evidently, the Russian bureaucracy and the emerging new class in the West.

As the highest stage of capitalism, bureaucratic state capitalism is, Cliff contended, the antithesis of socialism. Like Burnham, he believed that socialism puts an end to the workers' treadmill of exploitation: "the workers' state raises the influence of the trade unions to a maximum . . . [and] brings the highest degree of democracy society has known."[50] But is this not a prime example of Marxist mythmaking, a socialism with illusions—unreal socialism?

Castoriadis went one step further. By workers' democracy, he meant self-management of the process of production in the form of soviets, or workers' councils. Representative democracy does not suffice. Workers must be able to rid themselves of both labor bureaucrats and managers at the enterprise level. In a three-part essay entitled "On the Content of Socialism," published in serial form between 1955 and 1958, he said, "The abolition of exploitation is only possible when *every separate stratum of directors* ceases to exist, for in modern societies it is the division between directors and executants that is at the root of exploitation." Direct democracy demands the "dismissal of all managers . . . [and] full equality of wages and salaries"—a program for the present rather than the future.[51] But is this not another example of Marxist mythmaking?

"State capitalism"—a general description of twentieth-century society? "Bureaucratic State Capitalism"—a shorthand for real socialism? Both characterizations fly in the face of not only current usage but also the scholarly community and the principal political actors and ideologies. At the very least, they are confusing.

In taking their cue from Marx, both Cliff and Castoriadis mistakenly identified accumulation as uniquely capitalist. But as Max Weber observed, the ethic of accumulation for its own sake was a specific feature of capitalism mainly during its early or formative stage; it survives "precisely in those countries whose bourgeois capitalistic development, measured according to Occidental standards, has remained backward."[52] It does not define managerial capitalism. Nor was the Soviet emphasis on accumulation an instance of Weber's spirit of capitalism. Accelerating the tempo of production was not an end in itself; it was a means only. That is why Lenin said, "Either perish, or overtake and outstrip the advanced capitalist countries." That is why Stalin said, "We are fifty or a hundred years behind the advanced countries. We must make good this distance in ten years. Either we do it, or they crush us."[53]

Disillusioned Trotskyists are not alone in confusing actually existing socialism with capitalism. Following the Sino-Soviet split in the early 1960s, the Chinese Communists began describing the Soviet Union's post-Stalinist leadership as a "bureaucrat-bourgeoisie" or "bureaucratic-capitalist class." The Yugoslav system of workers' self-management was likewise depicted as a cover for a class of post-Stalin bureaucrats who had restored capitalism in that country. The Khrushchev clique was said to be taking the road already traveled by the Tito clique, that of imposing a new system of social relations to the benefit of a new exploiting class, scuttling the dictatorship of the proletariat and transforming the socialist public economy into state-monopoly capitalism.[54]

Martin Nicolaus, an American purveyor of the Chinese line, described the new type of manager in Soviet enterprises in terms that recall Marx's description of Mr. Moneybags. Since the restless, never-ending process of profit making alone is what the manager of a Soviet enterprise aimed at, he was a "bureaucrat capitalist . . . put into his post in order to function as capitalist . . . [like] his twins in Western state and private corporations." Labor power continued to function as variable capital since, as Marx put it, the self-expansion of capital presupposes control over a definite quantity of other people's unpaid labor.[55]

The foregoing depictions of capitalism without capitalists border on semantic mayhem. Each of them requires either clinging to capitalism as an empty word or so twisting the word as to legitimize the widespread, if grudging, acceptance of socialism under another name. Burnham was right in not calling the new order capitalist. First, in the strict sense of private owners, shareholders, and bondholders, the capitalists were expropriated in the countries of actually existing socialism and have been effectively marginalized in the leading Western metropolises. Second, capitalism without private owners in the driver's seat, without the lion's share of the surplus in their grasp and egging them on, is an engine without a motor, a body without a brain.[56]

Socialism with and without State Ownership

History was more generous to the traditional Marxist expectation of a new postcapitalist society. But the Marxist prophecy was enveloped in a myth. If Marxist socialism were to prevail, argued Bakunin, the outcome would be an exploitative society radically different from the picture painted by socialist ideologues.

Bakunin has the distinction of being not only the first to define education as mental capital and the first to use this term but also the first to identify the rule of the educated, professional, or knowledge class as state socialism rather than state capitalism. Though he failed to shed his faith in a classless and allegedly higher stage of cooperative socialism, he had no illusions concerning what would eventually materialize under the name of actually existing socialism.[57]

Under state socialism, the educated class of scientists, engineers, and bureaucrats would manage everything. "All that will demand an immense knowledge," Bakunin wrote sarcastically, "and many 'heads overflowing with brains.'" He likened the new society to "the reign of *scientific intelligence,* the most aristocratic, despotic, arrogant, and contemptuous of all regimes." There will be a "new hierarchy of real and pretended scientists and scholars, and the world will be divided into a minority ruling in the name of knowledge, and an immense ignorant [and exploited] majority." It would be the rule of expertise, rule by a fourth governing class—*after* the priestly class, the landed aristocracy, and Marx's bourgeoisie.[58]

An obscure disciple of Bakunin, the Polish revolutionary Waclaw Machajski (pronounced Vatzlav Makhaysky), did more than anyone else to develop Bakunin's novel scenario of intellectuals on the road to class power. Machajski died in the Soviet Union in 1926 as an unheralded prophet of the new economic and political order. However, the specter of *Makhayevshchina*—the ideas of Machajski—rubbed off on Trotsky and later on Nikolai Bukharin, the only Bolshevik writer who discussed them seriously. Nor did his influence stop there. Wherever the issue of bureaucracy flared up—as in the Soviet Union during the great purges and Yugoslavia after the split with the Soviet Union in 1948—his theory momentarily revived and gained a hearing. He also acquired a following in the West.[59]

As Trotsky indignantly noted in his autobiography, Machajski reached the "amazing conclusion that Socialism is a social order based on the exploitation of the workers by a professional intelligentsia." The expropriation of the capitalists, Machajski wrote, "by no means signifies the expropriation of the entire bourgeois society." Exploitation continues under the control of new masters, the noncapitalist owners of education. From private hands, the economic surplus "passes into the hands of the State, as the fund for the parasitic existence of all exploiters." Although the surplus is "distributed in the form of high salaries paid to the intellectual workers," bourgeois society remains the same ruling society as it was before. By bourgeois society, Machajski meant not just the propertied and monied interests but also the owners of expertise. Hence his startling conclusion: "Modern socialism is unable and unwilling to abolish the age-long exploitation and slavery."[60]

Insofar as the state becomes the owner of all surplus value, Machajski argued, there is no essential difference between state capitalism and state socialism. The owners of intellectual capital own the state, and it is through the state rather than the direct sale of expertise that they become a new exploiting class.

According to Max Nomad (1881–1973), a former Machajski disciple, the socialist theories of the nineteenth century only nominally championed the interests of the exploited workers. He initially believed that the "socialism which the radical intelligentsia really aspired to was nothing but State Capitalism . . . a system of government ownership, under which private capitalists would have yielded place to office holders, managers, engineers."[61] Later, after socialism began blossoming in the Soviet Union, he dropped all references to state capitalism.

An Austrian expatriate, exrevolutionary, exconspirator, and ex-admirer of the Soviet Union, Nomad further developed the scenario of a socialist society that originated with Bakunin. Having lived and worked in the Soviet Union for a brief period in the 1920s and subsequently in the United States, he perceived the sprouts of a new society germinating in both.

"Sandwiched between the capitalists and the manual workers there has emerged an ever growing stratum of neo-bourgeois . . . engaged in mental or near-mental occupations," Nomad wrote. This new middle class includes "office-holders, teachers, professional men, technicians, clergymen, commercial and financial experts, journalists, writers, artists, politicians, professional revolutionists and agitators, trade union organizers and so on." This class first came into power in the Soviet Union, where it replaced the capitalists as the owners of privileged incomes. But in the West, where its status was still that of privileged employees of capital, it also presaged the death of capitalism.[62]

Unlike Burnham, who derived his scenario of a managerial revolution from Nomad but interpreted it according to his own lights, Nomad defined it as both bureaucratic and socialist—a society headed by a "hierarchy of intellectuals who are bureaucrats at the same time." Far from being a classless society, real socialism is a society in which "higher education or training guarantees its owner a soft job and a salary which is above the average wage of a manual worker." In the Soviet Union, this new class had become the collective owner of the country's socialized economy, thereby excluding ordinary workers from anything more than nominal ownership. Instead of shrieking betrayal, however, Nomad believed that the "Bolshevik form of class rule and inequality of income is not a distortion of the original equalitarian character of socialism, as some sentimental souls may believe." Reduced to its economic essence, socialism is not, Nomad contended, egalitarian: "socialism has always meant merely *government ownership of the means of production.*"[63]

Distribution has always been considered a secondary matter not just by Marxists but also by most socialist schools. Only in the very distant future, if at all, would the inequalities under socialism yield to the communist principle "from each according to his ability, to each according to his needs"—a principle as hazy as it is deceitful. What are a man's needs, and who is to determine them, Nomad asked, if not the professionals in charge? Thus, under actually existing socialism, "the real meaning of that formula is . . . 'from the workers according to their abilities, to the bureaucrats according to their needs.'"[64] In other words, socialism for the masses, communism for the elites.

Nomad conceded that income inequalities are minimized under socialism, the gap between top and bottom incomes being "'merely' one to one hundred, instead of being one to one thousand as in the typically capitalist countries." That is no mean accomplishment to be passed over as betrayal. As for the other glowing achievement of socialism—centralized economic planning—it, too, "represents a great step forward as compared with the productive process under private capitalism with its calamities resulting from the business cycles." Nonetheless, he asserted, the "Soviet example has proven that *exploitation is just as much possible under socialism as under any other previous social system.*"[65]

The competing socialist schools not only make distribution a secondary matter but also further insist that wage inequalities are *not* a result of exploitation. Differences in abilities and in the quality and quantity of work supposedly account for unequal wages. Because socialism abolishes the privileges derived from inheritance and ownership, Nomad characterized the new society as socialist rather than bureaucrat capitalist, managerial capitalist, or state capitalist, not to mention intellectual capitalist. The word *socialism* not only has the widest currency but also suggests a sharp break with the old order. Nomad thus anticipated that "*the coming universal form of exploitation of man by man, as foreshadowed by Russia's system of government ownership and inequality of incomes, will simply be called socialism.*"[66]

With the collapse of the Soviet Union, the term *socialism* fell by the wayside, but there are already signs of a comeback. What was called socialism is currently called pseudo-socialism by Marxists and former Communists—mainly because of the undemocratic rather than the inegalitarian features of the Soviet system. Schumpeter made a strong case for using the term: "A society may be fully and truly socialist and yet be led by an absolute ruler or be organized in the most democratic of all possible ways; it may be aristocratic or proletarian; it may be a theocracy and hierarchic or atheist or indifferent as to religion."[67] In these respects, socialism takes many different forms—as does capitalism.

Does *socialism* designate the social systems only in countries ruled by Marxist-Leninist parties or also those ruled by democratic parties under conditions of a market economy? Why should government ownership be the decisive criterion? Why not also collective ownership, as in Yugoslavia, and corporate ownership, as in the advanced countries of the West?

To follow Keynes instead of Nomad, modern corporations are quasi-public, semiautonomous enterprises. Because of the remarkable "tendency of big enterprise to socialize itself . . . we must keep our minds flexible regarding the forms of this semi-socialism," Keynes advised. In the West, as well as in the early days of the Soviet Union, Keynes wrote in 1926, "[t]he battle of Socialism against unlimited private profit is being won in detail hour by hour."[68] State socialism is therefore only one progeny of a bigger family that also includes municipal socialism and corporate socialism.

Contrary to Nomad's assertion, the minimum condition for the existence of socialism is *not* government ownership. For Marx, the abolition of bourgeois property sufficed.[69] But was Marx's definition of socialism more than sufficient? It assumes that socialism abolishes not only capitalist exploitation but all exploitation. *That* asks too much of socialism. Even to assert that socialism abolishes *all* capitalist exploitation is an overstatement. Capitalist exploitation need not be abolished at all. It suffices for bureaucratic or professional exploitation to catch up to and outstrip it for the socialist sector to prevail.

It is by no means settled that a strong private sector and the determination of incomes and outputs by market forces are incompatible with socialism. But is capitalism replaced when the surplus is pumped out of the same class of wage earners and continues to take the form of profit? Yes, when the labor contract is no longer between labor and capital but between labor and management, when the distributed surplus takes the form of mainly surplus wages, not private profit. Although profit in the Soviet Union survived as an index of industrial performance, it no longer took the form of capital income.[70]

The labor contract between bourgeois proprietors and propertyless wage earners, according to Marx, lies at the heart of the capitalist system. But the

buying and selling of labor power can take a form that is not specifically capitalist. Change one of the partners to the contract, and you have a different
social system. As Marx noted in volume 3 of *Capital:* "It is always the direct
relationship of owners of the conditions of production to the direct producers . . . which reveals the innermost secret, the hidden basis of the entire social structure, and with it the political form of the relation of sovereignty and
dependence, in short, the corresponding specific form of the state."[71]

Fascist Socialism

Turning next to fascism as a transition to socialism, Nomad noted that Joseph
Goebbels, the Nazi propaganda chief, and Otto Bauer, one of the leading theorists of European socialism between the two world wars, affirmed the same
principle of rewarding each according to his work. Although socialism abolishes classes, Bauer wrote, "it differentiates society by rewarding those whose
achievements . . . are particularly outstanding, and by raising them above the
masses in matters of *income*." Similarly, Goebbels asserted, "We say, 'to everyone his due.' Hence we take the *aristocratic* point of view: not according to
property or rank, but according to ability and achievement." As Nomad pointed out, at least Goebbels was honest in "frankly admitting the aristocratic
nature of this principle"—in contrast to Marxists, "who defend inequality of
rewards as a 'proletarian' theory."[72]

Goebbels was not alone in defining contemporary post-Marxist socialism
as aristocratic. That was also how Gottfried Feder defined it in his *Manifesto
against Usury and Interest Slavery.* As an alternative to what he called the strait-
jacket of state socialism, which swallows the individual, he envisioned the free
play of entrepreneurship under a socialism that privatizes the bulk of govern-
ment-owned property. A socialism that privatizes? Is that not a contradiction?
On the contrary, what is privatized would be turned over to owner-managers, to "workers," as Gesell and Feder defined them. The dynamism of independent proprietors competing in the market—Schumpeter's entrepreneurs—
would be saved, thereby averting economic stagnation plaguing other forms
of socialism.[73]

Far from visionary, this fascist socialism with private entrepreneurship has
become a living reality under another name. In the name of reforms designed
to save capitalism, Keynes among others contributed to a major shift toward
socialism throughout the Western world. Despite the survival of parasitic capital and rentier income, Keynes's closet socialism corresponds to the present
reality in the United States—fascist socialism.[74]

Although increasing numbers of intellectuals chose fascism in the 1930s,
they did so partly for the same reason that intellectuals joined the Commu-

nist ranks. According to Nomad, it was largely their impatience, their desire for a shortcut to power, that helped promote the new gospel: "Many of the fascist intellectuals would join the communist movement [as they did after World War II], if they saw that it had any chance, or at least intentions of winning *immediately*." The ideologies of communism and anticommunism come down to the same thing—a springboard to power. The reactionary features of fascist ideology were partly veneer, since once fascist parties were in command, they turned against their allies in big business. Rather than flunkies of the capitalist class, they were its *"major partners"* in a coalition leading beyond capitalism to socialism. There was no reason why job-hungry fascists should be opposed to the elimination of the capitalists—provided they got *"the best positions to the exclusion of their leftist competitors."*[75]

Nomad contended that as a new form of class rule, socialism is possible under a variety of competing ideologies. A social system predicated on the breeding of supermen, on the "mastery of the office-holders' class," on Nazi race theory or on a Mussolinian "glorification of the 'elite'" is therefore just as compatible with socialism as is a system based on a Marxist-Leninist vanguard or mass political party, "which takes for granted the higher incomes enjoyed by men of 'achievement' and 'prestige.'"[76]

That fascism is a shortcut to socialism was the thesis of Lawrence Dennis (1893–1977), a disillusioned foreign service officer, a no less disillusioned Wall Street broker, a cerebral fascist turned political economist, and a vigorous opponent of U.S. involvement in World War II. For Dennis, as for Burnham, Machiavelli is a better guide to contemporary politics than is Marx.[77] Unlike Burnham, however, Dennis had no illusions concerning socialism.

Mars is the midwife of the new socialist order, he argued in his major work, *The Dynamics of War and Revolution* (1940). Most socialists denounce war in almost the same terms they use to condemn capitalism for squandering the people's blood and treasure. But wars and preparations for war bring about interference of the state in the economy, and the longer and bigger they are, the more likely will the process of socialization continue. As Dennis concluded during the Vietnam War, "conscription, high taxation and extreme state controls . . . are socialistic in character and tend to bring on or force a steady transition or trend towards socialism."[78]

Two world wars "did, as a matter of historical record, enable the Communists to seize power in Russia in 1917 and greatly to enlarge their sphere of control over Eastern Europe and China from 1945 onward," Dennis pointed out. Unlike private investment that is subject to the ups and downs of the business cycle, in a state of permanent cold war there is no spending cycle any more than there is one in Soviet Russia. He thus concluded that for the United States to become socialist, it would suffice that the cold war continue and that defense spending replace private investment.[79]

Dennis made no attempt to forecast the outcome of the titanic struggle between liberalism and totalitarianism. At most, he took a stand on "the prediction that capitalism is doomed and socialism will triumph." In all the major European powers and in the United States, capitalism was giving way to a new society. What defined the new order were not the various theories, ideologies, or ideals of socialism but the different trends and working systems of socialism in practice. To be sure, Dennis's socialism was old-fashioned, based on more public ownership, more public control; but it did not require freedom and democracy any more than it hinged on peace among socialist countries. Considering the different systems of socialism and near-socialism competing for a place in the sun, a war between them was more than merely conjectural.[80]

Writing in 1940, Dennis declared that a world revolution was in progress, that communism, fascism, nazism, and the American New Deal were each local adaptations, some more developed than others, of just one revolution— socialism.[81] Here we have the same constellation of new social systems that Rizzi and Burnham identified as neither capitalist nor socialist. But their conceptions of socialism were founded on illusions—unlike the Soviet, Fascist, and Nazi versions.

For Dennis, the differences among these new systems were secondary; rival strategies were leading to the same end. "The vital element of the Fascist and Nazi way of coming to power was the taking of big businessmen and middle classes into the socialist camp," he wrote. By promising to smash the heads of local Communists, they deceived the monied interests into believing that they would preserve capitalism. But by averting civil war, "[t]he Fascist-Nazi method of transition from capitalism to socialism was obviously more humane for the capitalists and business executives and far better for the community than the communist way of sudden liquidation."[82]

As for the New Deal, a repetition of the Nazi experiment seemed unlikely in the United States. One reason, Dennis believed, is that anti-Semitism will not work in country that prides itself on being a melting pot of nations. Besides, Marx was right in dismissing anti-Semitism as "the socialism of fools . . . a manifestation of selective anticapitalism," in Dennis's words. Compelled by circumstances, the New Deal was only the first step in coping with the crisis of the capitalist system.[83] Unlike the Nazis and Fascists, the new class in the United States crept its way into power as a result of the tendency for big industry to socialize itself. In Germany and Italy, the new elites acquired political power and then took control of the economy. In the United States, this process was reversed.

From the passage of New Deal legislation, capped by the Wagner Act in 1935, to Lyndon Johnson's Great Society and its War on Poverty, the new elites got their first taste of power because of a tacit pact with organized labor. But what began as a social democratic strategy gave way in the 1970s and 1980s to a Yankee equivalent of the fascist road to power. Professionals shifted their allegiance from the Democrats to the Republicans in opposition to the escalating costs of the welfare state; from allies of labor, they became allies of the monied interests in a joint front against the rising tide from below. During the former stage, capitalists were trimmed of both political and economic power; during the latter, it was labor's turn to receive a knock-out blow. If socialism without socialists—creeping socialism—is an apt depiction of what happened in the United States, then so is fascism without fascists—creeping fascism.[84]

For the most part, socialists defined socialism as public ownership of the *means* of production, whereas fascists defined it as public control over the *agents* of production, over bourgeois *and* proletarians. As Hitler described his new order in private conversation, socialism meant rule by a new aristocracy of experts, a "professional class . . . [in which] each individual is separate, graded according to his ability and quality, to work for the general good." As he further observed in conversation with Herman Rauschning, ownership was of secondary importance: "Why need we trouble to socialize banks and factories? We socialize human beings!" How? By making owners de facto servants of the Nazi party and the state and by making wages exclusively a function of performance—a performance wage. As the key to Nazi labor policy, said Hitler to a party congress, "[i]t has been the iron principle of National Socialist leadership . . . to raise income solely by an increase in performance"[85]—piece rates for manual workers and merit increases for the professional elites.

Contrary to the contentions of Marxist ideologues, fascism is not the enemy of socialism; it is the enemy of nineteenth-century liberalism and democracy. As Hitler remarked to Rauschning, he had learned a great deal from Marxism. He had only to develop logically what Marxists repeatedly failed in because of their attempts to realize socialism within the framework of democracy. "National Socialism is what Marxism might have been if it could have broken its absurd and artificial ties with a democratic order," he declared. To the question, "What is fascism?" Charles Maurras, the ideologue of French fascism, answered in the same vein: "It is socialism emancipated from democracy"[86]—fascist socialism.

Maximal and Minimal Definitions of Socialism

The key to the new order is neither state control nor ownership but the composition of the ruling elite. Who are the directors, and who are the beneficiaries? Are they the *private* owners of capital? Or are they the *private* owners of expertise?[87] If expertise, then socialism is possible without benefit of either socialist ownership or fascist control.

Marxists and mainstream political economists alike believe that if socialist or labor parties are not at the helm politically, if the economy is not centrally planned, and if the big capitalists are not expropriated, socialism is not the dominant mode of production. At issue is a maximal definition of the new order that takes its most developed form as definitive.

But that form is a theoretical model that can be faulted for being ahistorical. For the most part, socialism does not develop from the top down but from the bottom up. The process can be speeded up with a Marxist-Leninist vanguard, but the conquest of power through a political revolution is the exception rather than the rule. Socialism develops through a series of stages that are recognized and delineated mainly in retrospect. To discover the moment of its emergence requires only a minimal—not a maximal—definition.

What, then, are the stages through which socialism developed in the United States? The first stage, prior to satisfying its minimal conditions, was the period in which wages caught up to and surpassed profits. The second, likewise transitional, was the period in which the surplus concealed in wages exceeded capital income. The third stage emerged when professional pelf surpassed capital income. That suffices for a minimal definition of socialism.

Reliance on a minimal definition of capitalism was Lenin's way of outmaneuvering and marginalizing the orthodox Marxists in his party. Because they relied on a maximal definition, they failed to perceive how far Russia had advanced toward capitalism—despite the hangovers of a semifeudal landholding system and the absence of a bourgeois political revolution. Lenin's masterpiece, *The Development of Capitalism in Russia* (1899), turned the tide against the orthodox Marxists, for in Lenin's accounting, the Russian proletariat did not number some two or three million but constituted half of the adult male population. Although most were semiproletarians, that signified capitalism had dissolved the old social relations dominant in the countryside.[88]

Among the foolish definitions of socialism are not only the Nazi half-baked version of the minimum conditions of the new order but also the Marxist variant based on its maximum conditions. In the first case, the foolishness was to accept as socialist a mode of production that had progressed no further than the second stage. In the second case, the foolishness was to accept as socialist only its full flowering, which meant that in the United States the dominant relations of production were still capitalist.

In *The Machiavellians,* Burnham explained how a science of politics is possible for both poor and rich, demoliberals and totalitarians. No matter what problems are posed by conflicting interests, the conclusions are testable by all. The Fascist-sympathizer Dennis and the anti-Fascist Nomad agreed on the evidence and arrived at the same conclusions. Nor was their agreement merely verbal. By the doom of capitalism, they meant the end of rule by the monied interests, the plutocracy; by the triumph of socialism, they meant rule by professionals, the bureaucratic elite.[89] But because Nomad delved deeper, he saw in the shift from old to new masters the emergence of a uniquely socialist mode of exploitation—his tour de force was to unmask the exploitative character of so-called earned as well as unearned income. On this score, Dennis was conspicuously silent.

Has the advent of the Information Age nullified Nomad's and Dennis's scenarios? Prior to World War II, the professional elites in Russia, Germany, and Italy were in the driver's seat, although in Germany and Italy the monied interests survived as a significant power. With the onset of the Information Age, the monied interests are no longer a threat. Because of mushrooming salaries and sheer numbers, the new class is the most likely beneficiary of the economic surplus.

But are *fascism* and *socialism* the most appropriate terms for describing the new society? To the objection that both categories have had their day and do not need to be revived, I reply that their neutral substitutes fail to plow beneath the surface. A stiff price must be paid in cutting off the present from its socialist and fascist past—the continuity between the knowledge society and its origins may be forgotten.

A Dictatorship of the Proletariat?

Today the proletariat, the class of wage earners, decides almost everything of political and economic importance. But *which* proletariat? As used in the *Communist Manifesto,* this term is as slippery as it is ambiguous.[90]

Loosely construed, it designates the class of wage earners without regard for fine distinctions. So used, the proletariat has finally come into its own in the name of all but in the interest of its elites. Even the United States has arrived at Marx's vaunted transition from capitalist to socialist society, in which the state can be nothing but a dictatorship of the proletariat.

A dictatorship of the proletariat in corporate America? Consider Marx's definition of proletarian rule. First, it is dictatorship by a class, not a party, much less a personal dictatorship. Second, the political form of proletarian rule is democratic. Third, its substance consists of despotic inroads on the rights of property.[91]

The thorny issue is which one of Marx's two proletariats would become the ruling class: working stiffs whose labor increases capital or the educated world of white hands. In the first case, we would have a dictatorship of labor, the scenario of Marx's rivals within the Communist League. In the second case, we would have what we actually got, a dictatorship of professionals over both labor and capital—a republic of experts.

There is little doubt concerning Marx's resolution of this world-historical ambiguity. In the first section of the Manifesto, he identifies the proletarian movement with the self-conscious, independent movement of the immense majority. In that majority, he includes professional workers, "the physician, the lawyer, the priest, the poet, the man of science."[92] The Marxist dictatorship of the proletariat is not a republic of labor. In practice, it is the perpetuation of what the Manifesto describes as privates of the industrial army under the command of a perfect hierarchy of officers.[93] Why did Bakunin reject the Marxist scenario? Because of the division into two proletariats, one ruling and the other ruled, one exploiting and the other exploited.

Marx was wrong, but not altogether. It was not the working class as a whole that would make the revolution; it was the privileged sector of proletarians who would replace the propertied interests. Recall Bazelon's definition of the new class: "The propertyless New Class is most broadly defined as that group of people gaining status and income through organizational position . . . mostly by virtue of educational status." Like the lower proletariat, the upper proletariat consists of jobholders—but that is where the similarity ends. As Bazelon asserted, "*The New Class is the cream of the proletariat; and the cream has been separated from the curd.*"[94] The new ruling class dictates what is and what shall be—a dictatorship of the proletariat, but not as Marx imagined it.

Phrased in more moderate terms, the United States has become a society of jobholders, "from the quarter-million-dollar-a-year executive to the subsistence laborer." Having said this, Bazelon added, "*In a certain fundamental sense,* both are proletarians: an increasingly comfortable proletarianization is America's gift to the world."[95] Aside from the fact that Bazelon's executive needs upgrading to $100 million a year, an increasingly comfortable proletarianization hardly fits the subsistence laborer.

To be sure, this gift to the world was only partly the transitional regime Marx envisioned. Besides hangovers from capitalism—a marginalized class of private entrepreneurs, shareholders, coupon-clippers, and real estate speculators—its ultimate beneficiary turned out to be the professional class. *That* was the socialist revolution that came stealthily during the night, an invisible dictatorship that arrived without any fanfare or mass demonstrations. It was a silent revolution made neither from above nor from below but from the bulging bell curve representing the middle ranks of society.

Such is the new reality revealed by post-Marxist political economy. Marxist forecasts of a classless society belong on the shelves of social science fiction. Even a refurbished Marxist political economy can no longer portray the world as it is. Labor is left holding an empty bag; what labor militants call the "class struggle swindle" is the socialist wool peeled from their eyes. The reality is a struggle for "class" by the new leaders of labor and by talented persons from the lower ranks seeking to detach themselves from their humble origins.

The Marxist strategy of class struggle became obsolete, not so much from having failed as from having succeeded. The irony is that from a revolutionary strategy for the transformation of society, Marxism became a conservative buttress of a new system of exploitation. In effect, capitalists are no longer labor's fundamental enemy, socialism no longer means the abolition of exploitation, and democracy no longer serves the cause of political liberation.

The battle of democracy has been won, but rule by the majority has brought only token benefit to labor. Tyranny of the majority originally signified expropriation of the idle rich. Today, it means tightening the screws on the laboring poor. Postcapitalist society is run by committees because people with expertise have to be consulted. Democracy means collective insurance for those at the top, a way of avoiding responsibility and preventing heads from rolling. At every level, majority rule plays into their hands. Initially, it paved the experts' road to power when they were still a tiny minority relying on the labor movement's numbers. Today, the professional class and its technical staff constitute a near majority and are making life increasingly difficult for their former ally.

Burnham identified managers, rather than a dictatorship of the proletariat qua class of professionals, as the successors to the monied interests. Almost four decades later, Barbara Ehrenreich and John Ehrenreich settled on an alternative characterization of the new class. They called it the "professional-managerial class," or PMC for short. Unlike Burnham's excessively narrow depiction to the exclusion of most professional workers, the PMC included them. "We define the professional-managerial class," the Ehrenreichs wrote, "as consisting of salaried mental workers who do not own the means of production and whose major function in the social division of labor may be described broadly as the reproduction of capitalist culture and capitalist class relations"—that is, prior to the advent of postcapitalist society.[96]

In view of this common denominator defining both managers and professionals, why hyphenate them? Because managerial roles are directly concerned with social control, while professional roles are less explicit.[97] Why make *that* a criterion? Presumably, because corporate managers have more power and command bigger salaries than other professionals. *That*, however, is a difference in degree, not in kind. So why not use the common denominator—the word *professional*—and dispense with *managerial* altogether?

As Robert Reich astutely observed, management is a profession in the United States: "It has its own graduate schools and advanced degrees; its own professional associations, conferences, and conventions; its own books, magazines, and professional newsletters; and a professional culture that distinguishes it from the general culture by language, clothing, income, and style of work." Although a relatively new profession dating from the first graduate school of business administration established in 1908, it is a profession not unlike the other professions that preceded it.[98]

Common sense dictates that Burnham's successors to the monied interests are simply professionals, owners of expertise. Precisely *their* dictatorship—a republic of experts—is the dictatorship of the proletariat in the United States.

7

the politics of the professional class

We were on the side of those who would collectivize. . . . The big financiers, the industrialists, and the national political leaders had not produced anything constructive to "solve the mess we are in . . . so why not go to the universities?"
—R. G. Tugwell, *The Brains Trust* (1968)

Their [the neoliberals'] willingness to accept the efficacy of market forces in promoting liberal goals . . . is perhaps their most significant departure from contemporary liberal theory: the shift from Keynes to Schumpeter.
—Randall Rothenberg, *The Neoliberals: Creating the New American Politics* (1984)

In the free societies of North America and Western Europe, the Age of Expertise can be dated roughly from the end of World War II. However, its first sprouts appeared in the command economies of the Soviet Union and Nazi Germany during the interwar years. Its intellectual roots go back even further, to the proliferation of socialist ideologies and Marxism in particular during the late nineteenth century. Marxism was the first consequential ideology of professionals on the road to class power. It was the first expression of the class struggle swindle by which professionals made common cause with labor to raise themselves to positions of power, pelf, and privilege.[1]

The swindle was getting labor to serve as a political pawn in a struggle that benefited the "working class." Marxist ideologues deceived labor into believing it would inherit the kingdom by dangling before labor's eyes the prospect of a classless socialist society and the mirage of a future communist society. The swindle lay in getting workers to believe that victory for the working class would be a victory for labor. The culture of the Left played into the hands of the new slavemasters.

In *The New Class: An Analysis of the Communist System* (1957), Milovan Djilas examined a contemporary version of this swindle by the new class in power. But as the subtitle of his work indicates, his analysis is confined to class politics in the mislabeled communist system. It remains to extend his analysis to the mislabeled capitalist system during the Information Age.

Divided on such domestic issues as the welfare state and a balanced budget, the new class favors bipartisanship in foreign policy. Under the leadership of professionals, the Democratic party reshaped society in their image. By the end of the century, the Republican party was also catering to professional interests, on the same side of the barricades opposite the underlying population. The cold war brought them together; the politics of anticommunism served the same ulterior purpose in the United States that the politics of communism did in the Soviet Union—keeping working stiffs at bay.

Pre–Information Age professionals were by and large economic Keynesians and political liberals. With the arrival of the Information Age, they gravitated toward a medley of Keynesian and Marshallian economics—the so-called neoclassical synthesis—while their political preferences shifted to the right. Originally in favor of the social pact between labor and management, they became increasingly divided over the Great Society and the Vietnam War. Neoconservatism appeared on the scene in response to New Left radicalism, while New Deal liberals opted for neoliberalism in response to the ebbing tide that threatened to lower all boats.

This transformation did not happen overnight. It came about through the evolution of the owners of expertise from an aspiring class intent on capturing the state to the leading class in power.

The Roosevelt Revolution

Labeled by its enemies a system of national economic planning and regimentation, the governmental structure of America's new order was shaped by the continuing New Deal launched by President Franklin D. Roosevelt. No less a dignitary than his immediate predecessor in the White House underscored the common denominator of the Roosevelt revolution and the revolutions in Communist Russia, Fascist Italy, and Nazi Germany. The system of national regimentation, wrote Hoover in 1934, not only is a "challenge to our American System" but also shares with socialism, communism, fascism, and nazism "the idea of the servitude of the individual to the state, and the denial of liberties unassailable by the state."[2]

Hoover itemized a list of centralized powers in the executive that filled nearly two pages. The executive powers most damaging to human liberty, he argued, were economic: the imposition of regulatory codes on industry and commerce enforceable by fine and imprisonment through the courts; the establishment of quotas on agricultural staples, curtailing production on fertile as well as marginal lands; the government's entry into business to compete with or replace private enterprise; the regulation of wages, incomes, and prices through managed currency and credit that transferred purchasing power from one group to another; and the control of foreign commerce through protective tariffs threatening to end free trade. The result was a virtual revolution in American institutions detrimental to human liberties, an erosion of representative government, and its replacement by the rule of bureaucrats.[3] Although Hoover did not speak with the voice of labor, he targeted its new enemy in the course of defending the old.

Was the system of national regimentation really collectivism? More than one New Dealer, notably members of Roosevelt's brain trust, claimed it was a giant step in that direction. As originally constituted in 1932, the brain trust consisted of three university professors: Raymond Moley (1886–1975), professor of government at Barnard College, Columbia University; Rexford G. Tugwell (1891–1979), professor of economics at Columbia; and Adolf A. Berle Jr. (1895–1971), professor of law at Columbia's Law School. According to Tugwell, the most radical member of the trio, he and Berle were on the side of the collectivizers. They favored a fairly extensive system of economic controls, a planned economy relying on entrepreneurial initiatives. "But we were always making such concessions to others," Tugwell recalled, "that our proposals fell into the background." As Berle remembered, Roosevelt knew better than they what could and could not be achieved: "The country was not ready to accept economic planning . . . though it already is on the verge of adopting such planning today."[4]

The New Deal planners, according to Robert Reich, wanted a system of industrial coordination that would give authority to professional managers in government and labor, but New Deal legislation represented a "compromise between the superstructures already in place and the vision of the new national planners." Nonetheless, for the first time during peace, the government managers were in charge, and the labor managers got a hearing. A tripartite system came into being, "transcending the disputes that still raged over the relative power of business, labor, and government within the superstructures of management."[5] The closest analogue was the system worked out by the Fascist state in Italy, where the government acted as moderator between the claims of business and labor.

"Among the least enchanting words in the business lexicon are planning, government control, state support and socialism," wrote John Kenneth Galbraith in *The New Industrial State*, but to consider the likelihood of these in the future "would be to bring home the appalling extent to which they are already a fact." A former New Dealer in the Roosevelt administration, he provided an insider's account of its support for what he called the new socialism.[6]

Galbraith was among the few non-Marxist political economists to tie together the theses of a new industrial order indissolubly linked to the state, the replacement of the market by the planning agencies of the modern corporation and big government, the euthanasia of stockholder power in conjunction with the tendency of the corporation to socialize itself, the eclipse of physical capital by professionally trained personnel, and the delegation of decision making to corporate professionals and their staffs. *The New Industrial State* became a landmark in its challenge to the conventional wisdom and in its suggestion that America's new economic order was not fundamentally different from the Soviet Union's. Although the American variant was democratic rather than totalitarian and compelled by circumstances rather than by ideology, the word *socialist* might credibly be applied to both.[7]

As early as World War I, the professional class captured the commanding heights of the economy through its control of the modern corporation. But it was not until the New Deal (1933–39) that it also captured the government. For the first time in U.S. history, an American president relied on a brain trust influenced by socialist ideology. Roosevelt responded favorably to local pressures not only from share-the-wealth movements sponsored by Huey Long, Father Coughlin, and Dr. Francis Townsend but also from organized labor galvanized by John L. Lewis's CIO. Yet it was not the vast array of New Deal social legislation and alphabet agencies and commissions that launched America's new economic order. Variously described as government planning, collectivism, state capitalism, and national socialism, the new order had Mars for its midwife. Only America's entry into World War II provided the stimulus for ending the Great Depression.[8]

Following World War II and the Korean War, full employment and the expansion of the wage surplus made the professional class the principal beneficiary of the knowledge society as well as its driving force. In response to the technological demands of a high-tech war and the scientific-technical revolution that enabled the United States to prevail over the Axis powers, the quality as well as quantity of employment broke all records. High-paid as well as high-skilled jobs enabled the country to cross the threshold from managerial capitalism to corporate socialism.

New Deal legislation, specifically the National Labor Relations Act of 1935 legalizing collective bargaining and the Fair Labor Standards Act of 1938 legislating a minimum wage, contributed to this transition. Noteworthy is the fact that the only occasion in which an increase in the hourly minimum topped 50 percent was in 1950, when it soared from 30 cents to 75 cents for a record-breaking 150 percent raise. New Deal legislation and the increasing strength of unions made it possible.

It was not just war, the scientific-technical revolution, and labor reforms that made a difference. Education also played a key role. More than 20 million veterans had their skills upgraded after Congress passed the Servicemen's Readjustment Act—the first G.I. bill—during Roosevelt's fourth term in office. Designed for veterans of World War II, it was followed during President Truman's Fair Deal by a second G.I. bill, covering veterans of the Korean War.

As Theodore Schultz noted in a 1961 article, "Investment in education has risen at a rapid rate and by itself may well account for a substantial part of the otherwise unexplained rise in earnings." His preliminary estimates showed that the stock of education in the work force rose about 8.5 times between 1900 and 1956, compared with the stock of reproducible capital that rose only 4.5 times, calculated in 1956 prices. He attributed nearly half of the overall increase in the national income between 1929 and 1956 to education. During the two decades from the start of World War II to 1960, the number of college graduates doubled, while the number of doctoral degree holders more than tripled.[9]

The Roosevelt revolution accounts for these startling figures. But were the original brain trust, the professionals in government who replaced it, and the lower-level bureaucrats in charge of implementing legislation responsible for the change? Surely, more so than most of the political leaders in the Democratic party. As Walter Dean Burnham observed on the blurb of Thomas Ferguson's path-breaking *Golden Rule* (1995), "You think politicians run the political system . . . forget it." Contrary to Schumpeter, it is not political candidates competing for the people's vote who determine the outcome of elections.[10]

As Ferguson concluded from his studies of the New Deal, "to discover who rules, follow the gold." Major blocs of private and institutional investors determined the outcome of the Roosevelt revolution. In politics, you get what you pay for: "The guiding principle is that selection of political parties is a special case of rational portfolio choice under uncertainty: one holds politicians more or less like stocks."[11] Although the Golden International originally represented rentier capitalists, the subordination of property to expertise vastly enlarged its membership.

The Roosevelt revolution hinged on not only a political coalition but also a particular bloc of corporate investors. By tracing how the Great Depression divided the business community that had once been solidly Republican, Ferguson explained its dissolution into "one part intensely nationalist, protectionist, and . . . generally labor-intensive; the other oriented to capital-intensive production processes and free trade." Although the first New Deal (1933–35) began with the nationalist bloc in control, the second New Deal (1937–39) witnessed a major shift toward multinational liberalism. The shrinking of international trade and the decline in national income account for the nationalist coalition during the first New Deal. But with partial recovery on both the domestic and international fronts during the second New Deal, the nationalist coalition blew apart over labor and foreign policy.[12]

At the center of the coalition that came together during the second New Deal—the coalition that dominated American politics from 1938 to 1980—were not labor bureaucrats and government planners, as liberal commentators initially supposed. At the center was a historically new bloc of capital-intensive firms that included local real estate interests, investment banks, and internationally oriented commercial banks. Ironically, Roosevelt's unique achievement—the welfare state—had been found to be good business for American firms with minuscule labor costs.

As Ferguson noted, "capital-intensive firms use relatively less direct human labor (and that often professionally and elaborately trained)." They alone had the resources for granting major concessions to organized labor. Since they were mostly world leaders in their respective industries, they stood to gain from global free trade and from an alliance with the international bankers. The bankers' minuscule work force presented few sources of tension, while their costs were overwhelmingly the costs of borrowed money.[13]

Opposed to this winning coalition or capital-intensive party were the labor-intensive industries. They found it difficult to accommodate mass movements for unionization. Because of weakness in the face of foreign rivals, they were driven, in Ferguson's words, "to embrace high tariffs, quotas, and other forms of government intervention to protect themselves." These were the industries—textiles, footwear, steel, rubber, chemicals—that had dominated the earlier Republican-led political system and that resisted the creeping socialism of the Roosevelt revolution in its various mutations after World War II.[14]

Among supporters of the Roosevelt revolution were big-time capitalists collaborating with corporate directors behind the scenes. Prior to World War I, the Republican coalition was dominated by the House of Morgan, whereas Rockefeller interests played a leading role in the new Democratic coalition. According to Ferguson's extensive data, Roosevelt's election in 1932 was in part a showdown between these two blocs of supercapitalists.[15]

Although Ferguson maintained that theories of a managerial revolution fail to account for the Roosevelt revolution, his investment theory of political competition holds up under both his model of corporate capitalism and our own model under a different name. Campaign contributions condition access to the political media. They also determine the principal planks in a party's platform, the selection of candidates for political office, the issues presented to the public for debate, and the electorate's final choices. Big money, both private and corporate, thus determined the outcome of the Roosevelt revolution. If Ferguson is right, capital-intensive industries paid the piper and called the tune.

Class War on Two Fronts

In *The Managerial Revolution,* Burnham outlined three problems the managerial elites face on the road to managerial society: "(1) To reduce the capitalists (both at home and finally throughout the world) to impotence; (2) to curb the masses in such a way as to lead them to accept managerial rule . . . ; (3) to compete among themselves for the first prizes in the world as a whole." In the Soviet Union, the first problem was addressed first; the second was addressed only after disposing of the common enemy; the third was left to the future. Nazi Germany reversed the order: a fairly rapid curbing of the working masses was followed by a more gradual reduction of the capitalists to impotence. The third problem was not postponed but faced during World War II.[16]

The American way was unique. "The New Deal has *simultaneously* been reducing capitalist institutions . . . making easier the rise of the managers *and* curbing the masses along lines adapted to the managerial future," Burnham wrote. Its attack on the monied interests went hand in hand with new labor legislation that tied the unions to the state as benefactor. Burnham attributed the slower pace of institutional change in the United States to its comparatively favored position in the capitalist world. America's problems were never as acute as those of the powers defeated in World War I, although World War II was expected to speed up the transformation. Burnham anticipated that the United States would "meet all three parts of the managerial problem—the reduction of the capitalists, the curbing of the masses, and the competition with the other sectors of the managers—more or less at once."[17]

Consider the evidence for and against Burnham's scenario. At the time he was writing in 1941, he had only the New Deal to go on. While Roosevelt gave relief and jobs to the unemployed and bolstered the right of labor to bargain collectively, the New Deal exempted from the requirements of the antitrust laws those industries that agreed to collaborate with the government. As Secretary of Labor Frances Perkins later acknowledged, the National Industrial Recovery Act of 1933 "rested on the idea of suspending the effect of the antitrust laws in return for voluntary agreements by industries for fair competition, minimum wage levels and maximum hours." It was a boon for management as well as for labor. But having established the rights of labor in the interest of industrial peace, Roosevelt in a radio appeal on 24 July 1933 warned the workers against aggression—that is, against resorting to strikes to implement their rights.[18]

The National Recovery Administration (NRA) fell short of labor's demands. Its proposed wage minimums were resisted by workers, who had to strike to get their unions recognized. In the six months following enactment of the National Industrial Recovery Act, recalled the labor historian Art Preis, "the number of strikes totaled 1,695 in 1933 compared to 841 in 1932, and the number of strikers almost quadrupled." When the coal miners struck in Pennsylvania, Roosevelt called for an investigation of communist infiltration and ordered the mine leaders to heel. The American Civil Liberties Union denounced the NRA as initiating the most ferocious assault on American labor in its history—that may have been an exaggeration. Nonetheless, as reported in the *New York Times* on 11 February 1934, "At no time have there been such widespread violations of workers' rights by injunctions, troops, private police, deputy sheriffs, labor spies and vigilantes."[19]

Roosevelt's advisers argued for a frank acceptance of the large corporation, which meant concessions to the managerial elites on the matter of strikes as well as trust-busting. They supported, in the historian William Leuchtenburg's words, the "two thousand men, who controlled American economic life [and] manipulated prices and production." Although critics branded the Roosevelt administration as prolabor, the New Dealers had far less interest in helping labor than in helping business. They felt more in common with the industrial czars. As Leuchtenburg observed, "The New Dealers wished to cooperate with business, but they distrusted financiers." The president talked repeatedly of a government-business partnership, by which he meant a pact with heads of the big corporations.[20]

We have seen how the New Deal both rescued and imposed economic controls on big capital. But did it not behave similarly in first raising up and then clamping down on big labor?

The notorious Smith "Gag" Act of 1940, the first legislative step indirectly aimed at organized labor, was rushed through by a Democratic Congress and signed into law by the president. Over the protests of the AFL, the CIO, and the ACLU, it was, according to Preis, the "first federal law since the infamous and quickly-repealed Alien and Sedition Act of 1798 to make mere advocacy of views a 'crime'"—in this case, the advocacy of communism. Eleven Communist leaders were convicted in the 1949 Smith Act trial not for conspiring to overthrow the government but for presumably advocating overthrow. The conviction, upheld by the Supreme Court, was a blow against not just the Communist party but also the trade unions for harboring its members. Since

Communist militants had played an important role in organizing the unorganized and in building the CIO, class-conscious unionism was being equated with communism. Thus, as David Milton pointed out, "anti-communism, which for many decades had provided the ideology for containing American labor under craft unionism, was once again linked with the ideology of nationalism to contain the radical impulses of industrial unionism."[21]

A second act of repressive legislation came in response to labor's offensive at the end of World War II. Within a week of V-J Day, mass demonstrations erupted in the major industrial centers. By the close of 1945, unions had launched the greatest wage offensive in U.S. history. Congress responded with the Taft-Hartley Labor-Management Relations Act of 1947. Section nine on the rights of employees stipulated that no action would be taken by the National Labor Relations Board in response to a labor organization unless there was on file with the board an affidavit executed by "each officer of such labor organization of which it is an affiliate or constituent that he is not a member of the Communist Party or affiliated with such a party." At first, labor leaders refused to sign the controversial non-Communist affidavit, but most eventually complied. As President Philip Murray of the CIO told union leaders at a meeting of its executive board, "If communism is an issue in any of your unions, throw it the hell out . . . and throw its advocates out along with it." Ten unions refused and were expelled.[22]

The Taft-Hartley "Slave-Labor Act," as it was called, further curbed the powers of union leaders and their constituencies by outlawing the closed shop, making it more difficult to establish the union shop, prohibiting recourse to secondary boycotts and sympathetic strikes, and authorizing the separate states to pass so-called right-to-work laws. It was a virtual declaration of war on organized labor that augured the end of the social pact.

A series of other repressive laws followed, mainly laws directed against Communists in the independent unions expelled by the CIO. The McCarran-Kilgore Internal Security Act of 1950 established concentration camps for political dissenters without trial during a national emergency. The Communist Control Act of 1954 outlawed the Communist party. The 1954 act immediately became a pretext for government intervention against the International Union of Mine, Mill and Smelter Workers. CIO and AFL leaders turned a deaf ear to the Justice Department's attempt to deprive the union of legal standing on the ground that some of its members belonged to the Communist party.[23]

In 1958, the Supreme Court handed down decisions on three cases known as the Steelworkers Trilogy. It ruled that every dispute during the life of a labor contract is subject to compulsory arbitration by a neutral third party. According to the labor lawyer Thomas Geoghegan, this signified in practice "mini-lawsuits, millions of them, jam-packed in big backlogs, going back for years." As a result, strikes were banned for all practical purposes except for periods between contracts. Although labor initially wanted arbitration, the price it had to pay became prohibitive. "An arbitrator, unlike a judge, can charge by the hour," Geoghegan wrote, "so for the union, which is broke, there are two meters running, the arbitrator's and its lawyers."[24]

In 1981, labor experienced another setback when President Ronald Reagan outlawed the striking Professional Air Traffic Controllers Organization (PATCO). Encouraged by the government's strike-breaking example, corporate managers succeeded in reducing the strength of America's trade unions by some three million members by the end of Reagan's second term. They also compelled the unions to sign contracts surrendering some of labor's most important gains. The concessions, known as "give-backs," were substantial, in some instances reducing union wages by as much as 25 percent. No wonder that by 1990 labor was flat on its back,[25] while capital remained standing—if only on one leg.

In retrospect, Burnham's scenario required revision. His chief amendment to it was to provide a leading role for professional soldiers. Throughout most of the capitalist era, they had played a decidedly secondary role. Not until World War II did war managers rise to the rank of civilian managers in determining national policy. As Burnham correctly anticipated, "the soldiers, the men of force, the Lions, will be much more prominent among the new rulers than in the ruling class of the past century." Thus to the other managerial elites—"the production executives and organizers of the industrial process, officials trained in the manipulation of the great labor organizations, and the administrators, bureau chiefs, and commissars developed in the executive branch"—he added the graduates of military academies and war colleges in the United States.[26]

"Never again, in our time or our children's," Burnham contended, "will the army dry up into a small puddle on the fringe of the social pond." The armed forces may be expected not only to increase in size but also to become a major arena of the ambitious and powerful and to "supply a considerable section of the ruling class of the future." This heightened influence of professionals in the military establishment, Burnham concluded, constituted one of the most significant features of the managerial revolution.[27]

Some two decades later, in his Farewell Address on 17 January 1961, President Dwight D. Eisenhower testified to the accuracy of Burnham's prognosis: "The conjunction of an immense military establishment and a large arms industry is new in the American experience. The total influence—economic, political, even spiritual—is felt in every office of the federal government." The so-called military-industrial complex had taken the initiative and was making many of the crucial decisions that Congress used to make. Military spending became, in Marty Jezer's words, "the pot of gold at the end of the corporate rainbow and even with the coming of peace corporate leaders were loathe to give it up."[28] It was a military-industrial complex, not a capitalist complex, that dominated the United States politically.

The cold war would become the road to preeminence of professional managers, professional bureaucrats in the federal government, and the professional military—at the expense of the monied and the propertied interests. Big military budgets made possible by the permanent threat of war translated into bigger salaries all around. Initially, leaders of organized labor shared the laurels with professionals in industry and government in what amounted to a social pact that benefited the working masses. Their place would be taken by the military professionals who rose to prominence during World War II.[29]

Burnham, taking his cues from the Soviet and Nazi examples, believed that America's new elites would develop a coherent ideology in place of the mishmash of the New Deal. Neoliberalism and neoconservatism only partly confirmed his expectations. Lacking a revolutionary vanguard, the new elites have yet to formulate an ideology expressive of their unique class interests. A full half-century after Burnham penned *The Managerial Revolution,* they were still floundering, no longer over the merits of laissez-faire but more or less evenly attracted to the Republican and Democratic parties. An economic revolution had taken place under their noses, which they only vaguely recognized. Efforts have been made to shape such an ideology, but on mainly capitalist premises.[30]

From the Social Pact to the Great Repression

For an alternative account of professionals on the road to class power, I turn to the single most important work by radical political economists since Paul Baran and Paul Sweezy's *Monopoly Capital* (1966): Samuel Bowles, David Gordon, and Thomas Weisskopf's *Beyond the Wasteland* (1984). As John Kenneth Galbraith noted on the blurb in an appraisal shared by two Nobel laureates in economics, "This book is by the three most interesting economists of the left in the United States—or anywhere—today." Unlike Burnham's account, which relied on foresight, the work of Bowles, Gordon, and Weisskopf had the advantage of hindsight. Although the authors failed to address the fundamental issues of the political economy of expertise and the rise to power of the professional class, their thesis of a counteroffensive against labor is borne out by the downturn in productivity, by workers' resistance to corporate control, and by global competition and global challenges to the Pax Americana.

No matter that the authors were mistaken in calling the U.S. economy capitalist, albeit a kind of capitalist system different from the prewar vintage. No matter that they identified the new capitalism with private corporate power in which private profit making still holds sway. No matter that they classified professional managers as corporate capitalists and the management-labor pact as a capital-labor accord. Their explanation of the erosion of the social pact and their account of the shift from the Great Society to the Great Repression is a veritable tour de force.[31]

According to Bowles, Gordon, and Weisskopf, the terms of the social pact with labor boiled down to the following. The corporations would retain control over fundamental decisions governing operations as "codified in the 'management rights' clauses of most collective bargaining agreements," and unions would be "accepted as legitimate representatives of workers' interests." In return for the unions' contribution to an orderly and disciplined labor force, the corporations would "reward workers with a share of the income gains made possible by rising productivity, with greater employment security and with improved working conditions." Such was the quid pro quo carrot offered by management; the stick inducing labor compliance was the continuing threat of cyclical unemployment, reminding workers to be thankful for their jobs.[32]

By 1965, this mutual nonaggression pact no longer held. Unauthorized strikes were proliferating, while resistance on the factory floor led to a downturn in productivity. The civil rights movement compounded the problem of extracting business profits from a minority work force that was no longer submissive. Worker resentment at mounting wage differentials, dissatisfaction with working conditions, and growing worker independence resulted in an erosion of corporate power to hold wages down. Thus the real cost of labor mounted, the share of capital in overall income declined, and the "fiscal costs of pacifying this mounting rebelliousness—through the War on Poverty and the other Great Society programs—began to soar."[33]

Previously, the cost of rising wages had been passed to consumers through equivalent price increases. The erosion of U.S. international domination, however, signified "a growing penetration of U.S. domestic markets by imported foreign goods" that made it increasingly difficult for American corporations to raise prices. To make matters worse for big business, a hike in the effective corporate profit tax rate became a means of financing the welfare state, while "the fall in unit profits contributed to the crushing 1966 decline in the after-tax profit rate."[34]

Observers of the labor-management scene reported increasing intentional work slowdowns and growing absenteeism. In response, management in 1970 launched a workplace counteroffensive that included speedups and increased surveillance of shop operations. Accident rates soared as a result of the speed-ups, while U.S. Department of Labor data on job satisfaction showed a marked decline. The managerial counteroffensive accelerated as employers sought to change the rules of the game by getting rid of unions altogether. Union deau-thorization cases filed with the National Labor Relations Board more than doubled between 1960 and 1979.

Besides this direct onslaught against labor, the corporations lobbied for a change in macroeconomic policy. This second prong of the business counter-offensive, the authors contended, dealt the social pact its coup de grâce. Gov-ernment officials joined the antilabor brigade with a sustained ice-water dous-ing of the economy beyond its 1974–75 downturn. "Restrictive fiscal policy—the deliberate generation of high levels of unemployment—became a permanent feature of the macroeconomic terrain in the late 1970s." The logic of an artifi-cially extended recession is that it brings relief from both insubordination and wage pressures. Although most economists blame global competition for Amer-ica's economic reversals, Bowles, Gordon, and Weisskopf maintained that "avail-able data suggest that domestic factors have been much more important in causing the employment slowdown."[35]

Contrary to mainstream economics, the authors pointed to "the *costs of corporate power* as the fundamental source of the crisis in the U.S. economy." The economic success of the postwar period prior to 1965 depended on the social pact with labor. However, resistance to corporate domination spread with the escalating costs of the Vietnam War and the mounting demands of social movements for a redistribution of the economic pie. The costs of keeping peo-ple down therefore escalated. Too many demands on the corporate order were being made by too many interested parties simultaneously. "The resistance that eroded the postwar corporate system could not simply be quashed by a new display of political and economic muscle . . . [without] continuing escalation of the costs of corporate power," the authors concluded.[36]

To the authors' credit, they acknowledged that the corporate solution to declining profit rates and falling investments is not the only one. Rather than induce an artificial recession needed to discipline the work force, curb wage gains, and trim entitlements, the democratic solution is to induce economic growth by restoring material incentives, improving working conditions, and forging a new pact with labor, one that would do away with the mounting costs of surveillance and repression. But is that what the new professional elites wanted? On the contrary, for them the benefits outweighed the costs.

On the same wavelength as this radical overview of the American econo-my is Frances Fox Piven and Richard A. Cloward's *The New Class War: Reagan's*

Attack on the Welfare State and Its Consequences (1982). According to them, the Reagan presidency was the culminating point in the combined plutocratic and business elites' class war against labor's gains embodied in the welfare state. The corporate mobilization against labor took the form of cutbacks to the national minimum-income floor as "part of a larger strategy to increase business profits." The other parts of the strategy included (1) measures for reorganizing the tax structure that promoted a massive upward redistribution of income; (2) new corporate investment and depreciation write-offs; (3) personal income and estate taxes slashed by formulas that gave 85 percent of the benefits to those with annual incomes exceeding $50,000; and (4) directives for deregulating American business that relaxed enforcement standards and lowered the penalties for violations.[37]

The Reagan administration became, in their words, the "voice of a decade-long campaign waged by the large corporations" in such business publications as the *Wall Street Journal, Fortune,* and *Business Week.* In the early 1980s, corporations were spending roughly one-third of their tax-deductible advertising dollars to influence citizens, not just consumers—that is, for political purposes. The enemy of the American public was defined by Mobil Oil in one of its regular advertisement-editorials as "'negative growth'—growth in taxes, government spending and burdensome regulations"—resulting from "the era when government grew so fat and flabby that its weight pulled the private sector right into the ground."[38]

Corporate strategy, the authors argued, called for downsizing the federal government as a means of balancing the budget. First, because government borrowing in the capital markets crowds out corporate borrowers by driving up interest rates. Second, because a balanced budget is an excuse for slashing income-maintenance programs that indirectly jack up wages in the labor market. Almost half of the aggregate income of the bottom fifth of the population derives from social welfare, so that an unemployed work force with monetary benefits and food stamps cannot afford to take such punishment lightly.[39]

As Piven and Cloward summed up the consequences of Reagan's assault on the welfare state, the state rather than the factory floor has become the principal arena of class conflicts between big business and a labor movement in retreat. The Reagan administration's efforts to reverse past welfare policies resulted in a "crisis of power whose dimensions are comparable to the earlier struggle by capital to win control of the state from the . . . landed classes." But will this corporate-led assault succeed? Whatever the outcome, the authors declared, "the informal alliance among hard-hit racial minorities, the unem-

ployed and the working poor virtually insures that the politicization of economic issues involving income-maintenance programs . . . is not about to
disappear."[40]

Is the class war between capital and labor the only class war, as these radical critiques assume? When included among the major contenders for pelf and
power, the professional elites figure as the propellants of two additional class
confrontations. There is the class war with the former ruling class and the war
of professionals with organized labor. More than one zero-sum game is at stake:
a professional as well as a capitalist one. After all, the top professionals are only
slightly less hostile toward labor than are the capitalists they displaced.

To be sure, the top dogs are not the only professionals. The unions that still
flourish are mainly those of professional workers. In 1997, over half of all union
members had attended college, almost 28 percent with baccalaureates and
roughly the same percentage with some college education. According to Andrew Hacker, in the 18 February 1999 *New York Review of Books,* union members with degrees averaged an income of $45,400 in round numbers—well over
the national average. Because of collective bargaining, top reporters at the *New
York Times* received over $100,000 with overtime pay; senior professors at New
York's City University received even more for only 140 hours a year in the classroom; pilots with only fifteen years of service at Northwest, American, United, and US Airways earned *on an average* over $175,000 annually; and physi-
cians were becoming unionized, the better to bargain with the HMOs under
pressure from the insurance companies and the escalating costs of health care.[41]
Understandably, union leaders prefer to organize their fellow professionals,
whose high salaries and membership dues contribute to raising their own pay.
Labor's pact with management is thus being eroded from within the labor
movement, not just from outside it.

Beyond the Wasteland and *The New Class War* called for amendments to
Burnham's scenario of a class war on two fronts. Although the professionals'
zero-sum game targets both labor and capital, the rupture of the social pact
and the ensuing repression show that labor has become the principal enemy.
Like the original New Dealers, professionals feel more threatened from below
than from above. The balance of forces has changed; professionals resist the
encroachments of labor even more than they do the privileges of capital.

Overall, the United States followed a zig-zag path in implementing its new
economic order. Initially, both capital and labor were constrained by New Deal
legislation. Then, despite Taft-Hartley and McCarthyism, labor became the
prime beneficiary of the welfare state. More recently, with the shift from the
Great Society to the Great Repression, labor became the principal target of
government cutbacks and business layoffs.

Contemporaneous with the class war in the United States during the 1980s, the restructuring of the Soviet economy in the name of freedom and competitiveness represented a similar shift away from organized labor. While professionals in the United States were decrying welfare for indirectly sapping their privileged salaries, professionals in the Soviet Union were demanding an end to wage-leveling for having narrowed the gap between their incomes and those of manual workers. Mikhail Gorbachev's perestroika aimed at, among other things, scuttling Stalin's "utopian/voluntarist" legacy of "crude egalitarianism." As noted by Gorbachev's principal adviser, Alexander Yakovlev, Stalin failed to understand that the favorite child of socialism is not labor but the intelligentsia, indeed, that "Socialism *is* Knowledge"—a knowledge society ruled by intellect.[42]

As allies in World War II, both the United States and the Soviet Union contributed to the death of fascism. But with the onset of the Great Repression and its Soviet counterpart (perestroika) in the 1980s, fascism made a startling comeback without the benefit of fascists. By a route different from the one Fascists traveled in the 1930s, both the United States and the Soviet Union converged on the same goal—that of disciplining labor in a graded society governed by a performance wage.

Neoliberalism and the Zero-Sum Society

By the mid-1970s, the social pact between management and labor had eroded, leaving in its wake a new ruling class of professional workers as chief beneficiary. No longer required to stand together, professional workers became divided over the increasing costs of welfare under conditions of exploding entitlements coupled with economic downturn. The economic miracle—a postwar boom that had broken all previous records over a period of almost three decades—was over. As the economic slowdown transformed what had been a positive-sum into a zero-sum game, neoconservatives joined ranks with the monied interests against the perceived threat of a welfare state. Confronted with the fiscal crisis, neoliberals also beat a retreat from the web of special interests they had once championed.

President Johnson's Great Society represented both the climax and the end of the New Deal. Its public image of a positive-sum society promised not only the end of poverty but also the end of scarcity. As Robert Reich recalled, the liberalism of the 1960s was fueled by two intellectual currents: Keynesianism and pluralism. Keynesianism legitimized government intervention as a means of stabilizing the economy. Pluralism—the doctrine that there is no public or national interest apart from individual and group interests—justified government intervention as a way of pacifying social discontent. "Both currents,"

Reich wrote, "were ultimately propelled by the comforting notion that some people could be helped without imposing costs on others." Full employment would take care of the economic problem; the accommodation of interest groups through entitlements would defuse most political problems. It was an unreal world without hard choices and priorities. In such a sheltered and rich environment, unlike anything the United States had ever experienced or would likely ever experience again, "postwar liberalism was doomed to excess."[43]

As the economy slowed and global competition began to plague American industry, Keynesianism was challenged for promoting inflation, while pluralism was questioned for ignoring the national interest. "By the late 1970s," Reich observed, "liberalism and, inevitably, the Democratic Party, too, appeared less the embodiment of a shared vision and more a tangle of narrow appeals from labor unions, teachers, gays, Hispanics, blacks, Jews, the handicapped, the elderly, women." The disastrous 1972 presidential campaign of George McGovern confirmed the public impression that the Democratic party had become dominated by partisan concerns.[44] That Jimmy Carter's presidency made an about-face by adopting some of the central precepts of the new conservative public philosophy signified the end of the Roosevelt era. The sun had set on the Great Society, and a new age had dawned—that of the zero-sum society.

With good reason, Lester Thurow's *Zero-Sum Society* (1980) became the bible of neoliberal economics and of the new liberalism challenging the entitlements version. The first major shift in the new class had occurred over the Vietnam War and Students for a Democratic Society (SDS), pitting a younger generation of professionals and preprofessionals against the Democratic establishment. But the New Left never amounted to much, while its allies among New Deal holdovers soon changed their tune in response to Nixon's overwhelming victory at the polls and their own candidate's abysmal defeat.

Thurow had worked for McGovern during the debacle that foreshadowed an end to the old liberalism. Once Thurow realized that New Deal thinking had become exhausted, he began charting a new politics for professionals focused on economic growth instead of handouts. By bringing the productivity problem to national attention, he gave new life to the Democratic party. Neoliberalism as a full-fledged political and economic philosophy dates from his *Zero-Sum Society*.[45]

Thurow's key message for Americans was that for every economic solution to major national problems, there will be losers as well as winners. To get the economy going, the wealthiest taxpayers must foot the bill. Not just the robber barons' heirs but also CEOs and other extravagantly paid professionals. When neoliberals singled out recipients of the big salaries as potential targets, the professional class became additionally divided.

Faced with an economy that no longer performed, Thurow called for investment-stimulation in high-productive sunrise industries and for disinvestment in low-productive sunset industries. His neoliberal stress on the supply side of the public ledger became a counterweight to Keynesian demand-stimulation strategies. His new orientation stressed savings in new plants and equipment. It encouraged free trade and an end to subsidies as a means of making American industry more competitive. If neoliberals had their way, many industries, the oil industry in particular, would be deregulated to bring down prices. Corporate taxes would be reduced as an incentive to corporate research and development, antitrust legislation would be scrapped, and idle capacity would be discouraged. Flexible employment was another neoliberal policy, but with compensation for the victims of downsizing.[46]

Although these neoliberal policies had the backing of conservatives in both parties, the flip side of the neoliberals' hard choices was to compensate the losers. The safety net would be expanded; basic medical care for every American would become a top priority. Wage and price controls would be retained, but only as a last-ditch alternative to fighting inflation through unworkable fiscal and monetary controls and artificially induced recessions. Redistribution policies on behalf of those near the poverty level would be retained. The tax structure would be reformed as a means of reducing income inequalities; tax loopholes would be blocked. "When one reviews what must be done—massive public investment, budget surpluses to generate more savings, large compensation systems, increases in income transfer payments, and tax cuts for the lower middle class—it is clear that one of the basic ingredients of future progress is a tax system that can raise substantial amounts of revenue," Thurow contended.[47] That meant making the rich bear a bigger share of the burden.

Thurow pinpointed two principal causes of America's decline: global competition and domestic gridlock. America's competitors did not acquire an economic advantage by cutting taxes on the rich or by reducing wages as the conservatives would have liked. Sixteen countries, Thurow noted, collect a larger fraction in taxes than the United States does. The American economy is "one with the fewest rules and regulations . . . nowhere in the world is it easier to lay off workers." America's competitors have not unleashed incentives and savings by increasing income differentials—"they have done exactly the opposite." Nor are huge welfare expenditures an impediment to their global competitiveness.[48]

Domestic gridlock prevents the political system from working. Loss allocation is, Thurow declared, "precisely what our political process is least capable of doing." Special interest lobbies prevail. The ability to decide collapses into lengthy adversary procedures. "Costs rise, new projects cannot be undertaken, and old projects cannot be transformed," he observed. Candidates are elected to office on the promise of benefits for everyone, but there is no electoral mandate to impose losses on anyone.[49]

Thurow's work is impressive, but it fails on two counts. First, in leaving the determination of a fair distribution to be settled by government, he underestimated the role of special interests in determining the public's notion of fairness. Second, rather than focus on class politics and class struggle, he settled for conflicts among special interests, to which he assigned roughly equal weights even though they are decidedly unequal. His hard choices turn out to be soft, while his solutions to the productivity crisis reflect the special interests of owners of expertise.

Professionally considered, neoliberal policies are an improvement over the shibboleths of the New Deal, but the biggest loser promises to be labor. "In the old implicit post–World War II social contract," Thurow observed, "major employers paid what economists came to call efficiency wages . . . above-market wages [that] gave workers an incentive to voluntarily cooperate with their employers, an incentive to work hard." Without the economic threat of powerful unions, however, efficiency wages fell by the wayside. In the future, the motivation for cooperation is going to be not efficiency wages but fear, he declared, "the fear of being fired into an economy of falling real wages."[50]

Following on the heels of Thurow's book, Robert Reich's *Next American Frontier* underscored the same two causes of American decline: global competition and domestic gridlock. On the one hand, he faulted corporate managers and the conglomerate enterprise for becoming disconnected from the everyday process of production, for relying on financial and legal virtuosity and the "manipulation of rules and numbers as the primary means of maintaining the profitability of their firms." On the other hand, he blamed America's political leaders for refusing to make the hard choices necessary to get the economy going again.[51]

George Gilder, the conservative guru of supply-side economics and the darling of the two Reagan administrations, found little to dispute in Reich's presentation. In a review for the *Wall Street Journal* on 10 June 1983, he was even laudatory: "After a decade of Democratic fantasies about the end of economic growth, the 'threat' of new technology, the exhaustion of natural resources, the impending great depression, the need for 'reindustrialization,' the mandate for a 'new protectionism,' Mr. Reich is making an unabashed case for Schumpeterian 'creative destruction' and economic rivalry and growth." This represented "a turning point in American liberalism," the title of his review. But it hardly did justice to Reich's parallel contention, that profit seeking and investment in growth are compatible with claims for participation and fairness and that "American statesmanship must rise above . . . the myth of the unmanaged market."[52]

Neoconservatism cum Neoliberalism

Professionals no longer fit the pre-1970s descriptions of the new class. Initially, large numbers of professionals made common cause with the political left—in the sense of left-liberal rather than socialist. As New Deal and Great Society Democrats, they were concerned about the condition of labor and the poor and in favor of government intervention in the economy. Recent surveys support a different appraisal. Politically, as Steven Brint pointed out, "the liberal professional sphere is not decidedly left-of-center." Professionals in general are "moderately conservative on issues having to do with business, labor, and the welfare state"; they are liberal mainly on social issues concerning race and gender.[53]

Because of their conservatism on economic issues, professionals in the aggregate "look most like liberal Republicans or 'neoliberal' Democrats," Brint observed. These are the political groups that most consistently combine "generally conservative views on economic issues with relatively liberal views on social issues." Survey evidence in the early 1990s indicated that only 40 percent of professionals favored current or higher levels of spending on government welfare programs and that barely 20 percent showed significant interest in reducing income inequalities. Professionals trusted business more than they did labor, while they considered government more of a problem than a solution to the nation's ills.[54] This suggests that the gulf between liberals and conservatives is not as wide as their respective philosophies would have us believe.

Ferguson gave his assessment of the Democratic party's comeback in the 1992 and 1996 presidential elections as a key example. That neoliberalism has become a major force in American politics is traceable to the economic forces that backed Bill Clinton's candidacy. Although more than twice as many firms contributed to George Bush's campaign than to Clinton's in 1992, Clinton had support from among the biggest and most influential. As Ferguson pointed out, the Clinton coalition included the biggest investment bankers—notably Goldman, Sachs, whose leading figure, Robert Rubin, and other members of the firm contributed more than $100,000 for Clinton's campaign. It also included a bloc of businesses that were prepared "to countenance a cautious public rejection of laissez faire"—that is, the state-dependent capital-intensive exporters, the oil and gas industries, aircraft, computers, transportation, and tobacco. Not surprisingly, the Associated Press reported that there were more millionaires among President Clinton's top advisers than there were among either Reagan's or Bush's.[55]

Whatever may be said for liberal social values, they are little more than icing on the political cake. Thus Charles Peters, founder and editor of the iconoclastic *Washington Monthly* in the nation's capital, quipped in the February 1979 issue celebrating its tenth anniversary, "A neoconservative is someone who took a hard look at where liberalism went wrong, and became a conservative. A neoliberal is someone who took that same hard look at what was wrong with liberalism, and decided to correct it, but still retain his liberal values." Since the main point Peters and his fellow neoliberals hoped to correct was the liberal ardor for government intervention in disregard of the interests of entrepreneurs and private investors, on this score they shared the same political beliefs that neoconservatives held.[56]

Neoconservatism arose as the New York intellectuals' challenge to the left-liberal opposition to the Vietnam War and to the student counterculture's rejection of the so-called Establishment. Similarly, on rethinking what liberalism had led to, former liberals began to question the system of entitlements and the social disorders in their wake. Since government intervention had failed to overcome stagflation, it, too, came under criticism. Belatedly, on the heels of their neoconservative cousins, liberals became critical of the legacy of President Johnson's Great Society. While they remained true to some liberal beliefs, they chose to implement them with moderation.

While labor unions have retreated, professionals have advanced in political and economic influence. From 1960 to the mid-1980s, membership in professional associations grew from 7 to 16 percent, while union membership fell. Paradoxically, neoconservatives lament the growing influence of the professional class. As members of the new class, they claim that professionals are too often hostile to traditional institutions and values and that professionals are responsible for a new class conflict with profit-oriented capitalists.[57]

Irving Kristol (1920–), ex-Trotskyist, former welfare liberal, editor of the leading neoconservative journals—beginning with *Commentary,* then *Encounter,* the *Reporter,* and the *Public Interest*—and publisher of the *National Interest,* is the standard-bearer of neoconservatism in the United States. As executive secretary of the American Committee for Cultural Freedom during the early 1950s, he helped establish the ground rules for the cold war anticommunism of the professional class.

Having graduated from Marxism to cold war liberalism, Kristol declared himself a Humphrey supporter in 1968. Two years later, he was dining with President Nixon in the White House. Their common fear and loathing of the New Left had brought them together. He was not alone in this about-face. Many of his fellow professionals—especially those in academia—had become profoundly disturbed by the classroom takeovers by SDS and campus riots.[58]

Kristol's first collection of essays, *On the Democratic Idea in America* (1972), reads like an updating of José Ortega y Gasset's *Revolt of the Masses*, translated into English in 1932. Like Ortega, Kristol traced the moral and political malaise in Western culture to an excess of democracy and a break with traditional beliefs. Ortega was among the first to excoriate the slow erosion of traditional beliefs and institutions following the "accession of the masses to complete social power . . . not solely political, but equally, and even primarily, intellectual, moral, economic, religious." For Kristol, as for Ortega, mass production, mass society, mass politics, and mass culture were the culprits. Kristol ascribed the causes of the malaise to the rootless impression that life is easy, plentiful; to the expectation that our every demand and desire will be fulfilled; and to the youthful challenge to adult authority. Ortega had summed it up in the syndrome of the spoiled child.[59]

In a second collection of essays, *Two Cheers for Capitalism* (1979), Kristol specifically targeted the new class—ironically, the class he, too, represented— "those college-educated people whose skills and vocations proliferate in a 'post-industrial society.'" As he portrayed his own kind, they are disproportionately powerful. They are less interested in money than in "the power to shape our civilization . . . which, in a capitalist system, is supposed to reside in the free market." Professionals want power redistributed to government, he complained, where they can sit at the controls: "The simple truth is that the professional classes of our modern bureaucratized societies are engaged in a class struggle with the business community for status and power."[60]

That same year, Kristol published his "Confessions of a True, Self-Confessed—Perhaps the Only—'Neoconservative.'" It summed up the distinctive features of neoconservatism under eight headings: (1) disillusionment with contemporary liberalism; (2) disgust with political romanticism and utopianism; (3) kinship with the political philosophies of Aristotle and John Locke but distrust of Rousseau; (4) attachment to the bourgeois civic ethos and to liberal-democratic capitalism as the best of all existing worlds; (5) belief in a market economy as a necessary condition of a free society; (6) commitment to economic growth as indispensable to social and political stability; (7) support for a conservative welfare or social insurance state; and (8) defense of family and religious values as the pillars of a decent society. To this list, he added a critique of socialism, whether liberal or authoritarian, as a kind of barbarism incompatible with political stability and economic justice.[61]

For Kristol, neoconservatism is a revival of nineteenth-century, old-fashioned liberalism. But why should New York intellectuals turn their backs on the ideology of a new class of experts? Because of its association with Marxism, with Socialists, and with Communist fellow travelers; because, in Peter

Steinfels's words, "the 'new class' is essentially radical or adversarial in its politics."[62] This accounts for neoconservatives' hostility toward social engineers, rootless reformers, and members of the new class who one-sidedly defend its partisan interests.

No less than neoliberals, neoconservatives belong to the new priesthood of action-intellectuals, the policy professionals, the new brotherhood of experts who hope to shape public policy—but along quite different lines and with a broader social consensus that includes the business community. Neoconservatives are, Steinfels observed, "prominent operators in the 'knowledge industry'—in the universities, the think tanks, publishing, and journalism."[63] The difference between neoconservatives and neoliberals boils down to different winning strategies and to whether Republicans or Democrats can best promote their interests.

Members of the professional class make up a motley group. The class includes the policy professionals, both neoliberal and neoconservative; the pure professionals or career professionals, who steer clear of the temptation to change the world; and the alienated professionals of the Old Left and the New Left, who personify the totalitarian temptation. Their party allegiance and voting patterns are different. But the issues dividing them pale by comparison with the privileges they have in common and their underlying hostility toward labor as the chief threat to those privileges.

Professional Status and Political Profile

The key to understanding the political differences between the liberal and conservative wings of the professional class may be found in the different places they occupy in the economy and in their comparative market values. Those employed in the government and nonprofit sectors share a set of political interests different from those employed in the private and quasi-public sectors. According to one study, it is this sectoral connection that is most relevant in explaining the political differences among professionals.[64]

Survey data indicate that no other group in the United States changed its perception of political matters so quickly since the late 1960s. "The population explosion in higher education and in the professions between the 1960s and the 1980s," Brint pointed out, "led to a decidedly greater explicit interest in the marketability of educational resources." In 1969, what had been a shortage of college-educated specialists became a glut as university enrollments expanded faster than job opportunities for new graduates. This resulted in a startling shift in motivations among all students. Business and engineering degrees increased by 15 percent over the next decade; liberal arts degrees declined in the same proportion.[65] This new market orientation of college graduates partially accounts for professionals' shift from New Deal liberalism to neoliberalism and neoconservatism.

From the mid-1980s to the mid-1990s, over half of baccalaureate-level professionals were members of the human services sector. They were united by a common focus on maintaining minimal standards for individuals as functioning members of society. While many business professionals have a decidedly entrepreneurial outlook, human service professionals are usually employed by government or nonprofit organizations. This sector includes doctors, dentists, nurses, schoolteachers, clergy, social workers, and professionals specializing in the treatment of personal problems. "Expansion of education, health, and social services is, as the economists note, 'very much a reflection' of the state's emphasis on investment in human capital"—of prime importance in an age of experts, according to Brint. Unlike the dominant ethos of business professionals—a profit-centered focus—the guiding principle of the human service professionals is to improve the quality of life of the individuals being served.[66]

The difference between a professional-career orientation in the private and the quasi-public sectors and a professional-service orientation in the public and nonprofit sectors translates into different political profiles. "While the public sector displays the more traditionally Democratic and liberal profile," Brint observed, the nonprofit sectors are "moderately Democratic in profile." As for the private and the quasi-public sectors, they have more in common with the market-oriented neoliberalism of new Democrats and liberal Republicans concerned with American competitiveness in the global economy. Even so, as Ferguson noted, there is a marked difference between the borderless world and invisible hand of the Republicans and the bordered world with managed trade of the Democrats.[67]

More important than sectoral differences in explaining the class politics of professionals is the relative market value of different kinds of expertise. In approximate order of importance, there are five sources of market advantage: (1) private and group practice; (2) employment in state-of-the-art industries; (3) decision-making positions within organizations; (4) skill, legal, and market monopolies; and (5) male-predominant occupations. These factors make possible above-average incomes for professionals and are among the strongest predictors of their political preferences. Those who earn high incomes are mainly in business. "Professionals who fall lower in the ladder of economic success are more often the carriers of the 'public service' ethic," according to Brint.[68] While the "winners" typically throw their weight behind the Republican party, most of the "losers" are dedicated Democrats.

The political profile of professionals reflects their economic stratification. At the top of the new class are the for-profit experts—the "haute expertoisie"—

partners in the major accounting and corporate law firms. In the middle registers are the partners in small professional firms and sole practitioners, followed by "lesser specialists" in technical support, education, and human services. Below this stratum is the lumpen element among professionals, an apprentice sector of graduate students, research assistants, interns, and the like, not all of whom can be expected to pass muster and move up the professional ladder. The "haute expertoisie" continues to gravitate toward the Republicans. Politically, these top professionals are "worlds apart from the lower-income, nonprofit sector [of] social and cultural professionals, who are stalwarts of the Democratic party," according to Brint.[69]

During the late 1970s and throughout the 1980s, there were three Democrats for every two Republicans. But the decisive voices in American politics were not the Democrats' mid-level professionals. As Brint observed, "On the national level, the decisive leadership is provided by political appointees who come from the president's party." During the quarter-century from Nixon to Bush, the most influential professionals politically were Republicans. Defense and law enforcement were conservative Republican preserves, while the foreign policy establishment remained closely associated with the liberal wing of the Republican party. Highly educated professionals favored the Democrats, but high-income executives, managers, and the traditional monied interests continued to dominate Republican policy.[70]

Through the Reagan years, the Republican party remained a party where big property interests, the capitalists proper, held sway. That was what galled so many lesser and nonprofit professionals about President Reagan: the so-sincere repetition of business drivel about free markets and free enterprise. That the big problem was big government suggested that laissez-faire was the solution, as if that experiment had not been thoroughly tried and found wanting. Since Reagan, the dominance of this group has diminished, but it remains influential in Republican inner circles, alongside the radical right and the Republican professionals. The big private money among the nouveau bourgeoisie and the heirs of the robber barons has been funneled mainly into Republican coffers, even though Clinton received more golden backing all told.

In contrast, the Democratic party is the party where professionals rule unchallenged, having bested labor and kept African Americans in their place. In part, this followed the great split between liberals and labor over the Vietnam War, which gave the party back to the conservatives. After leading the party to the right-to-work South during the Carter presidency, the conservatives then lost it in 1984, 1988, and 1992 to the neoliberals. With President Clinton in the Oval Office, the Democratic party was truly the party of, by, and for professionals both big and small, though mainly big. Only by a stretch of the imagination can one visualize a prolabor candidate in the White House. Meanwhile, the perennial African American candidates, with or without labor backing, are unlikely to get beyond the convention stage.

The professional class is no more a homogeneous entity than any other social class. When it comes to political power, the fractures are often deep. With a few exceptions, the professorate does not rise to the positions in the political world held by investment bankers, corporate executives, and media personalities. Within the professional class, most professors live out their lives on the political sidelines, while most lawyers are drudges without any influence on legal developments. Mathematicians, chemists, physicists, and biologists outside the academy are no better situated to exert political clout; nor are schoolteachers, social workers, or even high-paid surgeons. For the most part, intellectuals are political zeros. If they have leading positions, it is mainly within their occupational bailiwick—in which case their status is that of big fish in little ponds.

"Professionals, it is said, operate in a 'culture of critical discourse' and project a high-minded moral idealism that stands in sharp contrast to the utilitarianism of business elites," Brint noted, but he went on to present survey evidence indicating that while analytical rationality is common among the professional class, "critical rationality is not." Critical rationality demands an examination and critique of prevailing assumptions that is conspicuously absent among professionals constrained to adapt in order to survive. As for moral commitment, most professionals "now justify their work on the basis of its technical complexity, not its social contribution . . . [and] are becoming less likely to emphasize selfless service to clients than to emphasize the market demand for expert services," Brint concluded.[71]

According to Brint, the common thread in the political preferences of professionals must be sought elsewhere, in the inordinate value set on higher education that "provides the credentials, skills, and training that allow for opportunities . . . and authority within organizations." No other class in society values education as highly. Academic meritocracy is the professionals' credo, "the practice of distributing scarce rewards principally on the basis of intellectual tests and academic qualifications at each succeeding level."[72] By comparison, the differences between neoliberals and neoconservatives fade into insignificance. To recall Eugene Debs's famous quip, "There are two wings to every bird of prey"—the Democratic and the Republican wings of the single party of expertise.

During the 1990s, the professional elites in both parties raised their voices against the high costs of traditional welfare and health insurance in particular. Why, then, did they support corporate welfare through outright subsidies, grants, price supports, low-interest loans, and tax breaks? From an investigative report in *Time* magazine on 9 November 1998, we learn that the "Federal government alone shells out $125 billion a year in corporate welfare."[73] The usual justification is that government handouts to corporations create new jobs. The real justification is that fewer expenses for firms receiving federal aid mean bigger budgets for professional salaries.

Making It

Norman Podhoretz (1930–), the editor of *Commentary* since 1960, thought his "dirty little secret" should be exposed to the world. In the first installment of his autobiography, *Making It* (1967), he recalled the sinister trinity that appeared to him in the form of a revelation: "Money . . . was important: it was better to be rich than to be poor. Power . . . was desirable: it was better to give orders than to take them. Fame . . . was unqualifiedly delicious: it was better to be recognized than to be anonymous." The bargain he made with Mephistopheles was, in the idiom of the radical Left, a sell-out—the transition from the radicalism of the thirties to postwar liberalism and from there to neoconservatism.[74]

Nothing so clearly defines the spiritual predicament of American life, said Podhoretz, as the contradiction between what our contemporary culture teaches—"to shape our lives in accordance with the hunger for worldly things"—and what our religious and ethical precepts teach—to be "ashamed of the pressures of these hungers in us." On the one hand, we are under the spell of what William James called "the exclusive worship of the bitch-goddess success." On the other hand, we feel a certain contempt for success because of the belief in human equality instilled in us at an early age.[75]

Podhoretz's way of escaping from this dilemma was to opt for the ways of the world. For Podhoretz, nobody is so naive as to believe that the force of egalitarianism, or communism, "has ever been [or will ever be] powerful enough to wipe out class distinctions altogether." So why court failure by championing it?[76]

No wonder Podhoretz's self-portrait and picture of his fellow intellectuals horrified them. He not only had exposed their secret thoughts but had broken ranks by casting a floodlight on their persistent hypocrisy. Nor was he satisfied with his devil's bargain. In the second installment of his memoirs, he had the gall to claim that the unabashed pursuit of success might be justified on moral grounds and that it need not be a corrupting force in American culture.[77]

Jeane Kirkpatrick, President Reagan's ambassador to the United Nations who shares Podhoretz's neoconservatism, coined the term *totalitarian temp-*

tation—the political temptation of the new class in "believing that its members' intelligence and exemplary motives equip them to reorder the institutions, the lives, and even the characters of almost everyone."[78] Although they are not given this opportunity in the United States, there are other ways the hunger for power expresses itself. Podhoretz's *Making It* is an ideal case, as are his courting of favors from people in high governmental positions and his efforts to influence them. Nor is it surprising that his so-called family of New York intellectuals ended up following him, if they had not already reached the same conclusions. So why focus on the totalitarian temptation when American intellectuals are no more immune to the allurements of power than were their Soviet or Chinese counterparts?

It is demonstrable, said Kirkpatrick, that "the new class has become in the last decade or so [1970s] progressively important to the American political elite and mid-elite and that its increased role has had observable consequences in government, political parties, and pressure groups."[79] The record of Podhoretz's New York intellectuals suggests that they were no less power-driven within the context of American liberal institutions than were their Marxist-Leninist cousins under conditions of a political monopoly by a vanguard party.

It is worth remembering that New York intellectuals during the thirties made their literary and artistic debut under the influence of socialists with Stalinist and predominantly Trotskyist persuasions. That they subsequently evolved into cold war liberals and ended up as neoconservatives is a testimony to their adaptation to their political milieu. Evidently, they made the best of the opportunities available under conditions in which total power was unobtainable.

The story of how they did so can be briefly summarized. From representing an adversarial culture on the margins of political power, they graduated to positions of responsibility as a loyal opposition. The "knowledge industry," wrote Kristol in 1967, had become "a kind of permanent brain trust to the political, the military, the economic authorities . . . men who commute regularly to Washington, who help draw up programs for reorganizing the bureaucracy . . . who analyze the course of economic growth." As cold war liberals, they had hoped for roles in government throughout the 1950s. The opportunity came a decade later when the more prominent among them became advisers to liberal presidents, after which they became neoconservatives and advisers to admittedly conservative ones.[80]

"All of us in the family knew and were even friendly with members of the White House staff," Podhoretz recalled; "they read our magazines and the pieces and books we ourselves wrote, and they cared . . . about what we thought." Although they received the cold shoulder from earlier administrations, President Kennedy seemingly cared. Kennedy, Podhoretz reported, was the first president "to give intellectuals a sense of connection to power." They had been nobodies; suddenly they became somebodies. Following Burnham's example, some took jobs in Washington, notably Arthur Schlesinger Jr., Daniel Patrick Moynihan, and Nathan Glazer. Others were periodically invited to Washington and even had supper with Kennedy. As Norman Mailer recalled, "We became just a touch like minor royalty." Thus did intellectuals move out of their ghetto to join the American mainstream—liberal in the 1960s, conservative in the 1980s.[81]

Burnham was not only the first of the tribe to make his mark on the nation's capital but also the single most influential member among them in shaping American foreign policy. "More than any other single person," wrote George Nash, "Burnham supplied the conservative intellectual movement with the theoretical formulation for victory in the Cold War." The first volume of his trilogy on World War III, *The Struggle for the World* (1947), served as the conceptual basis of his monthly column in the *National Review,* of which he was a founding editor. His column ran as "The Third World War" from November 1955 until April 1970 and thereafter as "The Protracted Conflict," until he retired as senior editor in December 1978. As William Buckley acknowledged, "Beyond any question, he [Burnham] has been the dominant intellectual influence in the development of this journal."[82]

In Washington, Burnham acted as a consultant to the Office of Strategic Services (OSS), the country's first central intelligence agency, and afterward to the CIA's Office of Policy Coordination. His writings and lectures on World War III received a sympathetic hearing among influential officials in the State Department, the National War College, the Air War College, and the Naval War College. Besides serving as an aide to Senator Joseph McCarthy's witch-hunt of native Communists, Burnham played a key role in the CIA-sponsored plan that overthrew President Mosadegh of Iran and installed Shah Mohammad Reza Pahlavi. In acknowledgment of his many services to the nation, President Ronald Reagan awarded him the Presidential Medal of Freedom in February 1983. The citation read, "As a scholar, writer, historian and philosopher, James Burnham has profoundly affected the way America views itself and the world."[83]

New York intellectuals first came to national prominence with the founding of the Congress for Cultural Freedom in 1950 and the American Committee for Cultural Freedom in 1951. Burnham and his colleague at New York University, Sidney Hook, were active promoters of both. The most prolific among the first generation of cold war liberals, Hook would also be honored by President Reagan with the Presidential Medal of Freedom in May 1985.[84]

Why did New York intellectuals evolve from one or another variant of Marxism in the 1930s to liberal anticommunism in the 1950s and 1960s and from there to neoconservatism and neoliberalism in the 1970s and 1980s? According to Alan Wald, in repudiating their former convictions in the name of rebelling against leftist ideological dogmatism, they created a "new world outlook as narrowly ideological and at least as dogmatic." Their own explanation of their ideological turnabout is less than convincing. They do not like to be charged with apostasy, but Wald believed it is a far more credible explanation of their behavior than is heresy. As he summed up Burnham and Shachtman's astonishing foresight, the kind of thinking that later engulfed the New York intellectuals consisted of "a series of abstractions, devoid of precise content, about the need for 'freedom' and 'democracy,'" in conjunction with a "revulsion against Stalin's macabre system of frame-ups and purges."[85]

The vital core of these New York intellectuals consisted of former Trotskyists who had first banded together as students at New York's City College. Why were they drawn to revolutionary socialism in the first place? A graduate of City College but of an earlier generation, Sidney Hook was drawn to it on ethical grounds: "This I believe was true of all the leading Socialists of our time . . . I know of none who majored in economics who, unless he was already committed to socialism on moral grounds, was converted to socialism in consequence of his economic studies." It is safe to say that, because their support of socialism was not based on an understanding of what it means to be exploited, the property question was incidental from the beginning. It became relatively easy to abandon serious advocacy of collective ownership of *all* the means of production because, like socialists elsewhere, they were "more wedded to political democracy than to any totally planned economy." As Burnham acknowledged, socialism meant a society that would be "free, classless, and international."[86] That is to say, it would be founded on America's widely shared values of liberty, equality, fraternity—the bourgeois gospel dating from the Declaration of Independence and the Great French Revolution.

The primary value in this established bourgeois trinity is liberty—also known as freedom and democracy. "Though freedom and democracy were never very extensive in revolutionary Russia," Burnham wrote, "there was a considerable measure during the first years of the revolution." Legal opposition parties, the existence of organized factions within the ruling party, and "important rights possessed by local soviets, workers' committees in factories, [and] trade unions" were features of the first experiment in socialism that elicited his initial sympathies for the Bolsheviks. But under Stalin there was even less freedom than under Hitler: "Every shred of freedom and democracy has by now [1941] been purged from Russian life."[87] Burnham's Marxism, like that of Hook and the rest of the New York intellectuals, was predicated on a belief in freedom. Why freedom? Because it lies at the core of the intellectual's world, the free exchange of ideas—cultural laissez faire—which is hardly a concern of labor.

The New York intellectuals' devotion to free and critical discourse goes a long way toward explaining what otherwise might appear as simple apostasy. Although they shared common ground with Marx's demoliberalism, they had little in common with Lenin, had nothing in common with Stalin's methods, and even suspected Trotsky of harboring dictatorial tendencies. At New York University from 1944 to 1947, both Hook and Burnham were my teachers. Not once in Burnham's course on ethics or in Hook's course on the philosophy of democracy were their interests or sympathies directed to labor's door. As Wald explained the intellectuals' about-turn, ingrained prejudice and social pressure played a role, as did "the postwar prosperity that resulted in a loss of ability to view the world from the class perspective of the oppressed." Hook was therefore continually "finding social democratic reasons for adapting to the tide of opinion while depicting himself as 'out of step.'"[88]

There were only a few rare exceptions to the prevailing tide. Dwight MacDonald, Mary McCarthy, Fred Dupee, and Philip Rahv reneged on their cold war liberalism and opposed the war in Vietnam. The emergence of a New Left revived their hope in socialism, encouraging them to take the route back to their intellectual origins, although they never arrived there. These obvious dents in the Establishment provided the objective grounds for their switch from hard to soft anticommunism. "Had the postwar labor upsurge sustained itself in the 1940s," Wald speculated, "at least some of the radical intellectuals would have remained on the left."[89]

Do not be fooled by political labels. Beneath the facade of American Trotskyists was a group of mainstream American liberals. Liberalism remained the common denominator of the New York intellectuals' peregrinations from self-styled revolutionary socialism through liberal anticommunism to both neoconservatism and neoliberalism. Rather than apostates, they were opportunists uncritical of their underlying motives; the apostates were their sworn enemies on the left, the Communists and the fellow travelers of the Communist party who ended up denouncing Stalin's crimes and supporting first Khrushchev and then Gorbachev.

Podhoretz was at any rate honest. His "dirty little secret" exposed the members of the family as they really were—social climbers hoping to be accepted by the Establishment. Unlike Podhoretz, the other members failed to probe the causes and circumstances behind their shifts in ideology.

Rather than money or power, which initially eluded them, fame drove them. As Podhoretz assessed it, the aggressive and acquisitive features associated with both money and power were enough to incline him in favor of fame: "Fame . . . does no one any direct harm; it cannot be transferred or inherited and can therefore be thought to inhere in the person." What he failed to note is that intellectual celebrity comes from writing for a mainly powerful or monied audience. To be published on Main Street, not in some dark alley, to be read by "society" rather than in the "privatized universe of most current American fiction," and to influence people who really count for something were really important because that was how and "where history was being made."[90]

In a nutshell, the New York intellectuals were condemned to choose between recognition or anonymity. As writers, they had to say something, and they had to please their audience. The trick was to find the "right" material, to say the "right" thing to the "right" people at the "right" time. That rules out writing for a truly adversary culture. In short, they learned how to conform, which raised them from the relative obscurity of the little magazines to the Big Time.

Such was the fate of the New York intellectuals whose politics were those of the professional class as a whole. They both mirrored that politics in microcosm and followed it faithfully to the end.

postscript

> The rise of informationalism in this end of millennium is
> intertwined with rising inequality and social exclusion
> throughout the world.
> —Manuel Castells, *End of Millennium*, vol. 3 of *The Age of
> Information* (1998)

In Christopher Lasch's last challenging work before he died, *The Revolt of the Elites and the Betrayal of Democracy,* he lashed out against the class warfare practiced by America's professional elites. Lasch showed how meritocracy, with its selective elevation into the elites, has replaced the democratic ideal of concern for each and all; how the elites define democracy not as making the good life accessible to everybody but as replacing an aristocracy of wealth with an aristocracy of talent; how the replacement of inherited privilege by careers open to all through higher education is mistaken for a classless society; and how the surviving body of socialists in the United States still targets the inequalities of unearned income with little regard for the inequalities of earned income.[1]

Democracy has thus been reduced to a system for recruiting professionals under conditions in which equality of opportunity presupposes hierarchy and subordination. Contrary to what socialist ideologues insist, democracy is no boon to labor, for the brain drain into the professional class virtually guarantees that labor will no longer have eminent leaders of its own. The new stratification provides the professional elites with fresh talent, while it simultaneously legitimizes their privileges on the grounds of merit instead of birth. The routine acceptance of professionals as a superior class, a class apart from the vulgar herd and secured from the unpredictable hazards of everyday life, legitimizes both their revolt against the masses and their subtle new system of class apartheid.

Lasch found support for his thesis in sociologist Michael Young's *Rise of the Meritocracy, 1870–2033,* on the growing power of professional elites and the betrayal of equality through educational selection based on merit. As Lasch concluded, the general course of recent history runs counter to the belief in social progress and more in the direction of a two-class society in which the new elites monopolize the advantages of money, power, and education. Such is the distinguished historian's intuition corroborated by our own research—the triumph of expertise over both capital and labor.[2]

This sociological route to an understanding of America's Information Age economy barely penetrates the tip of the political-economic iceberg. Missing is detailed statistical information concerning changes in the relative shares of capital income and wages, plus a conceptual apparatus that can unravel not only the share of professionals relative to that of both labor and capital but also the ratio of profits to professional pelf.

In *The State of Working America, 1998–99* by a trio of labor economists with the Economic Policy Institute in the nation's capital—both Lester Thurow and Robert Reich were among its founding scholars—we find further confirmation of our thesis of preferential treatment in distribution. The authors reveal a wage-privileged distribution not just at the bottom of the income pyramid but also at the top.[3]

Astonishing is the ratio of wages to capital income for each family income group in their sample year 1989. The surprising news is the breakdown of the wage/profit ratio within the top one-fifth: more than 9:1 for family incomes in the 81–90 percent group; around 6.5:1 for those in the 91–95 percent group; and almost 4:1 in the 96–99 percent group. Most astounding of all, it was almost 1.5:1 at the summit. The typical top family income earners did not derive the bulk of their income from property, real or otherwise. They were not capitalists—they were professional workers.[4]

The irony is that the authors—Lawrence Mishel, Jared Bernstein, and John Schmitt—call this wage share labor income. That is tantamount, in the Marxist idiom, to saying that the top 1 percent of family income earners were proles. But do the authors really believe that a proletarian revolution has occurred in the United States? On the contrary, they deny that the Information Age economy marks a decisive break with the past—that is, with the postwar system traditionally known as capitalism.

That the Marxist version of a proletarian revolution would mean rule by a fourth governing class—the owners of expertise—was the thesis first set forth by Bakunin in "The International and Karl Marx" in 1872.[5] More than a century has passed since his initial deconstruction of the so-called working class. Meanwhile, his followers have added fuel to his basic thesis, and, independently of Bakunin, more savants have come to agree with it. Where, then, do they part company?

That professionals are on the road to class power or have already arrived there is in large measure conceded. What has not been conceded is, first, that they form a new exploiting class, and, second, that their newly won preeminence constitutes a revolution, not a further stage, evolution, or metamorphosis of capitalism. These claims are controversial for the reasons proffered in the opening chapter. Another stumbling block is that so many of the key concepts in a critical analysis of contemporary society are antithetical to the conventional ones.

For example, the United States is not capitalist but socialist. We finished a half-century of cold war, but socialism instead of capitalism emerged victorious—a socialism without socialists. The privatization of industry is not privatization but destatification. The private sector is only partly private; its core enterprises are quasi-public and managerial. Today's imperialism is not Lenin's invasion of capital; it is the destruction of capitalism. Fascism was defeated in World War II, but the United States is fascist—a fascism without fascists. And so on.

In threatening cherished notions, a full-scale scrutiny of American reality is bound to meet resistance. Even a minor dent in the demoliberal armor may turn friends into enemies. Podhoretz felt the heat when New York intellectuals learned of his intentions and pressured him not to publish his dirty little secret.

But why target all professionals instead of the obvious goons among them? Because virtually all get something for nothing. Generally speaking, because they pretend to be what they are not and because their superior knowledge makes them stuffed shirts. They need to be brought down a peg.

Nobody suspects Irving Kristol or Jeane Kirkpatrick of harboring sympathies for Bakunin. Yet their critique of Marxist intellectuals follows in his footsteps. In a partial rehash of the Russian's animadversions a century earlier, they trimmed the radical intellectuals down to size, but they did not target the liberal and conservative ones. It remained only to turn their critique against themselves—against the demoliberal counterpart of the totalitarian temptation—and to expose professional exploitation through a political economy of expertise.

notes

Chapter 1: The Politics of Political Economy

1. Robert L. Heilbroner, "Reflections: The Triumph of Capitalism," *New Yorker* 64, no. 49 (23 January 1989): 98.

2. Paul A. Samuelson, *Economics: An Introductory Analysis*, 7th ed. (New York: McGraw-Hill, 1969), 48, 50.

3. Adam Smith, *An Inquiry into the Nature and Causes of the Wealth of Nations*, ed. Edwin Cannan (New York: Modern Library, 1937), 80; David Ricardo, *The Principles of Political Economy and Taxation*, 3d ed. (London: J. M. Dent and Sons, 1948), 52–53; Thomas R. Malthus, *The Principles of Political Economy*, 2d ed. (New York: Augustus M. Kelley, 1951), 224–28, 234.

4. Thomas Balogh, *The Irrelevance of Conventional Economics* (New York: Liveright, 1982), 141–44, 152–53.

5. Smith, *An Inquiry into the Nature and Causes of the Wealth of Nations*, 352, 397, 642–43.

6. W. Stanley Jevons, *The Theory of Political Economy*, 5th ed. (New York: Augustus M. Kelley, 1965), vii, xiv, xl–xli.

7. Alfred Marshall, *Principles of Economics*, 8th ed. (New York: Macmillan, 1948), 1, 4, 40, 43.

8. John Neville Keynes, *The Scope and Method of Political Economy*, 4th ed. (1963; reprint, New York: Augustus M. Kelley, 1965), 1–2, 53n.1.

9. Ibid., 92–93, 268–69.

10. E. Ray Canterbery, *The Literate Economist: A Brief History of Economics* (New York: HarperCollins, 1995), 174, 288 (Kalecki quote).

11. Joan Robinson, *Economic Philosophy* (London: C. A. Watts, 1962), 74, 75, 76. See John Maynard Keynes, *The General Theory of Employment, Interest and Money* (New York; Harcourt, Brace, 1936), 213, 359–62.

12. J. M. Keynes, *The General Theory of Employment, Interest and Money,* 214–15, 375–76.

13. Samuelson, *Economics,* 5.

14. Balogh, *The Irrelevance of Conventional Economics,* 1, 12–17. For a similar critique of conventional economics, see the introduction by the editors, E. K. Hunt and Jesse Schwartz, and E. K. Hunt's article, "Economic Scholasticism and Capitalist Ideology," in *A Critique of Economic Theory* (Baltimore: Penguin, 1972), 7–35, 186–93.

15. Karl Marx, "Manifesto of the Communist Party," in *The Communist Manifesto,* ed. Frederic L. Bender (New York: W. W. Norton, 1988), 62, 63, 75 (quote), 86.

16. Mao Tse-tung, "Analysis of the Classes in Chinese Society" (1926), in *Selected Works,* 4 vols., ed. Commission of the Central Committee of the Communist Party of China (Peking: Foreign Languages Press, 1965), 1:13; Carl Schmitt, "The Concept of 'The Political'" (1927), in *Modern Political Thought: The Great Issues,* ed. William Ebenstein (1947; reprint, New York: Rinehart, 1957), 326, 328.

17. Harold Lasswell, *Politics: Who Gets What, When, How* (New York: Meridian, 1965), 13.

18. Karl Marx, *Capital,* vol. 1, ed. Frederick Engels; rev. ed. Ernest Untermann; trans. Samuel Moore and Edward Aveling (New York: Modern Library, n.d.), 19–20; Karl Marx, *Capital,* vols. 2–3, ed. Frederick Engels (Moscow: Foreign Languages Publishing House, 1961–62), 3:772.

19. Harry Cleaver, *Reading "Capital" Politically* (Austin: University of Texas Press, 1979), 64–70, 171–73; Karl Marx, "Inaugural Address of the Working Men's International Association" (28 September 1864), in *Selected Works,* by Karl Marx and Frederick Engels, 2 vols.; ed. Institute of Marxism-Leninism (Moscow: Foreign Languages Publishing House, 1958, 1962), 1:383.

20. L. Afanasyev, N. Andreyev, M. Avsenev, et al., *The Political Economy of Capitalism,* ed. M. Ryndina and G. Chernikov; trans. Diana Miller (Moscow: Progress Publishers, 1974), 15, 16. See also Academía de Ciencias de la U.R.S.S., Instituto de Economía, *Manual de economía política,* 3d ed., trans. Wenceslao Roces (Mexico City: Grijalbo, 1966), 18–21.

21. Marx, *Capital,* 1:19.

Chapter 2: The Political Economy of Expertise

1. Marx, *Capital,* 1:189, 1:558.

2. Ibid., 1:168, 1:171–73, 2:47–48, 2:55 (quote).

3. Ibid., 3:427, 3:431.

4. Ralf Dahrendorf, *Class and Class Conflict in Industrial Society* (Stanford, Calif.: Stanford University Press, 1959), 40, 43, 44.

5. Ibid., 91, 255 (quote), 256 (quote), 297.

6. V. I. Lenin, "Imperialism, the Highest Stage of Capitalism," in *The Lenin Anthology,* ed. Robert C. Tucker (New York: W. W. Norton, 1975), 223, 243, 244 (quote), 245, 272–73.

7. Academía de Ciencias de la U.R.S.S., Instituto de Economía, *Manual de economía*

política, 255 (quote), 256 (quote); Frederick Engels, "Karl Marx," in *Selected Works*, by Marx and Engels, 2:164, 2:165.

8. Marx, *Capital*, 1:14–15; Frederick Engels, "Karl Marx, *Das Kapital*," in *On Marx's "Capital*," ed. Institute of Marxism-Leninism (Moscow: Foreign Languages Publishing House, n.d.), 33, 38.

9. Marx, *Capital*, 1:707; Marx, "Manifesto of the Communist Party," 66.

10. Marx, *Capital*, 1:678–79 (quote), 1:681 (quote), 1:689.

11. Ibid., 3:239, 3:240.

12. Ibid., 3:208–9.

13. Ibid., 3:241.

14. Marx, "Manifesto of the Communist Party," 60; Marx, *Capital*, 3:246, 3:249 (quote), 3:251 (quote).

15. Marx, *Capital*, 3:245, 3:254.

16. Ibid., 1:836–37, 3:258.

17. Joseph A. Schumpeter, *Capitalism, Socialism, and Democracy*, 3d ed. (New York: Harper and Row, 1950), 121, 129, 130.

18. Ibid., 131–32.

19. Ibid., 136 (quotes), 139.

20. Ibid., 140, 140–41.

21. Ibid., 140, 141, 142.

22. Ibid., 143, 144.

23. Ibid., 145, 146.

24. Ibid., 146.

25. Ibid., 146–47, 150–51, 152, 153 (quote).

26. Ibid., 156, 157, 158, 159, 160–62.

27. Marx, *Capital*, 1:220–21, 1:836–37.

28. Ibid., 3:862.

29. Ibid., 1:51.

30. François Noël "Gracchus" Babeuf, "From the Trial at Vendôme, February–May 1797," in *Socialist Thought: A Documentary History*, ed. Albert Fried and Ronald Sanders, rev. ed. (New York: Columbia University, 1992), 65; Auguste Blanqui, "The Man Who Makes the Soup Should Get to Eat It," ibid., 193; P. J. Proudhon, *What Is Property: An Inquiry into the Principles of Right and of Government*, trans. Benjamin R. Tucker (London: William Reeves, n.d.), 145, 150.

31. Marx, *Capital*, 3:862.

32. Michael Bakunin, *The Political Philosophy of Bakunin: Scientific Anarchism*, ed. G. P. Maximoff (Glencoe, Ill.: Free Press, 1953), 189, 355; Michael Bakunin, *Marxism, Freedom, and the State*, ed. and trans. K. J. Kenafick (London: Freedom, 1950), 32, 38, 47.

33. Waclaw Machajski, "On the Expropriation of the Capitalists," trans. Max Nomad, in *The Making of Society: An Outline of Sociology*, ed. V. F. Calverton (New York: Modern Library, 1937), 427–28.

34. Silvio Gesell, *The Natural Economic Order*, rev. English ed., trans. Philip Pye (London: Peter Owen, 1958), 117, 412.

35. Ibid., 36, 411.

36. Ibid., 27, 38.

37. Ibid., 38, 39.

38. J. M. Keynes, *The General Theory of Employment, Interest and Money,* 355.

39. Thorstein Veblen, *The Theory of Business Enterprise* (1904; reprint, New York: Charles Scribner's Sons, 1932), 312–13, 314–15.

40. Ibid., 317, 318.

41. Thorstein Veblen, *The Engineers and the Price System* (1921; reprint, New York: Harcourt, Brace and World, 1963), 58–59, 72–77, 81–84, 89, 97, 127, 129, 148.

42. Ibid., 56, 57.

43. Ibid., 132 (quote), 144–45, 150 (quote).

44. Ibid., 112, 132, 151.

45. Johannes Alasco, *Intellectual Capitalism* (New York: World University Press, 1950), 38, 44–45.

46. Ibid., 88.

47. Marx, *Capital,* 1:397, 1:459. For examples, see ibid., 3:285–90, 3:375–80.

48. Ibid., 1:364, 1:397n.2.

49. Marshall, *Principles of Economics,* 138–39, 313.

50. Adolf A. Berle Jr. and Gardiner C. Means, *The Modern Corporation and Private Property* (New York: Macmillan, 1932); Robert J. Larner, "Ownership and Control in the 200 Largest Nonfinancial Corporations, 1929 and 1963," *American Economic Review* 56, no. 4 (September 1966): 777–87. For a Marxist critique of the "managerial revolution," see Victor Perlo, "Ownership and Control of Corporations: The Fusion of Financial and Industrial Capital," in *American Society, Inc.,* ed. Maurice Zeitlin (Chicago: Markham, 1970), 272–80.

51. Adolf A. Berle Jr., *The 20th Century Capitalist Revolution* (New York: Harcourt, Brace, 1954), 23 (quote), 24, 164.

52. Adolf A. Berle Jr., *Power without Property: A New Development in American Political Economy* (New York: Harcourt, Brace and World, 1959), 157 (quote), 157–58 (quote), 175.

53. A. A. Berle Jr., "Economic Power and the Free Society," in *The Corporation Take-Over,* ed. Andrew Hacker (Garden City, N.Y.: Anchor, 1965), 93, 94 (quote), 95 (quote).

54. Ibid., 94–95.

55. Peter F. Drucker, *Post-Capitalist Society* (New York: HarperBusiness, 1993), 77–78, 82.

56. David T. Bazelon, *The Paper Economy* (New York: Vintage, 1959), 289, 290.

57. Ibid., 291, 309 (quote), 310.

58. Ibid., 310, 311 (quote), 312 (quote), 313–15, 316.

59. Ibid., 316, 318–19 (quote), 319 (quote), 321.

60. Ibid., 359, 371 (quote), 393, 396, 398 (quote).

61. John Kenneth Galbraith, *The New Industrial State* (Boston: Houghton Mifflin, 1967), 60, 63–64, 66, 67, 69, 70.

62. Ibid., 67, 69.

63. Ibid., 70, 71.

64. Robert Reich, *The Next American Frontier* (1983; reprint, New York; Penguin, 1984), 83, 88.

65. Ibid., 89, 90.

66. Ibid., 93, 99 (quote), 102, 117–18 (quote).

67. Ibid., 121.

68. Ibid., 127, 128.

69. Ibid., 236, 246.

70. Alasco, *Intellectual Capitalism*, 14–15.

71. Ibid., 104.

72. Ibid., 103–4.

73. Ibid., 24–25, 28–29, 32, 38, 44–45.

74. Alvin W. Gouldner, *The Future of Intellectuals and the Rise of the New Class* (New York: Continuum, 1979), 19, 22, 99.

75. Ibid., 23, 24–25.

76. Ibid., 61, 62.

77. Ibid., 49–50, 53 (quote).

78. Ibid., 28, 50.

79. Alasco, *Intellectual Capitalism*, 86–87, 94.

80. Gouldner, *The Future of Intellectuals and the Rise of the New Class*, 108–9n.32. See Theodore Schultz, "Investment in Human Capital [1961]," in *Perspectives on the Economic Problem: A Book of Readings in Political Economy,* ed. Arthur MacEwan and Thomas E. Weisskopf (Englewood Cliffs, N.J.: Prentice-Hall, 1970), 160–65; and Theodore Schultz, *The Economic Value of Education* (New York: Columbia University Press, 1963).

81. Theodore Schultz, *Investing in People: The Economics of Population Quality* (Berkeley: University of California Press, 1981), 60.

82. Ibid., 6 (quotes), 61, 84.

83. Ibid., 60–61.

84. Ibid., 61, 63.

85. Ibid., 68–69, 74 (quote).

86. Simon Kuznets, *Modern Economic Growth* (New Haven, Conn.: Yale University Press, 1966), 181–83; Schultz, *Investing in People*, 76–77.

87. Schultz, *Investing in People*, 81, 83.

88. Lester C. Thurow, *The Future of Capitalism: How Today's Economic Forces Shape Tomorrow's World* (New York: Penguin, 1996), 282, 283.

89. Ibid., 282–83, 284 (quote), 285, 286–87, 288 (quote).

90. Ibid., 281, 282, 285 (quote).

91. Ibid., 279.

92. Ibid., 304, 305, 306, 308–9.

93. Ibid., 317, 325–26.

94. Ibid., 11.

95. Thomas A. Stewart, *Intellectual Capital: The New Wealth of Organizations* (New York/London: Doubleday/Currency, 1997), ix–x, 35.

96. Ibid., 44, 46.

97. Ibid., 86–87.

98. Samuelson, *Economics*, 550–51.

99. Ibid., 551.

100. Ibid., 551, 566.

101. Peter F. Drucker, *The New Society: The Anatomy of Industrial Order* (1950; reprint, New York: Harper and Row, 1962), 93.

102. Ibid., 278.

103. Ibid., 94, 95.

104. V. I. Lenin, "The Immediate Tasks of the Soviet Government," in *The Lenin Anthology*, 443, 444.

105. Peter F. Drucker, *The Concept of the Corporation* (1946; reprint, New York: Mentor, 1964), 44–45, 167.

106. Ibid., 168.

107. Drucker, *Post-Captialist Society*, 87–89, 91–93.

Chapter 3: The Legitimizing Myth

1. James Burnham, *The Machiavellians: Defenders of Freedom* (1943; reprint, Washington, D.C.: Gateway, 1987), 304.

2. Marx, "Manifesto of the Communist Party," 58, 55n.7 (quote), 61 (quote).

3. Marx, *Capital*, 2:132, 3:140–41, 3:152–55.

4. Ibid., 1:678.

5. Karl Marx, *The Grundrisse*, ed. and trans. David McLellan (New York: Harper and Row, 1971), 134, 135, 136, 141 (quote), 142 (quote).

6. Karl Marx, "Critique of the Gotha Programme," in *Selected Works*, by Marx and Engels, 2:24.

7. Robert Michels, *Political Parties: A Sociological Study of the Oligarchical Tendencies of Modern Democracy*, trans. Eden Paul and Cedar Paul (1915; reprint, Glencoe, Ill.: Free Press, 1958), 197, 311; V. I. Lenin, "What Is to Be Done?" and "Imperialism, the Highest Stage of Capitalism," in *The Lenin Anthology*, 27–28, 209, 256.

8. Marshall, *Principles of Economics*, 717.

9. Karl Marx, "Wage Labor and Capital," in *Selected Works*, by Marx and Engels, 1:82–83, 1:92–93; Marx, *Capital*, 1:185–86, 1:198, 1:237–39.

10. Marx, *Capital*, 1:198, 1:200.

11. Smith, *An Inquiry into the Nature and Causes of the Wealth of Nations*, 262, 263.

12. Bakunin, *The Political Philosophy of Bakunin*, 189, 191–92, 355; Marshall, *Principles of Economics*, 139, 313.

13. Smith, *An Inquiry into the Nature and Causes of the Wealth of Nations*, 101, 266–67.

14. Marx, *Capital*, 1:51–52. For a full account of the discrepancy between "socially equal labor" and "physiologically equal labor," see Isaak Ilich Rubin, *Essays on Marx's Theory of Value*, trans. Milos Samardzíja and Fredy Perlman (Detroit: Black and Red, 1972), 167–69.

15. Marx, *Capital* 1:190, 1:220.

16. Ibid., 3:140. See also 2:131–32.

17. Ibid., 2:133. See also 1:232–33.

18. Karl Marx, "Wages, Price, and Profit," in *Selected Works*, by Marx and Engels, 1:403–4.

19. Marx, *Capital*, 1:363–64, 3:372–73, 3:378–79 (quote), 3:380 (quote).

20. Ibid., 1:344, 3:382 (quote).

21. Karl Marx, *Theories of Surplus Value*, Part 1, ed. Institute of Marxism-Leninism; trans. Emile Burns and S. Ryazanskaya (Moscow: Foreign Languages Publishing House, 1958), 170 (quote), 195.

22. Eduard Bernstein, *Evolutionary Socialism*, trans. Edith C. Harvey (New York: Schocken, 1963), 211.

23. Marx, *Capital*, 1:605, 1:612.

24. See, for example, Sarah Riedman, *The Physiology of Work and Play* (New York: Dryden, 1950), 82, 120–23.

25. F. Cottrell, *Energy and Society* (New York: McGraw-Hill, 1955), 8, 17.

26. Riedman, *The Physiology of Work and Play*, 82.

27. Cottrell, *Energy and Society*, 51, 105, 108.

28. Ibid., 18.

29. H. C. Sherman, *Chemistry of Food and Nutrition*, 8th ed. (New York: Macmillan, 1952), 180.

30. Riedman, *The Physiology of Work and Play*, 127, 156–57; Sherman, *Chemistry of Food and Nutrition*, 176, 180.

31. F. G. Benedict and C. G. Benedict, "The Energy Requirements of Intense Mental Effort," in *Proceedings of the National Academy of Sciences* (Washington, D.C.: National Academy of Sciences, 1930), 438–43. Their later estimate was one whole peanut. See F. G. Benedict and C. G. Benedict, *Mental Effort in Relation to Gaseous Exchange, Heart Rate, and Mechanics of Respiration*, Publication No. 446 (Washington, D.C.: Carnegie Institution of Washington, 1933), 83. The examples are from R. M. De Coursey, *The Human Organism*, 2d ed. (New York: McGraw Hill, 1961), 482–43; and from Sherman, *Chemistry of Food and Nutrition*, 176.

32. W. W. Tuttle and B. A. Schottelius, *Textbook of Physiology*, 14th ed. (St. Louis: Mosby, 1961), 106; Riedman, *The Physiology of Work and Play*, 127, 466–72. Sherman arrives at a ratio of 6:1. See Sherman, *Chemistry of Food and Nutrition*, 176–77.

33. Tuttle and Schottelius, *Textbook of Physiology*, 82, 104; De Coursey, *The Human Organism*, 161; Riedman, *The Physiology of Work and Play*, 155.

34. Riedman, *The Physiology of Work and Play*, 144–45; Tuttle and Schottelius, *Textbook of Physiology*, 81.

35. Riedman, *The Physiology of Work and Play*, 124–25, 157, 467–68, 475–76.

36. Marx, *Capital*, 1:612.

37. Ibid., 1:605–8.

38. Sherman, *Chemistry of Food and Nutrition*, 180.

39. Ibid., 182.

40. Riedman, *The Physiology of Work and Play*, 127; Tuttle and Schottelius, *Textbook of Physiology*, 338.

41. Marx, *Capital*, 1:448, 1:450.

42. Ibid., 1:51.

43. Jack London, *War of the Classes* (New York: Macmillan, 1908), 274, 275.

44. On the last two feasible matchings, see B. F. Skinner, *Walden Two* (1948; reprint, New York: Macmillan, 1966), 51–52.

45. Cornelius Castoriadis, "On the Content of Socialism, II" (July 1957) and "Proletariat and Organization, I" (April 1959), in *Political and Social Writings*, 2 vols., ed. and trans. David Ames Curtis (Minneapolis: University of Minnesota Press, 1988), 2:126, 2:214.

46. Babeuf, "From the Trial at Vendôme, February–May 1797," 64, 65.

47. Joseph Stalin, "Report on the Work of the Central Committee to the Seventeenth Congress of the Communist Party of the Soviet Union," in *Leninism: Selected Writings* (New York: International Publishers, 1942), 344, 346; Joseph Stalin, *History of the Communist Party of the Soviet Union (Bolsheviks): Short Course*, ed. Commission of the Central Committee of the Communist Party of the Soviet Union (New York: International Publishers, 1939), 313–14, 338–39.

48. Stalin, *History of the Communist Party of the Soviet Union (Bolsheviks)*, 314–15, 337.

49. Marx, "Critique of the Gotha Programme," 2:23.

50. George Gilder, *Wealth and Poverty* (New York: Basic Books, 1981), 130.

Chapter 4: A New Class Structure

1. Ronald Meek, *Studies in the Labour Theory of Value* (New York: International Publishers, 1956), 172; Paul M. Sweezy, *The Theory of Capitalist Development* (1942; reprint, New York: Monthly Review, 1956), 43.

2. Bureau of the Census, *Statistical Abstract of the United States: 1996* (Washington, D.C.: Government Printing Office, 1996), tables 235 and 236. Earlier editions are referred to simply as *Statistical Abstract* with the date.

3. Marx, *Capital*, 3:193.

4. E. Ray Canterbery, "A Theory of Supra-Surplus Capitalism," *Eastern Economic Journal* 13, no. 4 (October–December 1987): 320–23; James K. Galbraith, *Balancing Acts: Technology, Finance and the American Future* (New York: Basic Books, 1989), 112 (quote), 121.

5. David Bazelon, *Power in America: The Politics of the New Class* (1964; reprint, New York: New American Library, 1967), 308.

6. Marx, "Manifesto of the Communist Party," 68–69; *Statistical Abstract: 1996*, table 658.

7. AFL-CIO Committee on the Evolution of Work, *The Future of Work* (Washington, D.C.: AFL-CIO, 1983), 8–9.

8. Jennifer Reingold, "Executive Pay: Special Report," *Business Week*, no. 3253 (21 April 1997): 58–59, 64, 66; "Executive Compensation Scoreboard," ibid., 67–102.

9. "Grand National Consolidated Trades Union Programme and Manifesto (London, 15 April 1834)," in *Revolution from 1789 to 1906,* ed. Raymond Postgate (1920; reprint, New York: Harper and Row, 1962), 99.

10. Marx, *Capital,* 3:431; Frederick Engels, "Socialism: Utopian and Scientific," in *Selected Works,* by Marx and Engels, 2:127; V. I. Lenin, "On Cooperation," in *The Lenin Anthology,* 708.

11. E. J. Hobsbawm, *Labouring Men: Studies in the History of Labour* (London: Weidenfeld and Nicolson, 1964), 297–98.

12. G. N. Ostergaard and A. H. Halsey, *Power in Cooperatives: A Study of the Internal Politics of British Retail Societies* (Oxford: Blackwell, 1965), xvi, 193–95, 199, 233.

13. *Cooperative Grocer* (Athens, Ohio), no. 65 (July–August 1996): 23.

14. Ibid., no. 62 (January–February 1996): 19.

15. Ostergaard and Halsey, *Power in Cooperatives,* 84–85, 141–42, 145–47, 155–60, 163; Donald C. Hodges, "Yugoslav Marxism and Methods of Social Accounting," in *Marxism, Revolution, and Peace,* ed. H. Parsons and J. Somerville (Amsterdam: Grüner, 1977), 56, 57–58.

16. Philip S. Foner, *History of the Labor Movement in the United States,* 4 vols. (New York: International Publishers, 1947–1965), 1:170–83, 2:76–78; Bakunin, *The Political Philosophy of Bakunin,* 385; Michael Bakunin, *Bakunin on Anarchism,* 2d rev. ed., ed. and trans. Sam Dolgoff (1980; reprint, New York: Black Rose Books, 1990), 399 (quote).

17. Sydney R. Elliott, *The English Cooperatives* (New Haven, Conn.: Yale University Press, 1937), 4, 129.

18. *Cooperative Grocer,* no. 65 (July–August 1996): 23.

19. Take, for example, North Florida's leading food cooperative, the New Leaf Market of Tallahassee, which opened in 1972 as a buyer's club under another name. In 1997, New Leaf had some 1,300 members and annual sales of almost $3,000,000. How much did owner-members siphon off the co-op's working members? In 1997, discounts amounted to some $50,000, of which only a tiny fraction was retrieved by co-op wage earners. How does this equivalent of stockholders' dividends compare with the tribute for co-op managers? Managerial salaries came to $155,792. The general manager was paid $32,000, leaving $123,792 to be shared by the five department heads. If each had been paid the co-op's average wage, collectively they would have pocketed $71,848—a little less than half. New Leaf's managerial surplus of $73,944 thus exceeded discounts—the capitalist surplus—by $23,944. Professionals were therefore the major beneficiaries. On this score, New Leaf was definitely a socialist enterprise. But considered nationally, the excess of the general manager's salary over the average wage of $30,000 amounted to a skimpy $2,000, while the remaining managers each received less than the average. New Leaf was therefore not a socialist but a capitalist enterprise.

20. Donald C. Hodges, "Cynicism in the Labor Movement," in *American Society, Inc.,* ed. Zeitlin, 439–46.

21. Marx, "Manifesto of the Communist Party," 62, 63; Karl Marx, *The Poverty of Philosophy* (Moscow: Foreign Languages Publishing House, n.d.), 195.

22. Henry Miller, *To Remember to Remember* (New York: New Directions, 1947), xviii.

23. Robert Tressell, *The Ragged Trousered Philanthropists,* with an introduction by Alan Sillitoe (London: Grafton, 1965), 147, 149 (quote), 203 (quote).

24. Ibid., 153, 364.

25. Ibid., 364, 365 (quote), 539 (quote), 542–44.

26. Gesell, *The Natural Economic Order,* 19.

27. Ibid., 20–21.

28. Merlin Thomas, *Louis-Ferdinand Céline* (Boston: Faber and Faber, 1979), 125–26 (from Céline's 1936 pamphlet *Mea Culpa*).

29. Quoted by Florence King, *With Charity toward None: A Fond Look at Misanthropy* (New York: St. Martin's, 1992), 131.

Chapter 5: From Professional Power to Professional Pelf

1. James Burnham, *The Managerial Revolution: What Is Happening in the World* (New York: John Day, 1941), 9, 92–93, 99 (quote).

2. Ibid., 94–95.

3. Ibid., 9; Ricardo, *The Principles of Political Economy and Taxation,* 225.

4. James Burnham, "What New Class?" *National Review,* 30, no. 3 (20 January 1978): 98–99.

5. Burnham, *The Managerial Revolution,* 143–49, 168–71.

6. Ibid., 82–83.

7. Christopher Lasch, *The Culture of Narcissism: American Life in an Age of Diminishing Expectations* (New York: Warner Books, 1980), 234.

8. Berle, *The 20th Century Capitalist Revolution,* 39.

9. See Phillip Burch, *The Managerial Revolution Revisited* (Lexington, Mass.: Lexington Books, 1972), 29–47; and Edward S. Herman, *Corporate Control, Corporate Power* (Cambridge: Cambridge University Press, 1982), 56–61, 89–93, 102, 302–3.

10. Paul Blumberg, "Another Day, Another $3,000: Executive Salaries in America," in *The Big Business Reader: On Corporate America,* ed. Mark Green, Michael Waldman, Robert K. Massie Jr. (New York: Pilgrim, 1983), 316–17, 320; Wilbur G. Lewellen, *Executive Compensation in Large Corporations* (New York: National Bureau of Economic Research, 1968), 141–42.

11. Robert J. Larner, "The Effect of Management-Control on the Profits of Large Corporations," in *American Society, Inc.,* ed. Zeitlin, 251–52, 261.

12. Perlo, "Ownership and Control of Corporations," 279, 280.

13. John Galbraith, *The New Industrial State,* 56–59; Drucker, *Post-Capitalist Society,* 19–20, 42–45.

14. John Kenneth Galbraith, *The New Industrial State,* rev. 2d ed. (Boston: Houghton Mifflin, 1971), 107.

15. Gesell, *The Natural Economic Order,* 27 (quote), 35, 112–13, 273–79, 300 (quote).

16. Ibid., 36–37.

17. J. M. Keynes, *The General Theory of Employment, Interest and Money,* 375–76, 378; Gottfried Feder, *Manifiesto contra la usura y la servidumbre del interés del dinero* (1919;

reprint, Buenos Aires: Maxim, 1984), 51–52, 78–79; Donald C. Hodges, *Argentina, 1943–1987: The National Revolution and Resistance,* 2d rev. ed. (Albuquerque: University of New Mexico Press, 1988), 279, 288.

18. Donald C. Hodges, *America's New Economic Order* (Brookfield, Vt.: Avebury-Ashgate, 1996), 51–52; *Statistical Abstract: 1996,* table 693.

19. Meek, *Studies in the Labour Theory of Value,* 172; Sweezy, *The Theory of Capitalist Development,* 43.

20. *Statistical Abstract: 1965,* table 320; *Statistical Abstract: 1982–83,* table 659; *Statistical Abstract: 1996,* table 652.

21. The data for 1950 and 1955 are from the *Statistical Abstract: 1965,* tables 314, 320, 455; and *Statistical Abstract: 1982–83,* table 699. The data for 1965 are from *Statistical Abstract: 1982–83,* table 659; and *Statistical Abstract: 1996,* table 652. The data for 1960 and 1970–95 are from *Statistical Abstract: 1982–83,* table 699; and *Statistical Abstract: 1996,* tables 630, 652, 667, 695.

22. Hodges, *America's New Economic Order,* 59.

23. *Statistical Abstract: 1982–83,* tables 648, 659, 677, 699.

24. Ibid., tables 648, 677, 724.

25. Ibid., tables 648, 659, 677, 699.

26. *Statistical Abstract: 1996,* tables 641, 652, 667, 693.

27. Ibid., tables 652, 667, 693.

28. Ibid., tables 641, 652, 667, 693.

29. See the tables in note 21.

30. William Greider, *One World, Ready or Not: The Manic Logic of Global Capitalism* (New York: Simon and Schuster, 1998), 27, 28–29, 199. See also John Galbraith, *The New Industrial State,* 1st ed., 71, 77.

31. Abraham Guillén, *El capitalismo soviético: Ultima etapa del imperialismo* (Madrid: Queimada, 1979), 41.

32. Roger Burbach, "The Epoch of Globalization," *URPE Newsletter* 29, no. 1 (Fall 1997): 3 (quotes); Roger Burbach, "The Rise of Postmodern Marxism: Or, Virtually Existing Socialisms," *URPE Newsletter* 28, no. 2 (Winter 1997): 4.

33. Burbach, "The Rise of Postmodern Marxism," 4–5, 11.

34. Hodges, *America's New Economic Order,* 60n.7.

35. Marx, *Capital,* 3:772.

36. Ibid., 3:320–21, 3:322 (quote), 3:324, 3:580 (quote).

37. Frederick Engels, introduction to Karl Marx's "The Class Struggles in France, 1848 to 1850," in *Selected Works,* by Marx and Engels, 1:125.

38. Burbach, "The Epoch of Globalization," 4–5.

39. Kevin Phillips, *Arrogant Capital* (Boston: Little, Brown, 1995), 97 (quote), 98 (quote), 102. On America's "casino economy," see Canterbery, *The Literate Economist,* 317–18, 344.

40. Phillips, *Arrogant Capital,* 105; *Statistical Abstract: 1996,* table 693.

41. Richard J. Barnet and John Cavanagh, *Global Dreams: Imperial Corporations and the New World Order* (New York: Simon and Schuster, 1994), 14–15.

42. Ibid., 15 (quote), 400, 407, 423.

43. Kevin Phillips, *Boiling Point* (New York: HarperCollins, 1963), 204. See also ibid., 196–203 and 204–11; and Marx, *Capital*, 3:429.

44. For the data on manufacturing, see *Statistical Abstract: 1996*, tables 1210, 1220; for the data on the securities industry, see tables 767 and 814.

45. Ibid., tables 767 and 814.

46. Phillips, *Arrogant Capital*, 100.

47. Roger Burbach, with Orlando Nuñez and Boris Kagarlitsky, *Globalization and Its Discontents: The Rise of Postmodern Socialisms* (London: Pluto, 1997), 66–73; Robert Kuttner, *The End of Laissez-Faire: National Purpose and the Global Economy after the Cold War* (Philadelphia: University of Pennsylvania Press, 1992), 7–8, 11, 114–16, 153, 157.

48. See the chapter "Managerial Imperialism" in Hodges, *America's New Economic Order*, 83–104.

49. Frances Fox Piven and Richard A. Cloward, *The New Class War: Reagan's Attack on the Welfare State and Its Consequences* (New York: Pantheon, 1982), 15.

50. *Statistical Abstract: 1996*, tables 667 and 732.

Chapter 6: A Republic of Experts

1. Burnham, *The Managerial Revolution*, 29–57, 118.

2. Ibid., 39, 45–46.

3. Cornelius Castoriadis, "The Problem of the USSR and the Possibility of a Third Historical Solution," in *Political and Social Writings*, 1:49–55; Bruno Rizzi, *The Bureaucratization of the World*, trans. Adam Westoby (New York: Free Press, 1985), 38, 64–65 (quote).

4. Burnham, *The Managerial Revolution*, 82–87, 123, 132–36; Rizzi, *The Bureaucratization of the World*, 87, 96, 99; Adam Westoby, introduction to *The Bureaucratization of the World*, by Rizzi, 13–14.

5. Leon Trotsky, "The USSR in War," in *In Defense of Marxism* (New York: Pioneer, 1942), 10–11, 13–16; Westoby, introduction to *The Bureaucratization of the World*, by Rizzi, 23–26.

6. Max Shachtman, *The Struggle for the New Course* (New York: New International, 1943), 234–39, 241, 242 (emphasis added).

7. Castoriadis, "The Problem of the USSR and the Possibility of a Third Historical Solution," 1:50, 1:51.

8. Trotsky, "The USSR in War," 10–11, 15 (quote).

9. Milovan Djilas, *The New Class: An Analysis of the Communist System* (New York: Praeger, 1957), 18–19, 33–35, 39–40, 56 (quote), 58, 171–72.

10. Ibid., 38, 40.

11. Ibid., 45.

12. Alfred D. Chandler Jr., *The Visible Hand: The Managerial Revolution in American Business* (Cambridge, Mass.: Harvard University Press, 1977), 4, 5, 11, 492–93.

13. Ibid., 6–11, 515n.5.

14. Ibid., 9–10, 490–91, 492, 493.

15. Ibid., 3, 492–93; Lenin, "Imperialism, the Highest Stage of Capitalism," 218–21, 223, 273–74.

16. Chandler, *The Visible Hand,* 492–93, 583–84n.3.

17. Daniel Bell, *The Coming of Post-Industrial Society* (1973; reprint, New York: Basic Books, 1976), xiii, 89–97, 106–12.

18. Ibid., xv–xvi.

19. Ibid., 119, 483.

20. Ibid., 11, 93–94, 298n.18 (quote), 372.

21. Ibid., xiv, 161–62, 163–64.

22. Drucker, *The New Society,* 28–29, 40–41, 62.

23. Ibid., 28–30, 61–63, 71–73.

24. Ibid., 100–101, 102 (emphasis added).

25. Ibid., 40, 42, 43.

26. Ibid., 355, 356.

27. Drucker, *Post-Capitalist Society,* 3, 5, 6.

28. Ibid., 65 (quote), 84–85, 169.

29. Ibid., 4.

30. Ibid., 68, 75 (quote), 78, 82.

31. Peter F. Drucker, *The New Realities: In Government and Politics, in Economics and Business, in Society and World View* (New York: Harper and Row, 1989), 85; Drucker, *Post-Capitalist Society,* 82.

32. Drucker, *The New Realities,* 85.

33. Ibid., 176.

34. Thurow, *The Future of Capitalism,* 11.

35. Ibid., 11, 279.

36. Ibid., 11, 280.

37. Ibid., 280–81, 285, 289, 325, 326 (quote).

38. Manuel Castells, *The Rise of the Network Society,* vol. 1 of *The Information Age: Economy, Society and Culture,* 3 vols. (Malden, Mass.: Blackwell, 1996–98), 14.

39. Ibid., 32 (quote), 204–5, 206 (quote).

40. Ibid., 16 (quote), 18, 81, 195, 471, 473.

41. Ibid., 7, 471–72, 475.

42. Ibid., 473, 474.

43. Manuel Castells, *End of Millennium,* vol. 3 of *The Information Age,* 342 (quote), 343 (quote); Castells, *The Rise of the Network Society,* 474 (quote).

44. Castells, *End of Millennium,* 345, 346 (quote).

45. Cornelius Castoriadis, "Socialism or Barbarism," in *Political and Social Writings,* 1:77, 1:78–79, 1:99, 1:101–2; Cornelius Castoriadis, "The Yugoslav Bureaucracy," in *Political and Social Writings,* 1:188.

46. Castoriadis, general introduction to *Political and Social Writings,* 9; Cornelius Castoriadis, "Socialism or Barbarism," in *Political and Social Writings,* 1:80, 1:97.

47. Tony Cliff, *State Capitalism in Russia* (1948; reprint, London: Pluto, 1974), 168–69.

48. Ibid., 157, 169–70, 200–202.

49. Ibid., 159–62, 168; Marx, *Capital,* 1:649, 1:650 (quotes).

50. Cliff, *State Capitalism in Russia,* 163 (quote), 266.

51. Castoriadis, "On the Content of Socialism, I," in *Political and Social Writings,* 1:296, 1:301; Castoriadis, "On the Content of Socialism, II," 2:149 (quote), 2:151 (quote).

52. Max Weber, "The Spirit of Capitalism," in *The Making of Society,* ed. Calverton, 509–13, 514 (quote).

53. Marx, *Capital,* 1:652; Joseph Stalin, "The Tasks of Business Executives," in *Leninism,* 200 (Lenin quote).

54. Editorial Departments of *People's Daily* and *Red Flag,* "Is Yugoslavia a Socialist Country?" and "On Khrushchev's Phoney Communism and Its Historical Lessons for the World," in *The Polemic on the General Line of the International Communist Movement* (Peking: Foreign Languages Press, 1965), 154–57, 174, 441–42; Martin Nicolaus, *Restoration of Capitalism in the USSR* (Chicago: Liberator, 1975), 79, 124, 182–83, 186.

55. Nicolaus, *Restoration of Capitalism in the USSR,* 123, 124 (quote); Marx, *Capital,* 1:585.

56. Burnham, *The Managerial Revolution,* 16–17.

57. Bakunin, *The Political Philosophy of Bakunin,* 189, 355; Bakunin, *Bakunin on Anarchism,* 121, 217.

58. Bakunin, *Marxism, Freedom and the State,* 32, 38, 47.

59. Max Nomad, *Dreamers, Dynamiters, and Demagogues: Reminiscences* (New York: Waldon, 1964), 165; Bruce McFarlane, "Jugoslavia's Crossroads," in *The Socialist Register: 1966,* ed. Ralph Miliband and John Saville (London: Merlin, 1966), 117, 129n.14; Alasco, *Intellectual Capitalism,* 16; Gouldner, *The Future of Intellectuals and the Rise of the New Class,* 99. For a sampling of the voluminous literature on the new class, see Gouldner's Bibliographic Note, in *The Future of Intellectuals and the Rise of the New Class,* 94–101.

60. Leon Trotsky, *My Life: An Attempt at an Autobiography* (New York: Charles Scribner's Sons, 1931), 129 (quote), 143; Machajski, "On the Expropriation of the Capitalists," 427–28 (quotes).

61. Max Nomad, *Rebels and Renegades* (1932; reprint, Freeport, N.Y.: Books for Libraries, 1968), 207.

62. Max Nomad, "Masters—Old and New: A Social Philosophy without Myths," in *The Making of Society,* ed. Calverton, 882, 884.

63. Ibid., 884.

64. Ibid., 885.

65. Ibid., 885, 886.

66. Ibid., 886.

67. Schumpeter, *Socialism, Capitalism, and Democracy,* 170–71.

68. John Maynard Keynes, "Laissez-Faire and Communism" (1926), included under the title "The End of Laissez-Faire," in *Great Political Thinkers: Plato to the Present,* ed. William Ebenstein, 3d ed. (New York: Holt, Rinehart and Winston, 1962), 663, 664.

69. Marx, "Manifesto of the Communist Party," 68.

70. Hodges, *America's New Economic Order,* 75, 79–80.

71. Marx, *Capital,* 3:772.

72. Nomad, "Masters—Old and New," 886 (Bauer quote), 886–87n (Goebbels quote).

73. Feder, *Manifiesto contra la usura y la servidumbre del interés del dinero,* 68–71, 78, 79.

74. Bertram Gross, *Friendly Fascism: The New Face of Power in America* (Boston: South End, 1980), xi, 1.

75. Nomad, "Masters—Old and New," 887, 888, 889.

76. Ibid., 889.

77. Lawrence Dennis, *The Dynamics of War and Revolution* (Washington, D.C.: Weekly Foreign Letter, 1940), 3.

78. Lawrence Dennis, *Operational Thinking for Survival* (Colorado Springs: Ralph Myles, 1969), 37–38, 136 (quote), 137.

79. Ibid., 139, 143–44.

80. Dennis, *The Dynamics of War and Revolution,* xvi (quote), xxiii–xxvii.

81. Ibid., 236.

82. Ibid., xxvii, xxix.

83. Ibid., xxix, xxx (quote), xxxi.

84. Gross, *Friendly Fascism,* 3, 5–6, 28–30.

85. Hermann Rauschning, *The Voice of Destruction* (New York: Putnam's Sons, 1940), 40–41, 190 (quote), 193 (quote), 253; Adolf Hitler, *Mein Kampf,* trans. Ralph Manheim (Boston: Houghton Mifflin, 1943), 431; Franz Neumann, *Behemoth: The Structure and Practice of National Socialism, 1933–1944,* 2d rev. ed. (New York: Harper and Row, 1963), 432 (quote).

86. Quoted in Rauschning, *The Voice of Destruction,* 186; Charles Maurras, epigraph to chapter 5 of Richard Pipes, *Russia under the Bolshevik Regime* (New York: Vintage, 1995), 240.

87. Mao Tse-tung, *A Critique of Soviet Economics,* trans. Moss Roberts (New York: Monthly Review, 1977), 47.

88. V. I. Lenin, *The Development of Capitalism in Russia,* 2d rev. ed., ed. Institute of Marxism-Leninism (Moscow: Progress Publishers, 1964), 194–97, 580–84; Neil Harding, *Lenin's Political Thought: Theory and Practice in the Democratic and Socialist Revolutions,* vol. 1 (Atlantic Highlands, N.J.: Humanities, 1983), 106, 107.

89. Burnham, *The Machiavellians,* 251–52; Dennis, *The Dynamics of War and Revolution,* 163–64, 186–89, 216–17.

90. Marx, "Manifesto of the Communist Party," 58, 61.

91. Marx, "Critique of the Gotha Programme," 2:32–33; Marx, "Manifesto of the Communist Party," 74.

92. Marx, "Manifesto of the Communist Party," 58 (quote), 65.

93. Ibid., 61.

94. Bazelon, *Power in America,* 308, 20.

95. Bazelon, *The Paper Economy,* 398 (emphasis added).

96. Barbara Ehrenreich and John Ehrenreich, "The Professional-Managerial Class," in *Between Labor and Capital,* ed. Pat Walker (Boston: South End, 1979), 12.

97. Ibid., 12, 13.

98. Robert B. Reich, *The Resurgent Liberal* (New York: Random House, 1989), 70 (quote), 71.

Chapter 7: The Politics of the Professional Class

1. Max Nomad, *Aspects of Revolt* (New York: Bookman, 1959), 57. For a systematic critique of the Marxist "class struggle swindle," see Donald C. Hodges, *The Literate Communist: 150 Years of the Communist Manifesto* (New York: Peter Lang, 1999), 1–86, 171–99.

2. Herbert Hoover, *The Challenge to Liberty* (New York: Charles Scribner's Sons, 1934), 49, 52.

3. Ibid., 77–78, 80–102, 114.

4. Rexford G. Tugwell, *The Brains Trust* (New York: Viking, 1968), xxv, xxvi (Berle quote).

5. Reich, *The Next American Frontier,* 99, 100.

6. John Galbraith, *The New Industrial State,* 1st ed., 389; John Kenneth Galbraith, *Economics and the Public Purpose* (1973; reprint, New York: New American Library, 1975), 266.

7. John Galbraith, *The New Industrial State,* 1st ed., 2–4, 115, 314–15, 391, 394–95, 403.

8. William E. Leuchtenburg, *Franklin D. Roosevelt and the New Deal, 1932–1940* (New York: Harper and Row, 1963), 32–35, 97–104, 180, 188; Albert U. Romasco, *The Politics of Recovery: Roosevelt's New Deal* (New York: Oxford University Press, 1983), 219, 245; Dennis, *The Dynamics of War and Revolution,* xxvi, 138, 236; Dennis, *Operational Thinking for Survival,* 27–37, 136–37, 142–45; Bernard Nossiter, "The Role of Arms Spending in the American Economy," in *Perspectives on the Economic Problem,* ed. MacEwan and Weisskopf, 149–50. For the data on unemployment from 1931 to 1940 (the Great Depression), from 1943 to 1948 (World War II and its aftermath), and from 1951 to 1953 (the Korean War), see Department of Labor, Bureau of Labor Statistics, "The Labor Force and Unemployment: Past and Present," in *Perspectives on the Economic Problem,* ed. MacEwan and Weisskopf, 131–32.

9. Schultz, "Investment in Human Capital," 163, 164; *Statistical Abstract: 1965,* tables 174 and 186.

10. Schumpeter, *Capitalism, Socialism, and Democracy,* 269, 270.

11. Thomas Ferguson, *Golden Rule: The Investment Theory of Party Competition and the Logic of Money-Driven Political Systems* (Chicago: University of Chicago Press, 1995), 8 (quote), 22, 42 (quote).

12. Bazelon, *Power in America,* 76; Ferguson, *Golden Rule,* 117, 131 (quote), 150, 159.

13. Ferguson, *Golden Rule,* 117 (quote), 121.

14. Ibid., 122, 123 (quote).

15. Ibid., 76, 146–49, 406.

16. Burnham, *The Managerial Revolution,* 208 (quote), 243–44.

17. Ibid., 258–59 (emphasis added), 270.

18. Art Preis, *Labor's Giant Step: Twenty Years of the CIO* (New York: Pioneer, 1964), 14 (Perkins quote), 16.

19. Ibid., 16 (quote), 17 (*New York Times* quote), 18.

20. Leuchtenburg, *Franklin D. Roosevelt and the New Deal,* 34, 36.

21. Preis, *Labor's Giant Step,* 133, 142 (quote), 458, 500; David Milton, *The Politics of U.S. Labor: From the Great Depression to the New Deal* (New York: Monthly Review, 1982), 77–78, 118, 144 (quote).

22. Marty Jezer, *The Dark Ages: Life in the United States, 1945–1960* (Boston: South End, 1982), 83 (Murray quote); Preis, *Labor's Giant Step,* 260, 262; "Labor Management Relations Act of 1947," in *Readings in the United States Economic and Business History,* ed. Ross M. Robertson and James L. Pate (Boston: Houghton Mifflin, 1966), 445 (quote).

23. Preis, *Labor's Giant Step,* 458, 497, 500.

24. Thomas Geoghegan, *Which Side Are You On? Trying to Be for Labor When It's Flat on Its Back* (New York: Farrar, Straus and Giroux, 1991), 55, 164.

25. Melvin Dubovsky, *The State and Labor in Modern America* (Chapel Hill: University of North Carolina Press, 1994), xii, 227.

26. Burnham, *The Machiavellians,* 261, 262.

27. Ibid., 262–63, 263.

28. Jezer, *The Dark Ages,* 17 (Eisenhower quote), 31 (quote), 32.

29. Ibid., 78–79, 203, 208–9, 215–16, 309.

30. Burnham, *The Managerial Revolution,* 190–92, 196–97, 201–2. See the effort by A. A. Berle Jr., the clergyman's son, to shape a distinctively American managerial philosophy in *The 20th Century Capitalist Revolution,* 164–88; *Power without Property,* 77–116; and *The American Economic Republic,* 189–212.

31. Samuel Bowles, David M. Gordon, and Thomas E. Weisskopf, *Beyond the Wasteland: A Democratic Alternative to Economic Decline* (Garden City, N.Y.: Anchor/Doubleday, 1984), 62–64, 72, 75, 83, 91.

32. Ibid., 73.

33. Ibid., 70, 72 (quote), 79–80, 91–92, 96.

34. Ibid., 102, 103.

35. Ibid., 107–8, 109, 110 (quote), 111, 112 (quote).

36. Ibid., 148–49.

37. Piven and Cloward, *The New Class War,* 7–8.

38. Ibid., 9.

39. Ibid., 10, 13, 15, 26.

40. Ibid., 127–28, 138–39.

41. Andrew Hacker, "Who's Sticking to the Union?" *New York Review of Books* 46, no. 3 (18 February 1999): 45–48.

42. Mikhail Gorbachev, "An Ideology of Renovation for Revolutionary Perestroika," *Information Bulletin* (Prague), 26, no. 8 (1988): 12–13; Mikhail Gorbachev, "On Progress

in Implementing the Decisions of the 27th CPSU Congress and the Tasks of Perestroi-ka," in *Documents and Materials: Nineteenth All-Union Conference of the CPSU* (Washington, D.C.: Soviet Life, 1988), 19, 91; Alexander Yakovlev, "The Humanistic Choice of Perestroika," *World Marxist Review* 32, no. 3 (February 1989): 12.

43. Reich, *The Resurgent Liberal,* 281.

44. Ibid., 281–82.

45. Randall Rothenberg, *The Neoliberals: Creating the New American Politics* (New York: Simon and Schuster, 1984), 164.

46. Lester C. Thurow, *The Zero-Sum Society: Distribution and the Possibilities for Economic Change* (New York: Penguin, 1981), 3, 77, 80–82, 91–92, 101, 146.

47. Ibid., 101–2, 192, 193 (quote).

48. Ibid., 7–8.

49. Ibid., 12 (quote), 24 (quote), 212–13.

50. Thurow, *The Future of Capitalism,* 27, 28.

51. Reich, *The Next American Frontier,* 145 (quote), 256, 269, 275.

52. George Gilder, "Turning Point in American Liberalism," *Wall Street Journal,* 10 June 1983, 30; Reich, *The Next American Frontier,* 275.

53. Steven Brint, *In an Age of Experts: The Changing Role of Professionals in Politics and Public Life* (Princeton, N.J.: Princeton University Press, 1994), 85–86.

54. Ibid., 86.

55. Ferguson, *Golden Rule,* 291, 298, 300 (quote), 322.

56. Rothenberg, *The Neoliberals,* 68–69 (Peters quote), 70–73.

57. Brint, *In an Age of Experts,* 4; Irving Kristol, *Two Cheers for Capitalism* (New York: Mentor, 1979), 25–26, 165–66.

58. Peter Steinfels, *The Neoconservatives: The Men Who Are Changing America's Politics* (New York: Simon and Schuster, 1980), 87–88.

59. Irving Kristol, *On the Democratic Idea in America* (New York: Harper and Row, 1972), 25–30; José Ortega y Gasset, *The Revolt of the Masses,* 25th anniversary ed. (New York: W. W. Norton, 1957), 11 (quote), 17–18, 58, 97–98.

60. Kristol, *Two Cheers for Capitalism,* 25–26, 165.

61. Irving Kristol, "Confessions of a True, Self-Confessed—Perhaps the Only—'Neoconservative' [1979]," in *Reflections of a Neoconservative: Looking Backward, Looking Ahead* (New York: Basic Books, 1983), 75–77.

62. Steinfels, *The Neoconservatives,* 279, 280, 281, 286 (quote).

63. Ibid., 283, 285 (quote).

64. Brint, *In an Age of Experts,* 13–14.

65. Ibid., 14, 42 (quote), 44.

66. Ibid., 46, 47, 48, 53, 54 (quote), 58.

67. Ibid., 63, 64–65; Ferguson, *Golden Rule,* 299, 301.

68. Brint, *In an Age of Experts,* 66–79, 80 (quote).

69. Ibid., 206, 207 (quote).

70. Ibid., 57, 58 (quote), 89 (table 5.1).

71. Ibid., 81, 82.

72. Ibid., 83.

73. Donald L. Barlett and James B. Steele, "Corporate Welfare," *Time* 152, no. 19 (9 November 1998): 38.

74. Norman Podhoretz, *Making It* (New York: Random House, 1967), xi, 356. On Podhoretz's post-Vietnam "neoconservatism"—he dislikes the term and prefers to be judged as an "old-fashioned liberal"—see Alexander Bloom, *Prodigal Sons: The New York Intellectuals and Their World* (New York: Oxford University Press, 1986), 370–71, 374.

75. Podhoretz, *Making It*, xiii.

76. Ibid., 6.

77. See the detailed commentary on Podhoretz's *Making It* in Bloom, *Prodigal Sons*, 359–65.

78. Jeane J. Kirkpatrick, "Politics and the New Class" (1979), in *Dictatorships and Double Standards: Rationalism and Reason in Politics* (New York: Simon and Schuster, 1982), 203.

79. Ibid., 187.

80. Irving Kristol, "American Intellectuals and Foreign Policy" (1967), in *On the Democratic Idea in America*, 85; Bloom, *Prodigal Sons*, 370.

81. Podhoretz, *Making It*, 313 (first quote); Bloom, *Prodigal Sons*, 324 (second Podhoretz quote and Mailer quote), 325.

82. George H. Nash, *The Conservative Intellectual Movement in America since 1945* (New York: Basic Books, 1976), 91; James Burnham, *The Struggle for the World* (New York: John Day, 1947); William Buckley quoted by Samuel T. Francis, *Power and History: The Political Thought of James Burnham* (Lanham, Md.: University Press of America, 1984), 127.

83. Nash, *The Conservative Intellectual Movement*, 92; Francis, *Power and History*, 67, 83n.4, 127 (quote).

84. Sidney Hook, *Out of Step: An Unquiet Life in the 20th Century* (New York: Harper and Row, 1987), 597–98.

85. Alan M. Wald, *The New York Intellectuals: The Rise and Decline of the Anti-Stalinist Left from the 1930s to the 1980s* (Chapel Hill: University of North Carolina Press, 1987), 280–81. See James Burnham and Max Shachtman, "Intellectuals in Retreat," *New International* 5, no. 1 (January 1939): 4–22.

86. Hook, *Out of Step*, 599; Burnham, *The Managerial Revolution*, 45.

87. Burnham, *The Managerial Revolution*, 46, 47.

88. Wald, *The New York Intellectuals*, 293, 294.

89. Ibid., 330, 368 (quote).

90. Podhoretz, *Making It*, 245, 262.

Postscript

1. Christopher Lash, *The Revolt of the Elites and the Betrayal of Democracy* (New York: W. W. Norton, 1995), 5–6, 33–40, 74–77.

2. Ibid., 29–30, 41–44. See Michael Young, *The Rise of the Meritocracy, 1870–2033: An Essay on Education and Equality* (1958; reprint, Baltimore: Penguin, 1961), 106–7.

3. Lawrence Mishel, Jared Bernstein, and John Schmitt, *The State of Working America* (Ithaca, N.Y.: Cornell University Press, 1999), 62–63.

4. Ibid., 63 (table 1.12).

5. Michael Bakunin, "The International and Karl Marx," in *Bakunin on Anarchism*, 294–95, 318–19.

bibliography

Academía de Ciencias de la U.R.S.S., Instituto de Economía. *Manual de economía política*. 3d rev. ed. Translated by Wenceslao Roces. Mexico City: Grijalbo, 1966.

Afanasyev, L., N. Andreyev, M. Avsenev, et al. *The Political Economy of Capitalism*. Edited by M. Ryndina and G. Chernikov; translated by Diana Miller. Moscow: Progress Publishers, 1974.

AFL-CIO Committee on the Evolution of Work. *The Changing Situation of Workers and Their Unions*. Washington, D.C.: AFL-CIO, 1985.

———. *The Future of Work*. Washington, D.C.: AFL-CIO, 1983.

Alasco, Johannes. *Intellectual Capitalism*. New York: World University Press, 1950.

Aron, Raymond. *The Opium of the Intellectuals*. Translated by Terrence Kilmartin. New York: W. W. Norton, 1957.

Babeuf, François Noël. "From the Trial at Vendôme, February–May 1797." In *Socialist Thought: A Documentary History*, edited by Albert Fried and Ronald Sanders, rev. ed., 56–71. New York: Columbia University Press, 1992.

Bakunin, Michael. *Bakunin on Anarchism*. 2d rev. ed. Edited and translated by Sam Dolgoff. 1980. Reprint, New York: Black Rose Books, 1990.

———. "The International and Karl Marx." In *Bakunin on Anarchism*, 2d rev. ed., 286–320. Edited and translated by Sam Dolgoff. 1980. Reprint, New York: Black Rose Books, 1990.

———. *Marxism, Freedom, and the State*. Edited and translated by K. J. Kenafick. London: Freedom, 1950.

———. *The Political Philosophy of Bakunin: Scientific Anarchism*. Edited by G. P. Maximoff. Glencoe, Ill.: Free Press, 1953.

Balogh, Thomas. *The Irrelevance of Conventional Economics*. New York: Liveright, 1982.

Baran, Paul A. *The Political Economy of Growth*. New York: Monthly Review, 1957.

Baran, Paul A., and Paul M. Sweezy. *Monopoly Capital: An Essay on the American Economic and Social Order*. New York: Monthly Review, 1966.

Barlett, Donald L., and James B. Steel. "Corporate Welfare." *Time* 152, no. 19 (9 November 1998): 36–54.

Barnet, Richard, and John Cavanagh. *Global Dreams: Imperial Corporations and the New World Order*. New York: Simon and Schuster, 1994.

Bazelon, David T. *The Paper Economy*. New York: Vintage, 1959.

———. *Power in America: The Politics of the New Class*. 1964. Reprint, New York: New American Library, 1967.

Bell, Daniel. *The Coming of Post-Industrial Society*. 1973. Reprint, New York: Basic Books, 1976.

———. Introduction to *Engineers and the Price System*, by Thorstein Veblen, 1–35. New York: Harcourt, Brace and World, 1963.

Benedict, F. G., and C. G. Benedict. "The Energy Requirements of Intense Mental Effort." In *Proceedings of the National Academy of Sciences*, 438–43. Washington, D.C.: National Academy of Sciences, 1930.

———. *Mental Effort in Relation to Gaseous Exchange, Heart Rate, and Mechanics of Respiration*. Publication No. 446. Washington, D. C.: Carnegie Institution of Washington, 1933.

Berle, Adolf A., Jr. *The American Economic Republic*. New York: Harcourt, Brace and World, 1963.

———. "Economic Power and the Free Society." In *The Corporation Take-Over*, edited by Andrew Hacker, 86–102. Garden City, N.Y.: Anchor, 1965.

———. *Power without Property: A New Development in American Political Economy*. New York: Harcourt, Brace and World, 1959.

———. *The 20th Century Capitalist Revolution*. New York: Harcourt, Brace, 1954.

Berle, Adolf A., Jr., and Gardiner C. Means. *The Modern Corporation and Private Property*. New York: Macmillan, 1932.

Bernstein, Eduard. *Evolutionary Socialism*. Translated by Edith C. Harvey. New York: Schocken, 1963.

Blanqui, Auguste. "The Man Who Makes the Soup Should Get to Eat It." In *Socialist Thought: A Documentary History*, edited by Arthur Fried and Ronald Sanders, rev. ed., 193–99. New York: Columbia University Press, 1992.

Bloom, Alexander. *Prodigal Sons: The New York Intellectuals and Their World*. New York: Oxford University Press, 1986.

Blumberg, Paul. "Another Day, Another $3,000: Executive Salaries in America." In *The Big Business Reader: On Corporate America*, edited by Mark Green, Michael Waldman, and Robert K. Massie Jr., 313–25. New York: Pilgrim, 1983.

Bowles, Samuel, David M. Gordon, and Thomas E. Weisskopf. *Beyond the Wasteland: A Democratic Alternative to Economic Decline*. Garden City, N.Y.: Anchor/Doubleday, 1984.

Braverman, Harry. *Labor and Monopoly Capital: The Degradation of Work in the Twentieth Century.* New York: Monthly Review, 1974.

Brint, Steven. *In an Age of Experts: The Changing Role of Professionals in Politics and Public Life.* Princeton, N.J.: Princeton University Press, 1994.

Burbach, Roger. "The Epoch of Globalization." *URPE Newsletter* 29, no. 1 (Fall 1997): 3–5.

———. "The Rise of Postmodern Marxism: Or, Virtually Existing Socialisms." *URPE Newsletter* 28, no. 2 (Winter 1997): 4–5, 11.

Burbach, Roger, with Orlando Nuñez and Boris Kagarlitsky. *Globalization and Its Discontents: The Rise of Postmodern Socialisms.* London: Pluto, 1997.

Burch, Phillip. *The Managerial Revolution Revised.* Lexington, Mass.: Lexington Books, 1972.

Bureau of the Census. *Statistical Abstract of the United States: 1965.* Washington, D.C.: Government Printing Office, 1965.

———. *Statistical Abstract of the United States: 1969.* Washington, D.C.: Government Printing Office, 1969.

———. *Statistical Abstract of the United States: 1982–83.* Washington, D.C.: Government Printing Office, 1983.

———. *Statistical Abstract of the United States: 1991.* Washington, D.C.: Government Printing Office, 1991.

———. *Statistical Abstract of the United States: 1996.* Washington, D.C.: Government Printing Office, 1996.

Burnham, James. *The Machiavellians: Defenders of Freedom.* 1943. Reprint, Washington, D.C.: Gateway, 1987.

———. *The Managerial Revolution: What Is Happening in the World.* New York: John Day, 1941.

———. *The Struggle for the World.* New York: John Day, 1947.

———. "What New Class?" *National Review* 30, no. 3 (20 January 1978): 98–99.

Burnham, James, and Max Shachtman. "Intellectuals in Retreat." *New International* 5, no. 1 (January 1939): 4–22.

Canterbery, E. Ray. "Galbraith, Sraffa, Kalecki and Supra-Surplus Capitalism." *Journal of Post-Keynesian Economics* 7, no. 1 (Fall 1984): 77–90.

———. *The Literate Economist: A Brief History of Economics.* New York: HarperCollins, 1995.

———. "A Theory of Supra-Surplus Capitalism." *Eastern Economic Journal* 13, no. 4 (October–December 1987): 315–32.

Castells, Manuel. *The Information Age: Economy, Society, Culture.* 3 vols. Malden, Mass.: Blackwell, 1996–98.

Castoriadis, Cornelius. General introduction to *Political and Social Writings,* 1:3–36. Edited and translated by David Ames Curtis. Minneapolis: University of Minnesota Press, 1988.

———. "On the Content of Socialism, I." In *Political and Social Writings,* 1:290–309.

Edited and translated by David Ames Curtis. Minneapolis: University of Minnesota Press, 1988.

———. "On the Content of Socialism, II." In *Political and Social Writings,* 2:90–154. Edited and translated by David Ames Curtis. Minneapolis: University of Minnesota Press, 1988.

———. "The Problem of the USSR and the Possibility of a Third Historical Solution." In *Political and Social Writings,* 1:44–55. Edited and translated by David Ames Curtis. Minneapolis: University of Minnesota Press, 1988.

———. "Proletariat and Organization, I." In *Political and Social Writings,* 2:193–222. Edited and translated by David Ames Curtis. Minneapolis: University of Minnesota Press, 1988.

———. "Socialism or Barbarism." In *Political and Social Writings,* 1:76–106. Edited and translated by David Ames Curtis. Minneapolis: University of Minnesota Press, 1988.

———. "The Yugoslav Bureaucracy." In *Political and Social Writings,* 1:179–97. Edited and translated by David Ames Curtis. Minneapolis: University of Minnesota Press, 1988.

Chandler, Alfred D., Jr. *The Visible Hand: The Managerial Revolution in American Business.* Cambridge, Mass.: Harvard University Press, 1977.

Cleaver, Harry. *Reading "Capital" Politically.* Austin: University of Texas Press, 1979.

Cliff, Tony. *State Capitalism in Russia.* 1948. Reprint, London: Pluto, 1974.

Collodi, Carlo. *The Adventures of Pinocchio.* Translated by E. Harden. 1944. Reprint, New York: Alfred A. Knopf, 1988.

Cooperative Grocer (Athens, Ohio). Nos. 62–65 (January–August 1996).

Cottrell, F. *Energy and Society.* New York: McGraw-Hill, 1955.

Dahrendorf, Ralf. *Class and Class Conflict in Industrial Society.* Stanford, Calif.: Stanford University Press, 1959.

De Coursey, R. M. *The Human Organism.* 2d ed. New York: McGraw-Hill, 1961.

Dennis, Lawrence. *The Dynamics of War and Revolution.* Washington, D.C.: Weekly Foreign Letter, 1940.

———. *Operational Thinking for Survival.* Colorado Springs: Ralph Myles, 1969.

Department of Labor, Bureau of Labor Statistics. "The Labor Force and Unemployment: Past and Present." In *Perspectives on the Economic Problem: A Book of Readings in Political Economy,* edited by Arthur MacEwan and Thomas E. Weisskopf, 131–33. Englewood Cliffs, N.J.: Prentice-Hall, 1970.

Djilas, Milovan. *The New Class: An Analysis of the Communist System.* New York: Praeger, 1957.

Drucker, Peter F. *The Concept of the Corporation.* 1946. Reprint, New York: Mentor, 1964.

———. *The New Realities: In Government and Politics, in Economics and Business, in Society and World View.* New York: Harper and Row, 1989.

———. *The New Society: The Anatomy of Industrial Order.* 1950. Reprint, New York: Harper and Row, 1962.

———. *Post-Capitalist Society.* New York: HarperBusiness, 1993.

Dubovsky, Melvin. *The State and Labor in Modern America*. Chapel Hill: University of North Carolina Press, 1994.

Eaton, John. *Political Economy: A Marxist Textbook*. New York: International Publishers, 1949.

Editorial Departments of *People's Daily* and *Red Flag*. "Is Yugoslavia a Socialist Country? (26 September 1963)." In *The Polemic on the General Line of the International Communist Movement*, 139–83. Peking: Foreign Languages Press, 1965.

———. "On Khrushchev's Phoney Communism and Its Historical Lessons for the World (14 July 1964)." In *The Polemic on the General Line of the International Communist Movement*, 415–80. Peking: Foreign Languages Press, 1965.

Ehrenreich, Barbara, and John Ehrenreich. "The Professional-Managerial Class." In *Between Labor and Capital*, edited by Pat Walker, 5–45. Boston: South End, 1979.

Elliott, Sydney R. *The English Cooperatives*. New Haven, Conn.: Yale University Press, 1937.

Engels, Frederick. Introduction to Karl Marx's "The Class Struggles in France, 1848 to 1850." In *Selected Works*, by Karl Marx and Frederick Engels, 1:118–38. Edited by the Institute of Marxism-Leninism. Moscow: Foreign Languages Publishing House, 1958.

———. "Karl Marx." In *Selected Works*, by Karl Marx and Frederick Engels, 2:156–66. Edited by the Institute of Marxism-Leninism. Moscow: Foreign Languages Publishing House, 1958.

———. "Karl Marx, *Das Kapital*." In *On Marx's "Capital*," 32–38. Edited by the Institute of Marxism-Leninism. Moscow: Foreign Languages Publishing House, n.d.

———. Preface (1888) to "Manifesto of the Communist Party," by Karl Marx. In *The Communist Manifesto*, 46–49. Edited by Frederic L. Bender. New York: W. W. Norton, 1988.

———. "Socialism: Utopian and Scientific." In *Selected Works*, by Karl Marx and Frederick Engels, 2:93–155. Edited by the Institute of Marxism-Leninism. Moscow: Foreign Languages Publishing House, 1952.

"Executive Compensation Scoreboard." *Business Week*, no. 3523 (21 April 1997): 67–102.

Feder, Gottfried. *Manifiesto contra la usura y la servidumbre del interés del dinero*. 1919. Reprint, Buenos Aires: Maxim, 1984.

Ferguson, Thomas. *Golden Rule: The Investment Theory of Party Competition and the Logic of Money-Driven Political Systems*. Chicago: University of Chicago Press, 1995.

Foner, Philip S. *History of the Labor Movement in the United States*. 4 vols. New York: International Publishers, 1947–65.

Francis, Samuel T. *Power and History: The Political Thought of James Burnham*. Lanham, Md.: University Press of America, 1984.

Galbraith, James K. *Balancing Acts: Technology, Finance and the American Future*. New York: Basic Books, 1989.

Galbraith, John Kenneth. *Economics and the Public Purpose*. 1973. Reprint, New York: New American Library, 1975.

———. *The New Industrial State.* Boston: Houghton Mifflin, 1967.

———. *The New Industrial State.* Rev. ed. Boston: Houghton Mifflin, 1971.

Geoghegan, Thomas. *Which Side Are You On? Trying to Be for Labor When It's Flat on Its Back.* New York: Farrar, Straus and Giroux, 1991.

Gesell, Silvio. *The Natural Economic Order.* Rev. English ed. Translated by Philip Pye. London: Peter Owen, 1958.

Gilder, George. "Turning Point in American Liberalism." *Wall Street Journal,* 10 June 1983, 30.

———. *Wealth and Poverty.* New York: Basic Books, 1981.

Gillman, Joseph M. *The Falling Rate of Profit.* London: Dennis Dobson, 1957.

Gorbachev, Mikhail. "An Ideology of Renovation for Revolutionary Perestroika." *Information Bulletin* (Prague) 26, no. 8 (1988): 3–23.

———. "On Progress in Implementing the Decisions of the 27th CPSU Congress and the Tasks of Perestroika." In *Documents and Materials: Nineteenth All-Union Conference of the CPSU,* 5–93. Washington, D.C.: Soviet Life, 1988.

Gouldner, Alvin W. *The Future of Intellectuals and the Rise of the New Class.* New York: Continuum, 1979.

"Grand National Consolidated Trades Union Programme and Manifesto (London, 15 April 1834)." In *Revolution from 1789 to 1906,* edited by Raymond Postgate, 99–100. 1920. Reprint, New York: Harper and Row, 1962.

Gregor, James A. *The Ideology of Fascism.* New York: Free Press, 1969.

Greider, William. *One World, Ready or Not: The Manic Logic of Global Capitalism.* New York: Simon and Schuster, 1998.

Gross, Bertram. *Friendly Fascism: The New Face of Power in America.* Boston: South End, 1980.

Guillén, Abraham. *El capitalismo soviético: Ultima etapa del imperialismo.* Madrid: Queimada, 1979.

Hacker, Andrew. "Who's Sticking to the Union?" *New York Review of Books* 46, no. 3 (18 February 1999): 45–48.

Harding, Neil. *Lenin's Political Thought: Theory and Practice in the Democratic and Socialist Revolutions.* Vol. 1. Atlantic Highlands: Humanities, 1983.

Heilbroner, Robert L. "Reflections: The Triumph of Capitalism." *New Yorker* 64, no. 49 (23 January 1989): 98–109.

Herman, Edward S. *Corporate Control, Corporate Power.* Cambridge: Cambridge University Press, 1982.

Hirsch, Barry T., and David A. Macpherson. *Union Membership and Earnings Data Book.* Washington, D.C.: Bureau of National Affairs, 1998.

Hitler, Adolf. *Mein Kampf.* Translated by Ralph Manheim. Boston: Houghton Mifflin, 1943.

Hobsbawm, Eric J. *Labouring Men: Studies in the History of Labour.* London: Weidenfeld and Nicolson, 1964.

Hodges, Donald C. *America's New Economic Order.* Brookfield, Vt.: Avebury-Ashgate, 1996.

———. *Argentina, 1943–1987: The National Revolution and Resistance.* 2d rev. ed. Albuquerque: University of New Mexico Press, 1988.

———. "Calculating the Economic Surplus: Manpower versus Commodity and Wage Units of Account." *Manpower Journal* 2, no. 3 (October–December 1966): 7–30.

———. "Cynicism in the Labor Movement." In *American Society, Inc.,* edited by Maurice Zeitlin, 439–46. Chicago: Markham, 1970.

———. *The Literate Communist: 150 Years of the Communist Manifesto.* New York: Peter Lang, 1999.

———. "Yugoslav Marxism and Methods of Social Accounting." In *Marxism, Revolution, and Peace,* edited by H. Parsons and J. Somerville, 53–63. Amsterdam: Grüner, 1977.

Hook, Sydney. *Out of Step: An Unquiet Life in the 20th Century.* New York: Harper and Row, 1987.

Hoover, Herbert. *The Challenge to Liberty.* New York: Charles Scribner's Sons, 1934.

Hunt, E. K. "Economic Scholasticism and Capitalist Ideology." In *A Critique of Economic Theory,* edited by E. K. Hunt and Jesse Schwartz, 186–93. Baltimore: Penguin, 1972.

Hunt, E. K., and Jesse Schwartz. Introduction to *A Critique of Economic Theory,* edited by E. K. Hunt and Jesse Schwartz, 7–35. Baltimore: Penguin, 1972.

Jevons, W. Stanley. *The Theory of Political Economy.* 5th ed. New York: Augustus M. Kelley, 1965.

Jezer, Marty. *The Dark Ages: Life in the United States, 1945–1960.* Boston: South End, 1982.

Jones, R. J. Barry. "Political Economy: Contrasts, Commonalities, Criteria and Contributions." In *Perspectives on Political Economy,* edited by R. J. Barry Jones, 3–13. New York: St. Martin's, 1983.

Keynes, John Maynard. "The End of Laissez Faire." In *Great Political Thinkers: Plato to the Present,* edited by William Ebenstein, 3d ed., 654–66. New York: Holt, Rinehart and Winston, 1962.

———. *The General Theory of Employment, Interest and Money.* New York: Harcourt, Brace, 1936.

Keynes, John Neville. *The Scope and Method of Political Economy.* 4th ed. 1963. Reprint, New York: Augustus M. Kelley, 1965.

King, Florence. *With Charity toward None: A Fond Look at Misanthropy.* New York: St. Martin's, 1992.

Kirkpatrick, Jeane J. "Politics and the 'New Class.'" In *Dictatorships and Double Standards: Rationalism and Reason in Politics,* 186–203. New York: Simon and Schuster, 1982.

Kristol, Irving. "American Intellectuals and Foreign Policy." In *On the Democratic Idea in America,* 68–69. New York: Harper and Row, 1972.

———. "Confessions of a True, Self-Confessed—Perhaps the Only—'Neoconservative' [1979]." In *Reflections of a Neoconservative: Looking Backward, Looking Ahead,* 73–77. New York: Basic Books, 1983.

———. *On the Democratic Idea in America*. New York: Harper and Row, 1972.

———. *Two Cheers for Capitalism*. New York: Mentor, 1979.

Kuttner, Robert. *The End of Laissez-Faire: National Purpose and the Global Economy after the Cold War*. Philadelphia: University of Pennsylvania Press, 1992.

Kuznets, Simon. *Modern Economic Growth*. New Haven, Conn.: Yale University Press, 1966.

"Labor Management Relations Act of 1947." In *Readings in United States Economic and Business History*, edited by Ross M. Robertson and James L. Pate, 443–46. Boston: Houghton Mifflin, 1966.

Larner, Robert J. "The Effect of Management-Control on the Profits of Large Corporations." In *American Society, Inc.*, edited by Maurice Zeitlin, 251–62. Chicago: Markham, 1970.

———. "Ownership and Control in the 200 Largest Nonfinancial Corporations, 1929 and 1963." *American Economic Review* 56, no. 4 (September 1966): 777–87.

Lasch, Christopher. *The Culture of Narcissism: American Life in an Age of Diminishing Expectations*. New York: Warner Books, 1980.

———. *The Revolt of the Elites and the Betrayal of Democracy*. New York: W. W. Norton, 1995.

Lasswell, Harold D. *Politics: Who Gets What, When, How*. New York: Meridian, 1965.

Lebowitz, Michael A. *Beyond "Capital": Marx's Political Economy of the Working Class*. New York: St. Martin's, 1992.

Lenin, V. I. *The Development of Capitalism in Russia*. 2d rev. ed. Edited by the Institute of Marxism-Leninism. Moscow: Progress Publishers, 1964.

———. "The Immediate Tasks of the Soviet Government." In *The Lenin Anthology*, 438–60. Edited by Robert C. Tucker. New York: W. W. Norton, 1975.

———. "Imperialism, the Highest Stage of Capitalism." In *The Lenin Anthology*, 204–74. Edited by Robert C. Tucker. New York: W. W. Norton, 1975.

———. "'Left-Wing' Communism—An Infantile Disorder." In *The Lenin Anthology*, 550–618. Edited by Robert C. Tucker. New York: W. W. Norton, 1975.

———. "On Cooperation." In *The Lenin Anthology*, 707–13. Edited by Robert C. Tucker. New York: W. W. Norton, 1975.

———. "What Is to Be Done?" In *The Lenin Anthology*, 12–114. Edited by Robert C. Tucker. New York: W. W. Norton, 1975.

Leuchtenburg, William E., *Franklin D. Roosevelt and the New Deal*. New York: Harper and Row, 1963.

Lewellen, Wilbur G. *Executive Compensation in Large Corporations*. New York: National Bureau of Economic Research, 1968.

London, Jack. *War of the Classes*. New York: Macmillan, 1908.

Machajski (Makhaiski), Waclaw. "On the Expropriation of the Capitalists." Translated by Max Nomad. In *The Making of Society: An Outline of Sociology*, edited by V. F. Calverton, 427–36. New York: Modern Library, 1937.

———. *Le socialisme des intellectuals*. Edited and translated by Alexandre Skirda. Paris: Editions de Seuil, 1979.

————— [A. Volski, pseud.]. *Umstvennii Rabochii* (The intellectual worker). Geneva: n.p., 1905.

Machiavelli, Niccolò. *The Prince and the Discourses.* New York: Modern Library, 1950.

Machlup, Fritz. *The Production and Distribution of Knowledge in the United States.* Princeton, N.J.: Princeton University Press, 1962.

Malthus, Thomas R. *Principles of Political Economy.* 2d ed. New York: Augustus M. Kelley, 1951.

Mandel, Ernest. *Late Capitalism.* Translated by Joris de Bres. 1975. Reprint, London: Verso, 1978.

Mao Tse-tung. "Analysis of the Classes in Chinese Society." In *Selected Works,* 1:13–21. Edited by a Commission of the Central Committee of the Communist Party of China. Peking: Foreign Languages Press, 1965.

—————. *A Critique of Soviet Economics.* Translated by Moss Roberts. New York: Monthly Review, 1977.

Marris, Robin. *The Economic Theory of "Managerial" Capitalism.* New York: Free Press, 1964.

Marshall, Alfred. *Principles of Economics.* 8th ed. New York: Macmillan, 1948.

Marx, Karl. *Capital.* Vol. 1. Edited by Frederick Engels; rev. ed. edited by Ernest Untermann; translated by Samuel Moore and Edward Aveling. New York: Modern Library, n.d.

—————. *Capital.* Vols. 2–3. Edited by Frederick Engels. Moscow: Foreign Languages Publishing House, 1961–62.

—————. "Critique of the Gotha Programme." In *Selected Works,* by Karl Marx and Frederick Engels, 2:18–37. Edited by the Institute of Marxism-Leninism. Moscow: Foreign Languages Publishing House, 1962.

—————. *The Grundrisse.* Edited and translated by David McLellan. New York: Harper and Row, 1971.

—————. "Inaugural Address of the Working Men's International Association" (28 September 1864). In *Selected Works,* by Karl Marx and Frederick Engels, 1:377–85. Edited by the Institute of Marxism-Leninism. Moscow: Foreign Languages Publishing House, 1958.

—————. "Manifesto of the Communist Party." In *The Communist Manifesto,* 43–86. Edited by Frederic L. Bender. New York: W. W. Norton, 1988.

—————. *The Poverty of Philosophy.* Moscow: Foreign Languages Publishing House, n.d.

—————. *Theories of Surplus Value.* Part 1. Edited by the Institute of Marxism-Leninism; translated by Emile Burns and S. Ryazanskaya. Moscow: Foreign Languages Publishing House, 1958.

—————. "Wage Labor and Capital." In *Selected Works,* by Karl Marx and Frederick Engels, 1:70–105. Edited by the Institute of Marxism-Leninism. Moscow: Foreign Languages Publishing House, 1958.

—————. "Wages, Price and Profit." In *Selected Works,* by Karl Marx and Frederick Engels, 1:106–17. Edited by the Institute of Marxism-Leninism. Moscow: Foreign Languages Publishing House, 1958.

McFarlane, Bruce. "Jugoslavia's Crossroads." In *The Socialist Register, 1966,* edited by Ralph Miliband and John Saville, 114–31. London: Merlin, 1966.

Meek, Ronald. *Studies in the Labour Theory of Value.* New York: International Publishers, 1956.

Michels, Robert. *Political Parties: A Sociological Study of the Oligarchical Tendencies of Modern Democracy.* Translated by Eden Paul and Cedar Paul. 1915. Reprint, Glencoe, Ill.: Free Press, 1958.

Miller, Henry. *To Remember to Remember.* New York: New Directions, 1947.

Milton, David. *The Politics of U.S. Labor: From the Great Depression to the New Deal.* New York: Monthly Review, 1982.

Mishel, Lawrence, Jared Bernstein, and John Schmitt. *The State of Working America.* Ithaca, N.Y.: Cornell University Press, 1999.

Nash, George H. *The Conservative Intellectual Movement in America since 1945.* New York: Basic Books, 1976.

Neumann, Franz. *Behemoth: The Structure and Practice of National Socialism, 1933–1944.* 2d rev. ed. New York: Harper and Row, 1966.

Nicolaus, Martin. *Restoration of Capitalism in the USSR.* Chicago: Liberator, 1975.

Nomad, Max. *Aspects of Revolt.* New York: Bookman, 1959.

———. *Dreamers, Dynamiters, and Demagogues: Reminiscences.* New York: Waldon, 1964.

———. "Masters—Old and New: A Social Philosophy without Myths." In *The Making of Society: An Outline of Sociology,* edited by V. F. Calverton, 882–93. New York: Modern Library, 1937.

———. *Rebels and Renegades.* 1932. Reprint, Freeport, N.Y.: Books for Libraries, 1963.

Nossiter, Bernard. "The Role of Arms Spending in the American Economy." In *Perspectives on the Economic Problem: A Book of Readings in Political Economy,* edited by Arthur MacEwan and Thomas E. Weisskopf, 148–52. Englewood Cliffs, N.J.: Prentice-Hall, 1970.

Ortega y Gasset, José. *The Revolt of the Masses.* 25th anniversary ed. New York: W. W. Norton, 1957.

Ostergaard, G. N., and A. H. Halsey. *Power in Cooperatives: A Study of the Internal Politics of British Retail Societies.* Oxford: Blackwell, 1965.

Perlo, Victor. "Ownership and Control of Corporations: The Fusion of Financial and Industrial Capital." In *American Society, Inc.,* edited by Maurice Zeitlin, 265–82. Chicago: Markham, 1970.

Phillips, Kevin. *Arrogant Capital.* Boston: Little, Brown, 1995.

———. *Boiling Point.* New York: HarperCollins, 1963.

Pipes, Richard. *Russia under the Bolshevik Regime.* New York: Vintage, 1995.

Piven, Frances Fox, and Richard A. Cloward. *The New Class War: Reagan's Attack on the Welfare State and Its Consequences.* New York: Pantheon, 1982.

Podhoretz, Norman. *Making It.* New York: Random House, 1967.

Preis, Art. *Labor's Giant Step: Twenty Years of the CIO.* New York: Pioneer, 1964.

Proudhon, P. J. *What Is Property: An Inquiry into the Principle of Right and of Government.* Translated by Benjamin R. Tucker. London: William Reeves, n.d.

Rauschning, Hermann. *The Voice of Destruction.* New York: Putnam's Sons, 1940.

Reich, Robert B. *The Next American Frontier.* 1983. Reprint, New York: Penguin, 1984.

———. *The Resurgent Liberal.* New York: Random House, 1989.

Reingold, Jennifer. "Executive Pay: Special Report." *Business Week,* no. 3523 (21 April 1997): 58–66.

Ricardo, David. *The Principles of Political Economy and Taxation.* 3d ed. London: J. M. Dent and Sons, 1948.

Riedman, Sarah R. *The Physiology of Work and Play.* New York: Dryden, 1950.

Rizzi, Bruno. *The Bureaucratization of the World.* Translated by Adam Westoby. New York: Free Press, 1985.

Robinson, Joan. *Economic Philosophy.* London: C. A. Watts, 1962.

Romasco, Albert U. *The Politics of Recovery: Roosevelt's New Deal.* New York: Oxford University Press, 1983.

Rothenberg, Randall. *The Neoliberals: Creating the New American Politics.* New York: Simon and Schuster, 1984.

Rubin, Isaak Ilich. *Essays on Marx's Theory of Value.* Translated by Milos Samardzíja and Fredy Perlman. Detroit: Black and Red, 1972.

Samuelson, Paul A. *Economics: An Introductory Analysis.* 7th ed. New York: McGraw-Hill, 1969.

Schmitt, Carl. "The Concept of 'The Political.'" In *Modern Political Thought: The Great Issues,* edited by William Ebenstein, 326–28. 1947. Reprint, New York: Rinehart, 1957.

Schultz, Theodore W. *The Economic Value of Education.* New York: Columbia University Press, 1963.

———. *Investing in People: The Economics of Population Quality.* Berkeley: University of California Press, 1981.

———. "Investment in Human Capital [1961]." In *Perspectives on the Economic Problem: A Book of Readings in Political Economy,* edited by Arthur MacEwan and Thomas E. Weisskopf, 160–65. Englewood Cliffs, N.J.: Prentice-Hall, 1970.

Schumpeter, Joseph A. *Capitalism, Socialism, and Democracy.* 3d ed. New York: Harper and Brothers, 1950.

Shachtman, Max. *The Struggle for the New Course.* New York: New International, 1943.

Sherman, H. C. *Chemistry of Food and Nutrition.* 8th ed. New York: Macmillan, 1952.

Skinner, B. F. *Walden Two.* 1948. Reprint, New York: Macmillan, 1966.

Smith, Adam. *An Inquiry into the Nature and Causes of the Wealth of Nations.* Edited by Edwin Cannan. New York: Modern Library, 1937.

Stalin, Joseph. *History of the Communist Party of the Soviet Union (Bolsheviks): Short Course.* Edited by a Commission of the Central Committee of the Communist Party of the Soviet Union. New York: International Publishers, 1939.

———. "Report on the Work of the Central Committee to the Seventeenth Congress of the Communist Party of the Soviet Union." In *Leninism: Selected Writings,* 298–360. New York: International Publishers, 1942.

———. "The Tasks of Business Executives." In *Leninism: Selected Writings,* 194–202. New York: International Publishers, 1942.

Steinfels, Peter. *The Neoconservatives: The Men Who Are Changing America's Politics.* New York: Simon and Schuster, 1980.

Stewart, Thomas A. *Intellectual Capital: The New Wealth of Organizations.* New York/London: Doubleday/Currency, 1997.

Sweezy, Paul M. "The Illusion of the Managerial Revolution." In *The Present as History: Essays and Reviews of Capitalism and Socialism,* 39–66. New York: Monthly Review, 1953.

———. *The Theory of Capitalist Development.* 1942. Reprint, New York: Monthly Review, 1956.

Thomas, Merlin. *Louis-Ferdinand Céline.* Boston: Faber and Faber, 1979.

Thurow, Lester C. *The Future of Capitalism: How Today's Economic Forces Shape Tomorrow's World.* New York: Penguin, 1996.

———. *The Zero-Sum Society: Distribution and the Possibilities for Economic Change.* New York: Penguin, 1981.

Tressell, Robert. *The Ragged Trousered Philanthropists.* Introduction by Alan Sillitoe. London: Grafton, 1965.

Trotsky, Leon. *My Life: An Attempt at an Autobiography.* New York: Charles Scribner's Sons, 1931.

———. *The Revolution Betrayed.* Translated by Max Eastman. 1937. Reprint, New York: Merit, 1965.

———. "The USSR in War" (25 September 1939). In *In Defense of Marxism,* 3–21. New York: Pioneer, 1942.

Tugwell, Rexford G. *The Brains Trust.* New York: Viking, 1969.

Tuttle, W. W., and B. A. Schottelius. *Textbook of Physiology.* 14th ed. St. Louis: Mosby, 1961.

Veblen, Thorstein. *The Engineers and the Price System.* 1921. Reprint, with a new introduction by Daniel Bell, New York: Harcourt, Brace and World, 1963.

———. *The Theory of Business Enterprise.* New York: 1904. Reprint, Charles Scribner's Sons, 1932.

Wald, Alan M. *The New York Intellectuals: The Rise and Decline of the Anti-Stalinist Left from the 1930s to the 1980s.* Chapel Hill: University of North Carolina Press, 1987.

Weber, Max. "The Spirit of Capitalism." In *The Making of Society: An Outline of Sociology,* edited by V. F. Calverton, 506–31. New York: Modern Library, 1937.

Westoby, Adam. Introduction to *The Bureaucratization of the World,* by Bruno Rizzi, 1–33. New York: Free Press, 1985.

Yakovlev, Alexander. "The Humanistic Choice of Perestroika." *World Marxist Review* 32, no. 2 (February 1989): 8–13.

Young, Michael. *The Rise of the Meritocracy, 1870–2033: An Essay on Education and Equality.* 1958. Reprint, Baltimore: Penguin, 1961.

Index

DONALD CLARK HODGES is a professor of philosophy and an affiliate professor of political science at Florida State University. The founder of *Social Theory and Practice,* he served as secretary-treasurer of the Society for the Philosophical Study of Marxism from 1963 to 1987. He has lectured widely at universities and social science institutes throughout the United States, Eastern Europe, Latin America, and Australia. His previous publications include *Socialist Humanism* (1974), *The Bureaucratization of Socialism* (1981), *America's New Economic Order* (1996), and *The Literate Communist* (1999). His experience as a former industrial worker and shop steward of Local 201, United Electrical, Radio, and Machine Workers of America, in Bridgeport, Connecticut, is reflected in more than a hundred articles on socialism and the labor movement.